VENEZUELA

ALIVE

3rd Edition

Susan Brushaber & Arnold Greenberg

HUNTER
PUBLISHING

Hunter Publishing, Inc.
130 Campus Drive, Edison NJ 08818
(732) 225 1900, (800) 255 0343, fax (732) 417 0482

In Canada
1220 Nicholson Rd., Newmarket, Ontario,
Canada L3Y 7V1, (800) 399 6858

ISBN 1-55650-800-X

©1998 Alive Travel Books Ltd.

Maps by Desk Top Graphics (Marie Brown) and Kim André

For complete information about the hundreds of other travel
guides and language courses offered by Hunter Publishing,
visit our Web site at:

www.hunterpublishing.com

1 2 3 4 5

Contents

Preface

We first visited Caracas in 1966 to research the city for inclusion in an upcoming edition of our best selling guidebook *South America on $45 A Day* ($10 then). Although we spent some time visiting other parts of the country, space considerations did not allow us to include them in that guide. But we were so impressed with the variety of the experiences we had that a few years later we wrote *Caracas Alive*, followed by *Venezuela Alive*. Most travelers picked up a copy of *Caracas Alive*, visited that cosmopolitan city and its nearby beaches, then headed home, failing to appreciate that the "interior" (as Caraqueños call the rest of the country) can be a fascinating travel experience – albeit, at that time, an expensive one, since prices in Venezuela were among the highest in the world.

This new edition of *Venezuela Alive* proves us correct. It has become obvious from the calls and letters we've received that many more travelers looking for an exciting travel experience have explored this multi-dimensional country in depth. We feel sure you will agree with them and with Arthur Frommer, who dubbed Venezuela the next travel "must." Happily, at this writing the experience will be less costly since prices in Venezuela, due to currency fluctuations, are now moderate.

Other than Caracas, relatively little is known about Venezuela, whose attractions range from the 16,000-foot Espejo Peak (reached via the world's highest cable car in Mérida) to the jungle camps of Canaima; from the sparkling beaches of Margarita to the boom town of Maracaibo. Add to this the romantic beaches of Mochima. We will guide you to all of these exotic destinations and more.

Some of you may know us as the authors of *Rio Alive, Brazil on Your Own, Buenos Aires Alive, Aruba, Bonaire &*

Curaçao Alive and *The Virgin Islands Alive*. In the Alive series, we emphasize the best there is in the way of hotels, restaurants, clubs and shops. By "best" we do not mean the most expensive; we mean the **best value** in all price ranges.

To get the most benefit from our guides, carefully set a budget in advance. No matter what your budget, you can plan around our listings, for they include the widest possible range of accommodations and dining choices, as well as nightclubbing, sightseeing and shopping options. Now all you have to do is come alive in Venezuela!

Buen Viaje!

Arnold Greenberg

Dedication

To the heroes who have been my inspiration:
Clarence Darrow, William O. Douglas, Giuseppe
Verdi, Joe di Maggio, Groucho Marx.

An Acknowledgment

To my friend Bram Gunther,
my sincereest thanks for your help in
researching and writing this book.

Introduction

A quick 2½ hours from Miami and a scant 4½ hours from New York, this marvelously diverse country offers travelers a range of vacations. These can include sophisticated Caracas – a contemporary city that provides the added plus of a resort atmosphere with its deluxe hotels and beaches 45 minutes to the north – and the Caribbean island of Margarita, the oil-boom city of Maracaibo, the fisherman's nirvana of Mérida, the beach-rich historic city of Cumaná, the jungle village of Canaima with nearby wilderness camps, and the beautiful beaches of Los Roques and Mochima National Park.

For years Venezuela's reputation for sky-high prices was a deterrent to visitors. Happily, due to the devaluation of the Venezuelan currency, prices in Venezuela are now among the most reasonable in the world. That should entice anyone seeking a change of pace from the typical expensive large-city tour that snares most travelers to Europe or South America.

In this book, we have concentrated on the country's contrasting regions. In each area you will find a traveler's orientation, a summary of the best hotels, restaurants and nightclubs, sightseeing recommendations, and the best in shopping.

Getting to Venezuela

Chances are you will enter Venezuela by air (via **Avensa**, **Viasa**, **United** or **American**), which means you will come in at Maiquetía Airport outside of Caracas. From there you can pick up a domestic flight to your interior destination. US-Caracas airfares are quite low from New York and Miami. Package tours can cut

VENEZUELA

★ Caracas

THE GUIANAS

COLOMBIA

ECUADOR

PERU

B R A Z I L

BOLIVA

PARAGUAY

CHILE

ARGENTINA

URUGUAY

South
America

your costs even more, so check these out through your airline or travel agent. Avensa once offered an airpass for travel within Venezuela. However the recent proliferation of new domestic airlines has made air travel throughout Venezuela so inexpensive that the airpass is no longer necessary. Flights within Venezuela are generally under $100 round-trip.

Aqui Se Habla Inglés

The result of North American oil investment in Venezuela is reflected in a relatively high standard of living. A happy fact is that English is the number two language. Hotel clerks, shop managers and restaurant maitre d's often speak English. There are English-language TV and radio shows, as well as theater (though non-professional, the performers are highly regarded). Finally, the English-language daily, *The Daily Journal*, is one of Latin America's best. In short, you should feel comfortably at home.

Ready to Go

Happily, the Venezuelan government makes life easy for tourists. All you need is a valid passport and a tourist card, which will be issued by your carrier en route. You should keep your passport with you at all times.

A Monetary Note

Many years ago it seemed as if Venezuela's currency would hold fast at 4.3 bolívares to the US dollar forever. Those days are no longer. In February 1983 it was devalued to 14 bolívares to the dollar and that was just the beginning. Since then it skidded to 115 to the dollar and has been hovering just under 500 bolívares to the dollar since late 1996. How long will this last? Who knows? You should check the rate before you leave.

North Americans generally abbreviate bolívar to "B."

There is no black market or parallel market. As long as this weakness of the bolívar persists, Venezuela will be inexpensive for anyone arriving with dollars. For quick reference, here's a breakdown of Venezuelan currency:

Coins

5 céntimos
12½ céntimos (locha)
25 céntimos (medio), pronounced "medeeo"
50 céntimos (real), pronounced "rayal"
1 bolívar (1 B)
2 bolívares (2 Bs)
5 bolívares (5 Bs)

Bring about $40 in Bs with you into Venezuela to cover incidental arrival expenses.

Bills

Denominations are in 5, 10, 20, 50, 100 and 500 bolívares.

Try to avoid exchanging dollars at your hotel, which will invariably offer less for your money.

You can purchase Bs at Perera's (this international money dealer has offices in most major cities) or in the international department of any large US bank. Once in Venezuela, cambios (places where you can change money) are everywhere and all banks will offer the official exchange rate for your dollars. Shops too will gladly exchange your dollars for Bs with no discount.

The Cashless Society

Credit cards – MasterCard, American Express, Diner's Club, Visa and others – are widely used in Venezuela. You should carry traveler's checks; any will do.

Cash machines are now as commonplace in Venezuela as they are in the United States. Provided you have a PIN number, you can use your credit card or possibly even your bank card to withdraw bolívares. However, keep in mind that certain cards work only at certain banks:

❑   Banco Mercantil – MasterCard, Cirrus

❑   Banco de Venezuela – Visa, MasterCard

❑ Banco Unión – Visa, MasterCard
❑ Banco Consolidado – American Express

What to Pack

Stick to our suggestions and you will ease your life considerably. Don't – as most travelers do – overpack. Only in Caracas will you need somewhat dressy clothing, and even there you can do well on a minimum. In the other cities you will require only casual, comfortable lightweight outfits. Only in Mérida will warm clothing be necessary. These are our tips:

Women

Emphasize summer clothing. White dresses are popular from December to February. Pants are okay everywhere. Leave fur pieces home. No one wears them here. Two bathing suits and resort wear are a must for Margarita, Cumaná, Puerto La Cruz and Maracaibo. For Canaima you'll need slacks and comfortable shoes if you stay over. In Mérida you'll need a warm sweater or poncho for the trip up to Pico Espejo. A raincoat is important as well. In general, the sporty informal look predominates.

Men

Lightweight suits or jackets and slacks for evening wear. Better restaurants require jackets and ties. Bathing suits and beach wear are a must. Sport shirts and light cottons are ideal for the daytime. Travel light.

Sundries

Bring sunglasses and suntan lotions – widely available, but expensive in Venezuela. Pharmacies, plentiful in all cities, are well stocked with North American non-prescription items. Don't become a walking drugstore. US cigarettes and pipe tobacco are expensive. Bring your own poison or stick to local brands.

Luggage

You are allowed two suitcases and there's no reason to exceed that. One 26-inch bag per adult plus a small tote bag for cameras and such should do nicely.

Laundry

In most better hotels, laundry and valet service is fine. On a short trip, wash-and-wear is more convenient.

Hotels in Venezuela

Venezuela has many fine hotels, from deluxe down to basic hostelries. They are rated by the government on a one- to five-star scale. Prices are in tandem with their rating. Only five-star hotels can charge any rate they want, although by international standards the rates are low. Most are in the four- and three-star range, all of them clean, comfortable and private.

Our price scale is designed to give you a ballpark figure to plan with, based on the price for a double room. Single rooms are 20% less.

The Alive Scale

Deluxe	$125+
Expensive	$60
Moderate	$40
Inexpensive	$25 or less

Venezuelan Foods

Most traditional dishes of Venezuela have been adopted from Spanish foods. They lean to sharp tangy sauces – not as hot as in Mexico but sample before you plunge. Shrimp, lobster, beef and chicken are extremely popular; but most menus are extensive and you will find virtually any kind of food you get an urge for.

Ever have an avocado stuffed with shrimp or lobster? Or a shellfish casserole in a piquant creole sauce? You are in for an unusual gustatory experience. While certain foods are popular throughout Venezuela, every region adds a nuance. And there are many regions, styles and mini-cultures within Venezuela. But there is one dish that stands out everywhere: the *hallaca* – small pieces of pork, chicken, or beef, seasoned with olives, raisins, onions, and garlic rolled into a layer of corn dough and wrapped with plantain leaves. Corn bread *arepas* are also common throughout the country.

Venezuelans usually dine late in the evening, well after 8 pm. Lunch, served between noon and 3 pm, is usually a heavy meal. Tea at 5 pm is a local cusom that will hold you until the late dinner.

There are many regional specialties (they will be covered in corresponding chapters). Here is a brief survey to give you an idea of Venezuelan cuisine.

❐ The State of Zulia, whose capital is Maracaibo, specializes in meats cooked with coconut, chiefly rabbit. Fish dishes are especially popular since Lake Maracaibo is a fine source of fresh water fish. *Tostones*, round slices of green plantain, are also common to the region.

❐ In Caracas, international food dominates, but local cuisine is still popular. *Pabellón Criollo*, a mélange of shredded meat, black beans, boiled rice and fried slices of ripe plantain, is the most common dish.

❐ Since the trout of the Andean region is considered among the best in the world, it is not surprising that trout dishes are featured on restaurant menus in Mérida. Also popular is a dish called *mojos*, scrambled eggs with milk, tomato and Tabasco.

❐ Fish dishes are also quite popular in the northeast along the Caribbean. Be sure to sample local favorites such as *cuajao*, a dish made with mullet or loach roe, and *cuajao de chucho*, a similar dish. *Cachapas*, thin tortillas made with young corn, salt and sugar, are sold along the road between Puerto La Cruz and Cumaná.

Most restaurants charge a "cubierto," or cover, for bread, rolls, butter and other extras.

A 10% gratuity will be added to your bill. If service has been satisfactory, add another 10%. Venezuelans tend to give the waiter the benefit of the doubt.

Appetizers

A true local delicacy is *aguacate relleno con camarones*, avocado stuffed with shrimp and served with a sauce similar to Russian dressing. You can have your avocado stuffed with crabmeat or lobster as well. Tangier is *ceviche de mero*, uncooked grouper marinated in a vinaigrette or lime sauce. Often shrimp (camarones) are substituted. If you're partial to smoked salmon order *salmón ahumado*.

Soups

One of the most traditional dishes is a thick vegetable soup called *sancocho*, which is usually served as a main course and prepared with either fish or meat.

Main Courses

An extremely tender steak called *punta trasera* is a constant in most local restaurants. Sample it. Argentine-style steaks served with a hot red pepper relish and a cool green pepper relish are popular too. Common designations include *lomito, churrasco* and *baby bife*.

Turning from beef to seafood, there is a remarkable casserole, *cazuela de mariscos*, a perfectly baked blend of clams, mussels, lobster, shrimp and squid served in a hot creole sauce. Then too there is the ubiquitous *paella Valenciana* comprised of chicken, lobster, shrimp, clams, mussels, olives and saffron rice. Moreover, you can order *arroz con mariscos* (a mixed seafood platter with Spanish rice). Since seafood is extremely popular, here is a capsule vocabulary:

❑ Langosta – lobster served in many different ways

❑ Langostinos – large shrimp (crayfish)

❑ Cangrejo – crab

- Pargo – red snapper
- Mero – grouper
- Trucha – trout
- Lenguado – sole
- Mejillones – mussels
- Róbalo - sea bass

Desserts

Venezuelans adore strawberries and most restaurant menus include one strawberry dish, typically *fresas con crema*, strawberries with whipped cream. Guava is in demand too, and one popular dessert is *cascos de guayaba con queso crema* (red guava fruit in syrup with cream cheese). Ice cream is very good indeed and the *flan*, or caramel custard, is worth sampling.

Cocktails

Rum is the king of hard liquor here, and little wonder since Venezuela produces some of the world's best. Try *ponche crema*, an egg nog rum drink, a tall rum punch, *cuba libre*, or the daiquiris. Scotch, bourbons, and blends are available at relatively high prices. Local beers are quite good. The best of the premium beers is Solera, which you may even find in your local liquor store in the States. Popular everyday beers include Polar, Caracas, and Zulia. Brahma, a popular Brazilian beer which is lighter than the local brews, has opened a distillery in Venezuela. Do not drink the tap water in Venezuela. Bottled water is readily available

How Alive Restaurant Listings Work

We've scored Venezuela for the restaurants that offer the best values in all price ranges. Categories are arranged by nationality or type of restaurant (such as French, Chinese, fast food or cafés). Our price scale is based on the cost of a four-course dinner (per person) – appetizer or soup, main dish, dessert and coffee – and includes the cover and a 10% service charge. Cocktails and wine are extra.

Credit cards are accepted at most of the restaurants we have listed.

The Alive Scale (per person)

Expensive	$40+
Moderate	$25-$35
Inexpensive	$20 or less

Shopping Tips

Prices vary markedly so it is important to comparison-shop.

If you pay cash, many shops will offer you a "des-cuento." Ask about it.

In general your best buys are native handicrafts, which range from colorful wool ruanas in Mérida to rugs woven by the Guajiro Indians of Maracaibo. Margarita is the place for pearls and ceramics. Other items of interest include modern art, wood carvings, colorful devil masks, multi-hued, handwoven hammocks and many other unusual gift ideas. Leather goods cost a fraction of what they would in North America. As one example, a good pair of ladies dress leather shoes can be purchased at Charles Jourdan for around $60. Many people from Miami fly here to shop.

Most good shops accept credit cards, including Master-Card, American Express, Diner's Club, and Visa. Store hours are generally 9 am to 7 pm, including Saturdays, but most take a noon-3 break.

Sizes (Tamaños)

Sizes here differ from North America. Rely on the comparison chart below, but try everything on first to be safe. Below, the US size is shown, followed by its corresponding size in Venezuela.

Women

Shoes *(Zapatos)*   *Dresses (Vestidos)*

4 - 34	8 - 34
4½ - 35	10 - 38
5 - 36	12 - 42
5½ - 37	14 - 44
6½ - 38	16 - 46
7½ - 39	18 - 48
8½ - 40	20 - 50

Men

Shoes *(Zapatos)*   *Suits (Trajes)*

6½ - 39	40 - 32
7½ - 40	42 - 34
8 - 41	44- 36
8½ - 42	46 - 38
9½ - 43	48 - 40
10½ - 44	50 - 42
11 - 45	52 - 44
12 - 46	54 - 46

Climate

Located just north of the equator, Venezuela is always warm. Temperatures range from quite warm at sea level to moderate in more elevated sites. Venezuela's climate is generally perfect for vacationing.

Though the weather is constant all year round, there are three distinct high tourist seasons: Easter Week, the month of August when Europeans and Venezuelans are on vacation, and Christmas. During these periods reservations are advised if you are planning to visit Margarita, Mérida and Los Roques.

Sports

Baseball is the national sport. There is a Venezuelan professional season that lasts for four months and culminates with the Caribbean Series. Several Venezuelans play, or have played, in the US major leagues, including Dave Concepción, Luis Aparicio, Andres Galaraga, Tony Armas, Manny Trillo and Luis Salazar.

In recent years basketball has experienced enormous growth in popularity and is now a close second to baseball. Virtually every major city has its own team and games are frequently sold out. Soccer, boxing and horseracing follow in popularity.

History

Venezuela is one of Columbus' many children. Of course he was an absent, even indifferent father, but nonetheless Venezuela's modern history begins with Columbus' discovery of the islands of Margarita and Cubagua in 1498. A year later, Venezuela received her name when Alonso de Ojeda and Amerigo Vespucci, sailing along Venezuela's coast, encountered the Indians of Guajira, who lived around Lake Maracaibo in the northwest region of the country. Their houses, built upon piles over the water, inspired the two explorers to call the area Venezuela, Little Venice.

Venezuela's, and indeed South America's, first settlement of Europeans was founded on the island of Cubagua a year later by Cristobal de la Guerra and Pedro Alonso Niño. They chose this site because of its abundant pearls. The two men had returned to Spain a year earlier in 1499 with 80 pounds of pearls. Upon their return to Cubagua they wasted no time in beginning a frenzy of mining.

In 1501 the cartographer Rodrigo de Bastidas mapped Venezuela's shores. He used the name Venezuela on his map, thus ensuring its permanence.

In 1520 Fray Bartolomé de las Casas began a community on the northern coast of Venezuela, near present-day Cumaná. He envisioned the creation of a small society of artisans, including Indians. It failed, but the area remained populated and a structured society.

The province of Margarita was established in 1525. In 1527 Coro, in the modern State of Falcón, was founded and leased shortly thereafter to a family of German bankers named Welser. The contract allowed the Welsers control of the area, but they had to use their own money to make the region productive. For 17 years the bankers searched the northwest region of Venezuela for gold, diamonds and valuable raw materials, pillaging the earth in their quest for wealth. In 1546 the lease was not renewed and, although the Welsers had not come up with the envisioned natural factory of riches, the region had been explored and settled.

Cubagu came to an end in 1541 because of a massive earthquake and tidal wave. The waters had been pillaged of pearls, and the Indians drowned, en masse, as they dove, day after day, for the pink treasure.

Diego de Losada founded Caracas in 1566. Eleven years later the capital moved from El Tocuyo, set up by the Germans, to Caracas.

The next 100 years saw Venezuela forming, shifting, settling and expanding. This was still its childhood, the outline of the country being continually drawn and muddled. Maracaibo was established in 1574; Venezuela's main port, La Guaira, was begun in 1589; the Andean province of Mérida was unveiled in 1622; the Archbishop of Coro moved to Caracas in 1637, beginning the trend to centralize in that city; the Viceroyalty of Nueva Granada was formed in 1739, furthering the movements toward a centralized government. And finally the Captaincy-General of Venezuela was created in 1777, linking the country's six older provinces – Margarita, Mérida, Maracaibo, Nueva Andalucia, Guayana, Trinidad (which seceded in 1802) and Venezuela – into one territory.

The first rumblings of independence were felt in 1776. Francisco de Miranda traveled to Europe to muster up support for Venezuelan independence. But it was not until 1806 that he tested his might with the Spanish. With the assistance of American volunteers, Miranda's excited swing of the sword began; it was quickly dulled by the Spanish off the coast of Ocumare de la Costa. Vengeful, the Spanish hung 10 American officers (unimaginable today) and imprisoned 50 others. Slippery Miranda made it to the State of Falcón, where he briefly flew a Venezuelan flag of his design, and revved the engine for future events.

On April 19, 1810 a renegade commission declared that Venezuela was independent from Spain and thereby catapulted the country into civil war. On July 5, 1811 Venezuela's independence was reiterated, igniting rebellions throughout the territory. Almost a year later, Caracas and its periphery was leveled by an earthquake, and the Spanish tried to advertise this as an act of God. The fighting became even more heated, with Miranda battling on the western front and several generals sweeping the Spanish away from the eastern coast. Miranda eventually lost out and was imprisoned. But, simultaneously, Simón Bolívar, Venezuela's most famous and revered citizen, was thundering toward Caracas.

Bolívar initially entered Venezuela from Colombia (then Nueva Granada) in 1813. On June 15 he issued the "War to the Death" promise from Trujillo, and on August 7 entered and took Caracas for the first time. The tide eventually turned, and on June 15, 1814

Bolívar and General Mariño's forces were almost elimi-
nated, forcing him to flee.

Bolívar

Bolívar is the secular icon of Venezuela. His
name is glorified in every city and town across
the nation, and his name is invoked far more in
Venezuela than Roosevelt, Kennedy or Washington in America. Even the currency bears his
name.

He was born in Caracas on July 24, 1783. His
short life was a chain of liberations, starting
with Colombia and continuing to Venezuela,
Ecuador, Peru and Bolivia. Although Miranda
was the initial spark for Venezuela's independence, Bolívar was the dynamite. But his
role was not only a military one. He is famous
for several publications – the "Letter from Jamaica" and "Manifest" being the best known –
containing his speeches and political ideas. It
was his dream to see Colombia, Venezuela,
Ecuador and Panama united under one central
government; it was also his dream to be its
president. He died at the age of 47 in San Pedro
Alejandino, an estate on the outskirts of Santa
Marta, Colombia.

The Spanish tried to fortify in 1815, when 15,000 troops
from Spain arrived. On September 6, Bolívar reared his
head again with the publication of his "Letter from
Jamaica," which reiterated his, and the independence
force's, demands. Twice he tried to return to the mainland, but was repelled. Margarita was made the transitory capital on May 8, 1817. In the same year Bolívar set
up a provisional government in the jungle city of Angostura (now Ciudad Bolívar).

With the shroud of peace at Angostura, work started on a constitution, and so began the final push for independence. Yet this did not come until the independence of Colombia was secured on August 7, 1819. June 24, 1821 was recognized as Venezuela's independence day, with the battle of Carabobo; but it was not entirely secure until June 24, 1823, when the last of the Spanish loyalist forces were defeated on Lake Maracaibo. In between those dates Bolívar proposed the Grand Colombian Union, which included present-day Venezuela, Colombia, Panama and Ecuador. The Union, of course, was short-lived. Venezuela broke off on May 6, 1830, naming revolutionary star José Antonio Paez her first president.

On March 24, 1854 slavery was outlawed, and in 1864 the United States of Venezuela was constituted. From 1830 to 1958 Venezuela flip-flopped between democracy and dictatorship. Venezuela's most indelible period took place under the leadership of Antonio Leocadio Guzmán, who ruled intermittently in the second half of the 19th century. His initial rise to power came on the ruinous tail of a civil war, called the Federal War. When in power he began reshaping and rebuilding the country in his secular vision. He made education free and obligatory, and fostered an atmosphere of cultural excitement. He was no democrat, more like Venezuela's Perón, and he let little interfere with his goals; civil liberties were irrelevant. His reign, though, filled Venezuela out in many ways – architecturally, educationally and culturally.

The next three successors to Guzmán paled in comparison and in 1908 the country was taken over by Cipriano Castro, who fought his way to Caracas from the Andes. Yet his military might did not transfer to government, and the country began to crack under his incompetency. Arrogance and the military kept him politically alive, but he was immediately dethroned when he left for a trip to Europe.

His successor, Juan Vicente Gómez, rejuvenated the ailing governmental structure, paid off Venezuela's debt to Europe, and kept the country neutral in WWI. Gómez's term was undeniably autocratic, and the government became bloated while the infrastructure, civil services and regional communities were starved.

Gómez ruled until his death and was replaced by General López Contreras in 1936. He brought back a touch of democracy, which was furthered by General Isaias Medina Angarita, the next president. But then came a dictator, ironically in the year 1945. Romúlo Betancourt's rule was followed by a brief period of democracy under the famous writer Romúlo Gallegos. General Marcos Pérez Jimenez, next in line, ignored civil liberties, and built up the country's infrastructure with airports, roads, and hospitals – a legacy felt today. He was punted out in 1958, and since that date Venezuela has had an uninterrupted string of freely elected presidents, with the present one, Rafael Caldera, elected for a second, although non-consecutive, term in 1994. Despite recent unrest and attempted coups, Venezuela is one of South America's strongest democracies.

The Country Today

Venezuela is a large country with a population of 20,000,000. It is divided into 20 states, the Federal District around Caracas, two territories and 72 islands. Its borders are the Atlantic Ocean and Guyana on the east, Brazil to the south, Colombia to the west and the Caribbean to the north.

The government, like that of the US, has an executive, legislative, and judicial branch. Nineteen ministries, with their ministers, make up the executive branch.

The legislative branch is comprised of 50 senators (47 elected and three ex-presidents who became permanent) and a Chamber of Deputies that has 199 elected officials. The judicial branch has a reigning supreme court and 768 lower courts.

Demographically, the population is divided into 58% of mixed race, 29% white, meaning European, 11% black, of African descent, and finally 2% native Indian. There are 75,000 North Americans living in Venezuela. The country has 17 universities and 47 colleges. There is one English-language newspaper in Caracas, *The Daily Journal*.

Although Venezuela is considered a developing country by the UN, the standard of living is noticeably middle class. In Mérida, for example, the city is steadily growing, with its white clean houses, making it look more and more like a Swiss mountain town.

Yet the rich oil years have come to an end. Once terribly expensive, Caracas is now very affordable. When the city sat in that pool of affluence, tourism was virtually non-existent. Venezuela is now a tourist magnet, with prices astoundingly low – chic four-star hotels go for $60 a night. The country has also tried to diversify its economy into aluminum, metals, iron ore, and agriculture.

Venezuela's cultural pedigree is mainly European, with its art very heavily influenced by Christianity. Native Indian arts and crafts are widely available, yet the country is dominated by European-style art. This is seen in many of its churches, both architecturally and artistically.

Music bloomed in early colonial Venezuela. A school created by Father Pedro Sojor (1739-1799) became a breeding ground for young composers. With the rising hoots of independence, the school and its composers, began to express the atmosphere in music. Many of its students saw their music as rebellious and necessary. The most notable musicians of the time were José Angel Lamas, Cayetano Carreño, Mateo Villa Lobos and Juan Manuel Olivares.

Venezuela's most famous writer is Romúlo Gallegos, author of *Doña Barbara* (1929), *Cantaclaro* (1934) and *Canaima* (1935).

Geography

The country is divided geographically into the **coastal region**, which runs for a total of 300 miles; the **Andean region** of snow-capped peaks and temperate, deciduous forests; the tropical **Maracaibo region**; and finally the **southern region**, called the Gayana Shield. The Shield is made up of the State of Bolívar and the Amazonas Federal Territory. It is savannah and rain forest. The savannahs are great plains dotted with hulking mesas. The rain forests shelter most of Venezuela's wild animals, along with some untouched tribes.

The climate, nationwide, varies little, with the average temperature remaining around 80°. The two exceptions are Mérida, with minimal temperatures between 60 and 65°, and Caracas, with a slightly higher range of 65-70°. The rainy season is from June to November, with the dry season running from December to May.

Only 2½ hours from Miami, this cosmopolitan city of sophisticated women, chic boutiques and super highways rivals New York and Paris in its restaurants, shops and elegance. And all this within 45 minutes of superb beaches that are open the year round. Since this city of almost four million is just slightly north of the equator, the seasons hardly change – it seems like early summer much of the year – and with 3,000 feet of elevation, breezes dissipate the warmth of the afternoons.

Venezuela

Introduction to Caracas

Your first glimpse of Venezuela in all likelihood will be through the window of your jet as it approaches the modern Simón Bolívar International Airport. The airport is in the coastal town of Maiquetía on the Caribbean (2½ air hours from Miami and 30 minutes by cab from Caracas).

On the flight you will be given a tourist card that must be filled in. After claiming your baggage, head toward customs, which is perfunctory – but you must save the part of the tourist card that they hand back to you! It would be wise to leave the card in your passport. It can also serve as identification if necessary.

Those arriving by ship will land at the adjacent town of La Guaira, Venezuela's major port.

The airport is in mint condition, air-conditioned, and streamlined. Unlike JFK in New York, which can make you dizzy with its complications, Simón Bolívar Airport is laid out well. Baggage claim is never more than five minutes from the gate, all on the same level; and once you're out of customs, tourist services are immediately visible. Corpoturismo, Venezuela's tourist corporation, is marked by an orange-and-black sign. They will provide information on hotels, restaurants, trips, prices, crime, and other concerns; literature is available. To the right of Corpoturismo is a booth for hotel reservations, and next to that are several car rental outlets – Hertz, Avis, etc.

There are several cambios where you can change money. Rates are fairly comparable. However, lines may be long and sometimes they run out of money early in the day. It may be wise to change some money before you depart for the cab ride to your hotel. Also, exchange rates tend to be least favorable in the hotels. However, many cabs will accept dollars if you don't have bolívares.

If you are not staying in Caracas and are immediately leaving for another destination, there are free shuttle buses to the domestic terminal. They park immediately outside the terminal. Otherwise it's only a three-minute walk if your load is light. Exit the terminal and turn right.

Getting to Your Hotel

Two options exist for getting to the city. A *por puesto*, a public transportation van or bus, will take you to Parque Central, near the Hilton Hotel, for $2. There are a couple of metro stops along the way. A cab into the city will cost around $25; be sure to agree upon the fare before setting out.

Once outside the airport, the first charge of balmy air reminds you that you are now on the Caribbean. Were you in a bathing suit, you would be rejoicing. The taxi ride to Caracas is about 30 minutes, and it is a climb.

The ranchitos have been carved out of the mountains that encircle Caracas.

Caracas sits in a valley surrounded on the north and south by towering peaks. The highest, Mt. Avila, is on the north side of the city. A national park, it is a popular weekend retreat for hikers and nature lovers. A cable car, when operating, will put you on top in 15 minutes. The drive to Caracas is quite scenic, with green mountainsides eventually replacing the Caribbean Sea. As you near the city, cool breezes will provide some relief from the humidity and the small shacks and houses (*ranchitos*) dotting the mountainsides will grow more numerous. You'll drive through three tunnels before reaching Caracas.

Suddenly, as you come through the third tunnel, Caracas unfolds before you, a sea of tall, white high-rises and glass towers. It is both startling and spectacular to have just a split second separating darkness from a high-rise city. You are in the western section, El Silencio, the oldest and most commercial part of Caracas. As you head east,the city becomes more residential.

To the Beaches

Most beach hotels are within 20 minutes of the airport. The landing field is on the Caribbean, as are these hostelries. Look to your left as the cab speeds along the main beach road, Av Playa, and you'll to see the waves gently beating against the shore. The residents are more casually dressed and the pace more relaxed than in Caracas. This is the time for an attitude adjustment, where you will quickly find your approach to life becoming more casual. If you need to catch an early flight out of Caracas, you should consider staying at one of the hotels in this area. This area, known as El Litoral, "the Coast," is discussed in detail in a later chapter.

Orientation

Coming from the airport via the Autopista La Guaira-Caracas, your first sight is the El Silencio District, one of Caracas' oldest areas, with narrow streets and many government buildings. From here you will proceed along one of the three main east-west thoroughfares that cut through the city.

Neighborhood districts *(urbanizaciones)* change rapidly and even radically within a few blocks as you proceed through the city. Within minutes you leave El Silencio behind and enter El Conde, followed by San Bernadino and then Mariperez, each distinctive. To get to know Caracas quickly, keep in mind two facts:

The Cota Mil, the newest of the three thoroughfares, runs along the northernmost sections and because of the elevation offers a stunning view. Libertador runs through the center, while Autopista del Este serves the southernmost districts.

❑ First – Caraqueños rarely use street numbers. Rather, the location of a restaurant or hotel is noted in terms of the district and the street, sometimes the nearest intersecting avenue and occasionally the building. Therefore, the Hotel Avila address is Av Jorge Washington, San Bernadino. Period. Cabbies have no trouble at all with this system.

❑ Second – Each neighborhood district has one main street, invariably called "Avenida Principal," which is followed by the name of the district. Thus, La Estancia, a recommended restaurant, is located on the Avenida Principal de La Castellana, while the Hotel Tamanaco is on Avenida Principal de Las Mercedes. By the way, when you see a street designated "La Calle," that means it is "First *(primera)* Street" and usually is the initial street crossing the Avenida Principal.

Below, we have noted some important *urbanizaciones* for quick reference (west to east):

El Silencio

We recommend a walking tour through this area in the "Sun up to Sundown" section.

Important historically, this district is the first you see as you enter the city on your trip from Simón Bolívar International Airport. The area's landmark is El Centro Simón Bolívar, a large government office complex marked by twin 32-story towers that dominate the skyline nearby. The main plaza, Plaza Bolívar, is flanked by the gold-domed Congress Building, El Capitolio, and the Cathedral of Caracas.

El Conde

East of El Silencio, this district too is part of the city's colonial history. Heavily commercial, El Conde is home to the Caracas Hilton Hotel, the Museums of Art and Natural Sciences, a large amusement park and the Nuevo Circo Bull Ring.

Parque Central

This urban renewal area features some of the city's finest apartment houses (mostly condominiums), shopping centers, and the Museum of Contemporary Art. Located near the Hilton, "Central Park" is home to the Teatro Teresa Carreño, one of the most incredible cultural centers in the world, and the main office of the government tourist office.

San Bernadino

North of El Conde, and largely residential, San Bernadino is home to the Hotel Avila and the Colonial Art Museum. The higher area is lovely and is home to many Jewish families.

Mariperez

Just east and north of San Bernadino is this blue collar residential area. The cable car (Teleférico) terminal is here.

Plaza Venezuela

While not technically a district, Plaza Venezuela is important enough for separate mention. The plaza, which is the beginning of the Sabana Grande shopping district (below), houses many nightclubs, restaurants, movie theaters, and two of the city's tallest office towers, the Edificio Phelps and Centro Capriles.

Sabana Grande

Heading East from Plaza Venezuela, you come upon the city's true center, the large and bustling Sabana Grande shopping district. Shop after shop lines the main thoroughfare, Avenida Abraham Lincoln, known as Calle Real de Sabana Grande. Many of our recommended restaurants and nightclubs are here. The hotels Tampa, Kings Inn and Savoy are located in this section. Keep in mind when looking for a hotel, that

There is a Metro stop at each end for the subway that runs below.

this area tends to be noisier than some of the other districts.

Bello Monte

This tiny district on the southern edge of the Sabana Grande area is noteworthy as the home of the first-class Hotel Las Américas, and the former home of Sears, once considered a fine shop in Latin America.

Chacaíto

Bordering Sabana Grande on its east side, Chacaíto is home to the Centro Comercial Chacaíto, one of the city's poshest shopping centers, with fashionable boutiques, art galleries, outdoor cafés and nightclubs.

El Rosal

Just southeast of Chacaíto is El Rosal, home to splendid restaurants and popular night spots, as well as shops and banks.

Las Mercedes

Across the river just south of El Rosal is the North American-style residential area of Las Mercedes. Lined with lovely homes and fine shops and restaurants, the area's landmark is the magnificent Hotel Tamanaco on the Avenida Principal de las Mercedes, as well as the Hotel Paseo Las Mercedes and a shopping center. There is even an English-language theater group in nearby San Román.

Country Club District

This section, east of Chacaíto, is where wealthy Caraqueños reside in eye-popping mansions. The hub is an exclusive club called, appropriately, The Country Club.

La Castellana

Heading East from the Country Club this upper middle class residential area also houses a number of recommended restaurants and discotheques. Stop at the fountain in the plaza for a relaxing moment if you're in the neighborhood.

Altamira

Within walking distance of La Castellana is this section of modern high-rise apartment houses, fashionable nightclubs, Cleopatra's Obelisk, and a lovely park and fountain. The Hotel Continental Altamira is a few blocks north.

Los Palos Grandes

A short stroll from Altamira, the modern shopping center here was once the home of a large Sears.

Ciudad Universitaria

South of the Plaza Venezuela is the huge 500-acre University City campus, which embraces mammoth *futbol* (soccer) and *beisbol* stadiums, as well as the botanical gardens.

Two other areas of Caracas worth knowing are La Florida north of Sabana Grande, and Chacao, just before Altamira, where there is a twice-weekly flea market.

Getting Around Town

Cabs

Cabs are cheap, plentiful and most have meters. It should never cost more than $2-$3 dollars to get from one point to another within the city, and a bit more for the suburbs, beaches and airport. In fact, most rides within city limits will rarely be more than a dollar. A trip from El Conde to Altamira, not short, will be just about a dollar. Always negotiate the fare with the driver before getting into the cab, regardless of whether it has a meter or not. Cabs are not identified

Always agree on the fare before getting into the cab.

by color, but only by the exterior top light, reading "taxi" or "libre."

Por Puestos

Por puestos (literally translated, "by the place") are small buses that travel along fixed routes. A *por puesto* is identified by a sign in the front window indicating the last stop on its route. Routes include all major thoroughfares, and the fare is usually under 25¢.

Buses

Buses are also about 25¢ and routes are marked on the side of the bus. The bus sytem is extensive.

The Subway

Caracas has a fine subway system, El Metro. Built in 1976 by the French (obvious immediately if you have ever been to Paris), the subway system is eventually supposed to cover 51 stations and 32 miles. At this point it is much more abbreviated. The subway is surprisingly efficient and regular. It will seem even more so if you're coming from New York. It covers the main tourist sights of Caracas, from Bellas Artes, which is the stop for the Hilton, to Altamira and Parque del Este, and even further east.

The entrances are marked by a big orange M, and the ticket system is the same as the Parisian one. You can buy a ticket either from a manned booth or from a ticket machine that takes only exact change. No ride is more than 25¢. The yellow ticket that you receive is necessary to get in and to exit. You put it in the slot on the turnstile. When you enter it flips back out to you; when you exit it does not.

An arrow on a wall map will mark the station you are at, and all you have to do is find the direction of your destination. There are two lines, but Line One is probably all you will use. It travels east to west and is marked in orange. It covers the area from Propatria to Parque del Este.

The metro runs from 5 am to 11 pm and should be avoided late at night. The cars are clean, brand new and air-conditioned. Even if you don't need to use the metro, try it.

Following are the main stops:

□ Capitolio Station

In the center of Caracas, the Capitolio station is within walking distance of most monuments and historic sites, including the National Library, the Plaza Bolívar and the Cathedral, the Municipal Council and the Casa Amarilla, office of the Foreign Ministry. Both the National and Municipal Theaters are also nearby.

□ La Hoyada Station

From the Hoyada Station you'll step out into colonial Caracas. Nearby are the Casa Natal (birthplace of Simón Bolívar) and the Museo Boliviano.

□ Parque Carabobo Station

Just outside the station is the well-known fountain by Francisco de Narvaez, the design strongly influenced by native art. Parque Carabobo is the traditional meeting place for visitors from the provinces. The Plaza de la Candelaría, home to much of Caracas's Iberian population and, of course, numerous Spanish restaurants and cafés, is within walking distance.

□ Parque Bellas Artes Station

This station is in the midst of what is aptly known as "the cultural triangle." Not only is the Bellas Artes Museum here, so are the Museum of Contemporary Art, the Audiovisual Museum, the National Gallery, the Ateneo de Caracas and the Teresa Carreño Theater.

Caracas Metro

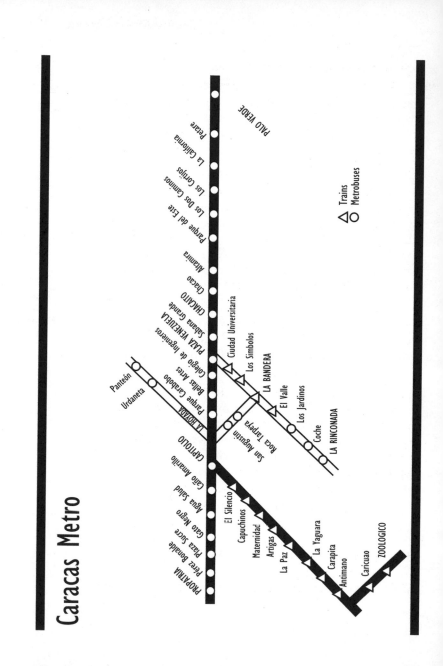

PALO VERDE

Petare
La California
Los Cortijos
Los Dos Caminos
Parque del Este
Altamira
Chacao
CHACAÍTO
Sabana Grande
PLAZA VENEZUELA
Colegio de Ingenieros
Bellas Artes
Parque Carabobo
LA HOYADA
CAPITOLIO
Gato Amarillo
Agua Salud
Gato Negro
Plaza Sucre
Pérez Bonalde
PROPATRIA

Ciudad Universitaria
Los Símbolos
LA BANDERA
El Valle
Los Jardines
Coche
LA RINCONADA

Panteón
Urdaneta

San Agustín
Roca Tarpeya

El Silencio
Capuchinos
Maternidad
Artigas
La Paz
La Yaguara
Carapita
Antímano
Caricuao
ZOOLOGICO

△ Trains
○ Metrobuses

❐ Plaza Venezuela Station

The Plaza Venezuela is a favorite meeting and studying place among students of the Central University. The Botanical Gardens and Sabana Grande are nearby.

❐ Sabana Grande Station

A great shopping stop, this station is located in the heart of the city's commercial district.

❐ Parque Del Este Station

Away from the noise and traffic of the city, this stop lets you off at the beautiful Romúlo Betancourt Park, better known as Parque del Este.

A Capsule History

Caracas was officially founded on July 25, 1567 by Diego de Losada. Its original name was Santiago de León de Caracas. The baby city was just a 25-block compound between the Catuche, Caroata and Guaire Rivers; it was home to only 60 families at the time.

Caracas was declared the capital of Venezuela in 1731, yet it was still a small city. In 1807 there were only 47,000 people, and the city was quiet. It wasn't until the end of the 19th century that the city began to grow. That growth was spurred by President Guzmán. He expanded its districts, adding schools, churches and theaters.

Around 1930, with oil's first discovery, Caracas took another leap forward. It began to modernize. Since World War II the city has grown exponentially. Thirty years ago there were 400,000 people. Now there are close to 4,000,000 people in the city, pushing its capacity to the limit, if not beyond.

Caracas is the capital of Venezuela and houses the important Federal Government buildings.

Caracas is part of the Distrito Federal (Federal District), which also includes the coastal region. Yet the city has now spilled over into the Sucre District of the neighboring State of Miranda.

Caracas Hotels

As befits a cosmopolitan city, Caracas has an abundance of good first-class hotels. But for purposes of this guide we have selected what we consider the best 20 or so hotels in Caracas. In our chapter on the beach area, we have included other recommendations. Many of you are coming to Caracas as part of a package tour that includes a hotel. Otherwise, read this and the beach chapter carefully to help you decide whether you wish to bed down in Caracas and make day trips to the beaches or split your visit between the city and the beach.

Most hotels are in the three- and four-star range – all of them clean, comfortable and private. The majority are more than just functional; they are quite nice. Recommended hotels are spread throughout the city.

As with all hotels in Venezuela, star ratings determine the prices. Only five-star hotels are free from this system and can charge any rate they want, though all rates are generally low.

Prices

Our price scale is designed to give you a ballpark figure to plan with. It is based on the price for a double room. Single rooms are 20% less.

The Alive Scale

Deluxe	$125+
Expensive	$60
Moderate	$40
Inexpensive	$25 or less

Caracas Hilton ☆☆☆☆☆
Av Libertador Sur, 25
(El Conde Section)
905 rooms, 20 suites, pool and tennis courts
☎ 503-5000
Fax 503-5003
US 800-HILTONS
Deluxe

The elegant Caracas Hilton has become a mecca for prominent international personalities in business, entertainment, the arts and Venezuelan society. Its convenient location, only a 10-minute drive from the shopping and business district and across the street from the city's major museums and cultural center, is attractive. The Caracas Hilton is a unique combination of cosmopolitan city hotel with good resort facilities, two adjacent swimming pools and terrace café, tennis court, and health club. La Rotisserie, its elegant restaurant which recreates the dining room of a Spanish hacienda, has repeatedly won the highest award for the best hotel restaurant in Venezuela since the hotel opened.

A fabulous urban mall, called Parque Central, is next to the Hilton, with shops, restaurants, the Museum of Contemporary Art and one of the most modern concert halls in S. America, the Teatro Teresa Carreño.

Be sure to try the Danish pastries and croissants in the hotel's Los Caobos coffee shop. On the premises, other facilities include a beauty salon and barber shop, gym, car rental, florist, photo shop, boutique, newsstand, bank and airline office. Handy for the business traveler is a secretarial service.

The Caracas Hilton is the nexus for activity in the El Conde/Parque Central area of Caracas. Identifiable all over the city by its tall white tower, its opulent lobby is marble. It is also busy, with a stream of people pacing the central hallway en route to any of several shops, the hotel's several restaurants, the pool, the bookstore, or merely criss-crossing between the two towers.

The rooms are plush and large. There is a minibar in each, along with in-room movies, direct dial telephones, 24-hour room service, and central air-conditioning. The majority of the rooms have spectacular views of the city.

Suites are large, roomy and homey, with kitchens, refrigerators and two bathrooms in each. The Presidential Suite is a majestic duplex.

The higher-priced executive floors are on the 22-29th floors of the new tower.

For those staying on the executive floors, a complimentary breakfast of coffee, tea, refreshments and sweets accompanied by a selection of international and local newspapers, magazines and television, is served between 6:30 and 11 am on the 22nd floor. There is a large conference room on the executive floors, and the hotel provides telex, fax and secretarial services.

The Hotel Tamanaco ☆☆☆☆☆
Av Principal de las Mercedes
(Las Mercedes District)
600 rooms, tennis courts, large pool
☎ 909-7111
Fax 909-7116
Deluxe

This is a true luxury resort hotel that still retains the flavor of Venezuela, part of the Inter-Continental chain and located in one of the city's poshest areas. Reminiscent of elegant hostelries in the Caribbean Islands, the Tamanaco is considered by many seasoned South American travelers to be the premier hotel, not only of Caracas, but of all South America. It is home to Le Gourmet, a first-class restaurant overlooking the city, La Brasserie, a large American-style coffee shop, several bars with phenomenal views of the city and a renowned nightclub, La Boite, where big-name stars have appeared, as well as banquet-convention rooms for 10 to 2,000 persons.

Virtually a small city unto itself, the Tamanaco is also home to a bank, beauty shop, boutique, giftshops, a branch of H. Stern, airline offices, Hertz Rent-a-Car, a cable office, a sauna and health club, and a bookshop that carries English-language periodicals, including *The New York Times*, *Newsweek* and *Time*.

Activities are available around the large pool, which also contains a children's area. A good value is the combination sauna, massage, and health club. Cocktails at sundown on the terrace of the El Punto (off the lobby) or the Cacique Bar overlooking the city are highly recommended. Located in the hilly Las Mercedes section where many North Americans live, the Tamanaco's views are spectacular.

Even if you are not a guest, hop a cab and stop in for a drink. Reservations can be made here for Inter-Continental hotels in Maracaibo, Guayana, Valencia, and elsewhere around the world.

Eurobuilding Caracas Hotel ☆☆☆☆☆
Calle La Guairita
(Chuao District)
473 rooms – main building; 180 suites – suite building
2 pools, tennis, spa
☎ 902-1111 or 902-2013
Fax 902-2189
Deluxe
From conception to completion and operation, the Eurobuilding Hotel was created to offer the ultimate in service, comfort and excellence. Looking out at Mt. Avila on one side and the skyline of Caracas on the other, this hotel is a welcome addition to the city.

Ideally located, the magnificent Eurobuilding Caracas offers everything for a complete vacation or business stay; it has two pools, tennis courts, a spa, a gym, panoramic elevators, and Carrara marble walls and floors. Varied dining options include Casandra, a gourmet restaurant offering Spanish nouvelle cuisine; Verde Lecho, a health food/vegetarian restaurant; and the Jardin de Cristal coffee shop. Or, if you don't want to miss a minute of that delicious Caribbean sun, you can dine in your swimsuit at Sol y Sombra, the poolside snack bar or have lunch at Il Forno, a pizzeria not far from the pool.

Rooms are tastefully decorated and feature built-in hairdryers, minibars and individual safety deposit boxes that permit guests to set their own combinations. Double-thick windows keep out street noises and provide quiet repose. Thoughtful extras include afternoon tea and pastries, a cocktail lounge and an executive bar.

For those guests interested in shopping – welcome to heaven. You are near the finest shopping center complex in Caracas, the Centro Ciudad Comercial Tamanaco (C.C.C.T.), featuring hundreds of shops and boutiques. On the premises is a good English-language bookshop and a host of other stores.

The service staff has been specially selected. Add to this an internationally trained team of management experts and you have all the ingredients for a perfect vacation or business trip.

Residencias Anauco Hilton ☆☆☆☆
Parque Central
(El Conde Section)
317 units, 44 floors
☎ 573-4111, 573-5702
Fax 573-7724
Expensive

A unique sister to the Caracas Hilton, the Anauco Hilton is a hotel for long-term residential stays, and is designed for large families or large groups. Doubling as a residence for Venezuelans, the atmosphere is much more like that of an apartment building than a hotel. Even more than the Hilton, the Anauco Hilton's long broad-shouldered profile is identifiable from most points in the city. Rooms range from studios to four-bedroom units, all with private baths and refrigerators (most have kitchens also).

The hotel is part of Parque Central, a sprawling urban complex that includes shops, restaurants, museums and a concert hall. The mall is under the hotel, and Hilton International runs several of the restaurants in the mall: La Canoa, La Pergola, and a snackbar.

An ideal choice for families or for long stays.

It is connected by a plaza to the Caracas Hilton and all facilities there are available for Anauco residents. A nice, more family-oriented stay is what the Anauco provides, but with all the trimmings of hotel excitement and opulence.

Hotel CCT ☆☆☆☆☆
Centro Ciudad Comercial Tamanaco
80 rooms, 122 suites; pool; tennis
☎ 959-0611
Fax 959-6697
Deluxe
Located in Caracas' best shopping center, this Best Western hotel is a hub of activity. A triangular gray structure, it features suites geared toward business people. The hotel has an exceptional conference center, with a private entrance, private access to its restaurants, soundproof walls, recording equipment, orchestra, telex and photocopy machines, and secretarial services.

Hotel Paseo Las Mercedes ☆☆☆☆
Av Principal de Las Mercedes
(Las Mercedes District)
200 rooms; pool
☎ 910-033
Fax 993-0341
Expensive
Formerly the Holiday Inn, the Paseo Las Mercedes is among the finest of the city's four-star hotels. Connected to the Paseo Las Mercedes shopping mall, the

hotel is smaller but no less comfortable or elegant than some of the five-stars. The rooms are spacious, and air-conditioned. There are several restaurants, a piano bar with occasional live music and a swimming pool. Soda machines are located on each floor.

The Hotel Avila ☆☆☆☆
Av Jorge Washington (San Bernadino District)
120 rooms, 4 floors; pool
☎ 515-119; Fax 523-121
Expensive

On 14 acres of land, the most relaxing hotel in town.

The relatively small Avila, founded by Nelson Rockefeller, offers one hard-to-match advantage – its natural setting. Situated high above the city amid 14 acres of trees, subtropical flowers and plants, this exquisite hotel is, in our opinion, the most thoroughly relaxing place to stay in Caracas. Early in the morning or at dusk, you can stroll through the grounds, marveling at the birds, mango trees, and ever-changing flowers. The modest pool is surrounded by beach chairs and a lawn perfect for sunning. You can enjoy breakfast and lunch at poolside. The absence of air-conditioning is no problem since evenings are always breezy and the nights are delightful for sleeping. Most rooms are terraced and face the pool. Furnishings are in charming Spanish colonial style with rich dark woods and wrought iron dominating. The ubiquitous TV set is standard, of course. A bookstore is off the lobby (English-language periodicals are sold). You will need a taxi to get around.

Lincoln Suites ☆☆☆☆
Av Francisco Solano
(Sabana Grande)
128 rooms
☎ 762-8575
Fax 762-5503
Expensive

Few hotels in Caracas can boast of a better location than Lincoln Suites. Nightclubs, restaurants and shopping are all within walking distance. And there's a metro stop nearby. Rooms are spacious and tastefully furnished. Restaurants, bar, beauty salon and a drugstore are on the premises. Very popular with business travelers.

Aventura Caracas ☆☆☆☆
Av Francisco Fajardo
(San Bernardino District)
93 rooms
☎ 514-844
Fax 519-186
Deluxe - Expensive
A hotel almost strictly for business people, the Aventura Caracas has four conference rooms, executive center, bar and restaurant, spa, swimming pool, English-language television stations, air-conditioning and two presidential suites.

A good value hotel located near the Avila Hotel and cable car terminal. But if you want to be close to the center of the city, rule the Aventura out.

Hotel Continental Altamira ☆☆☆
Av San Juan Bosco
(Altamira District)
Pool
☎ 261-6019
Fax 262-2163
Moderate
With super-modern furnishings and decor, this hotel is located near the nightlife district of Altamira, a desirable feature for nightowls. Appropriately, a prime draw is My Piano Bar, a delightful cocktail nook that pulls many Caraqueños as well as Continental guests. And for overcoming that morning-after hangover, the

Among the newer hotels in Caracas, the Continental resembles a luxury terraced apartment house more than a hotel. Most rooms are small suites.

pool and deck to the rear are ideal. We are partial to terraces and the Altamira has one for every room. That is comfort indeed.

Hotel Crillon ☆☆☆
Av Libertador & Av Las Acacias
(Sabana Grande District)
80 rooms, 13 floors
☎ 761-4411
Fax 761-6911
Expensive

For travelers who prefer roominess or who like to entertain in their hotel rooms, the plush Crillon is perfect. Most accommodations are two-room suites, complete with carpeting, refrigerator, couch, TV and terrace. Interestingly, each suite is different in decor and colors. Some are furnished in neo-Danish, while others are in more traditional style. In all rooms, the accent is on comfort. A couple of blocks away is the Sabana Grande shopping district. Since the hotel is near a main thoroughfare, try to avoid lower front rooms, opting instead for the quieter upper rear suites.

Hotel Tampa ☆☆☆
Av Francisco Solano Lopez No. 9
(Sabana Grande District)
135 rooms, 8 floors
☎ 762-3722
Fax 762-3771
Moderate

A clean, comfortable and pretty hotel, with more of a motel look. Once again, in the Sabana Grande area, the hotel is in the center ring of activity in Caracas. It is also a great base for exploring the many discos and bars in the area. The hotel has a restaurant and bar.

Hotel Savoy ☆☆☆
2a Av de las Delicias de Sabana Grande
(Sabana Grande District)
100 rooms
☎ 762-1971
Fax 762-2792
Moderate
The best value in Caracas is probably the Savoy, which is ideally located near the Centro Comercial Chacaíto. Rates are low. While the rooms are small, they are neat and clean, and some come with terrace, private bath (as do all our selections), wall-to-wall carpeting and piped-in music. The restaurant and bar are more than adequate. You should have a comfortable stay here.

Hotel Caracas Cumberland ☆☆☆
2a Av de las Delicias
(Sabana Grande District)
☎ 762-6606
Fax 762-5549
Moderate
Just steps from the Sabana Grande metro stop, the Cumberland is conveniently located in the heart of downtown Caracas. It caters primarily to business travelers, offering both suites with kitchenettes and jacuzzi and standard rooms, as well as secretarial services. Modern furnishings make this a fine downtown choice.

Hotel El Condor ☆☆☆
3a Av Las Delicias
(Sabana Grande District)
73 rooms
☎ 762-9911
Fax 762-8621
Inexpensive
A stocky brick building in the shopping area, the Condor is a deal. With a glassy neon look, the rooms are

large, and fitted with leather furniture. A restaurant and bar complement conference space for 30.

Hotel Las Américas ☆☆☆

Great for walkers, Las Américas caters to businessmen, who find the location convenient and the rates right.

Calle Los Cerritos
(Bello Monte District)
72 rooms, 7 floors
Small pool
☎ 951-7596
Fax 951-1727
Moderate

If you are a walker, Las Américas is for you. Ideally located in the geographic center of Caracas, Las Américas provides a focal point for sightseeing on foot, by *por puesto* or even bus. Rooms are small but adequate, with acceptable furnishings. The rooftop pool offers a pleasant interlude and a good view of Caracas. Try the poolside bar and restaurant. Nights are quiet since the hotel is not on a major traffic street.

Plaza Catedral Hotel ☆☆☆

Boulevard Plaza Bolívar
75 rooms
☎ 564-2111
Fax 564-1797
Inexpensive

Smack in the center of the financial and historical area, the hotel adopts its style from its colonial past. The colonial atmosphere is authentic. Its restaurant overlooks the Plaza Bolívar and serves international food.

King's Inn Hotel ☆☆☆

Calle Olimpio
(Sabana Grande District)
60 rooms, 6 floors
☎ 782-7033, 782-7532
Moderate

Small, informal and reasonably priced, this offers modest carpeted rooms that represent good value. All rooms are air-conditioned and have TV, along with piped-in music. There is free parking for guests. Location is convenient to the busy Sabana Grande District, where you will probably do most of your shopping.

A Couple of Residential Hotels

More like residences than hotels, these are fine for families or for longer stays

Hotel Residencia Montserrat
Av Avila Sur Altamira
(Altamira)
☎ 263-3533
Fax 261-1394
Moderate
In the nice Altamira district, this is a good comfortable place if you're staying for a week or more.

Hotel La Floresta ☆☆☆
Av Avila Sur Plaza Altamira
(Altamira)
☎ 263-1955
Fax 262-1243
Moderate
Like the Montserrat, this hotel is geared more for long-term stays than overnight visits. Fabulous location.

Some Final Choices

Hotel Sante Fe Suites Gardens ☆☆☆☆
Av José María Vargas
(Santa Fe Norte District)
100 suites
☎ 979-8355 or 979-8033
Fax 979-6580
Expensive

Excellent for families or groups, the hotel features a pool and restaurant – but the draw is the four-room suites with kitchen and three baths. Located in a quiet residential district between the Tamanaco Hotel and Prados del Este section. You can't go wrong here.

Hotel President ☆☆☆☆
Av Valparaiso
(Los Caobos District)
165 rooms
☎ 782-6622 or 708-8111
Fax 782-6458
Expensive
Near the Plaza Venezuela Metro station, the President offers large rooms with great views of Mt. Avila or the valley in which Caracas sits. The swimming pool is in constant use and the restaurant is excellent.

Caracas' Best Restaurants

Whether your taste leans to French, Italian, Spanish, Chinese, German, or Argentinean cuisine, you are only a cab ride away from a first-class restaurant. Venezuelan food can be excellent. What would life be without succulent avocados stuffed with shrimp? Or shellfish casserole in a blistering hot creole sauce? Or a delicate shredded beef dish served with black beans, white rice, and large fried plantains?

After Venezuelan-style places, Continental, Italian and steak restaurants are the most prevalent, and provide for the best meals in the city. Slightly less popular is French food. There is bound to be at least one restaurant serving every cuisine you can think of.

Colonel Sanders has invaded Venezuela with his Kentucky Fried Chicken. Pizza Hut, McDonald's and Burger King are here too.

Our price scale is based on the cost of a four-course dinner (per person) – appetizer or soup, main dish, dessert and coffee – and includes cover and a 10% service charge. Cocktails and wine are extra. Local liquors are much cheaper than imported brands. Make your choice known. Credit cards are accepted at practically all the restaurants we have listed.

The Alive Scale (per person)

Expensive	$40+
Moderate	$25-$35
Inexpensive	$20 or less

French & Continental

Caraqueños anxious to impress will escort a guest to one of the first-class French restaurants. We begin our tour of the city's best restaurants in the so-called French quarter. Our selections are elegant (coats and ties de rigueur) and reservations are a must. It's fashionable to dine after nine. Prices are high.

La Belle Epoque
French cuisine
Av Leonardo Da Vinci (Bello Monte)
Century Building
☎ 752-1342/2202
Lunch & dinner, Mon.-Fri.
Closed Sat. lunch, all day Sun.
Valet parking
Expensive
La Belle Epoque is a classic in every sense. The city's first French restaurant, it's been four decades since this Parisian gem first opened. Although chefs have come and gone, the owner's dedication to traditional French cuisine and attentive service has never waned.

Gazebo
Av Rio de Janeiro
(Las Mercedes District)
12 - 3 pm; 8 pm - 11:30 pm
Sat. dinner only
(Closed Sun.)
☎ 92-5568
Expensive
Formerly one of Caracas' finest French restaurants, Gazebo recently made the switch to Middle Eastern cuisine, though the French decor remains unchanged. Falafel, kibbe, labne and shish kabob dominate the menu, along with desserts that literally drip with

honey and pistachios. Belly dancers weave their way throughout the dining room.

Aventino
Av San Felipe
(La Castellana District)
Noon - 3 pm; 7 pm - midnight
(Closed Sun.)
☎ 32-2640
Expensive

A member of the prestigious Confrerie des Chevaliers de Tastevin.

On a magnificent private estate in the residential La Castellana District is Aventino, through whose massive doors you might expect Louis XIV to pass. Set amid flourishing trees, this restaurant is formal, with high ceilings, dark paneling, and chandeliers. The ambience is muted – you will find yourself speaking softly – and the food is appropriately splendid. The restaurant specialty is *caneton à la presse* (pressed duck), which Latin Americans travel great distances to sample. Other recommendations include the *fonds d'artichauts* (artichokes) as an appetizer; *bisque de langosta* (lobster bisque); *Chateaubriand Béarnaise*; beef filet Wellington; and for dessert, a *crêpe Suzette* or the *Georgette Romanoff* (a crêpe with cognac, Grand Marnier and almonds).

Presidents Leoni and Caldera have both signed the Gold Book (Livre d'Oro) here, reserved for those patrons ordering the pressed duck, who are also awarded a gastronomical diploma for their adventurous spirit.

The restaurant features 10,000 bottles of wine – ranging from such popular favorites as a Beaujolais to a 1966 Chateau Lafite Rothschild. Ask the owner, Dino Riocci, or his son, Giovanni, for a tour of their spectacular wine cellar. It is a grand experience.

Restaurant Lasserre
3a Av
(Los Palos Grandes)
12 - 3 pm; 6 - 12 am
(Closed Sun.)
☎ 283-3079
Reservations requested

Lasserre is a smaller version of the super-elegant Aventino. And that's no coincidence since two brothers independently operate these restaurants. Jimmy runs his own kitchen, which is fortunate for his patrons because the food is remarkable, in a city where good restaurants abound. A shade less formal than brother Dino's Aventino, this eatery features wine, cheese, and fruit carts that move up and down the aisles in the dining room. Organ music begins at 8 nightly. Jimmy wisely uses a tri-lingual (French-Spanish-English) menu. He is justly proud of his *Ostras Rockefeller* (Oysters Rockefeller served with spinach and cheese dressing); his *steak flambée poivre* (steak with pepper sauce); and his *brochette*. Jacket and tie required.

Le Petit Bistro De Jacques
Av Principal de Las Mercedes
(Las Mercedes District)
12 - 2:30 pm; 7:30 - 11:30 pm
Sat. dinner only
(Closed Sun.)
☎ 91-8108; 993-4093
Moderate
A small French bistro, this restaurant has specials each night. The service is personal and the menu is on the mirror. If this bistro doesn't make you believe you're back in Paris, nothing will.

Alfi's
Centro Comercial Chacaíto
Noon - 3 pm; 7 pm - 12 midnight
☎ 72-3509
Moderate
Well-kept and elegant, Alfi's has international food that ranges from *pato naranja* (duck in orange sauce), to *steak pimienta* (pepper steak) and *quiche Lorraine*. There is a piano bar.

Anatole
Av La Estrella (corner Av Avila)
(San Bernadino District)
Noon - 3:30 pm; 6 pm - 1 am
(Closed Sun.)
☎ 52-4353
Moderate
Considered one of Caracas' best restaurants, Anatole's offers eight private salons (one table per salon), as well as a large dining space furnished in imperial French style. Looking like a private club, the opulence verges on excess, but is tasteful.

The menu is bilingual and features *pato a la naranja* (duck with orange sauce), *frog legs Provencal*, *coq au vin*, and pork chops.

La Rotisserie
Hilton Hotel
Mon. - Fri.: Noon - 3pm; 7 pm -11 pm; dinner only on Sat.
Expensive
First-class dining is provided by the Hilton's premier restaurant. Primarily nouvelle cuisine, the menu ranges from typical French dishes to more arcane ones. Very formal. The lobby level L'Incontro, though less formal, features fine Italian cuisine. To satisfy its growing Japanese clientele, the Hilton has recently installed a sushi bar next to La Ronda jazz bar.

Venezuelan

You should savor at least one truly Venezuelan meal. This gastronomical experience cannot be duplicated in North America or Europe. Review our discussion of Venezuelan foods in the *Introduction*.

El Portón
Av Pichincha No. 18
(El Rosal District)
11 am - 1 am (daily)
☎ 952-0027
Inexpensive
Spanish-colonial in decor, El Portón is delightfully comfortable, especially the outdoor dining in the rear. Masks, hammocks and handwoven tapestries enliven the walls. High on our recommended list is *aguacate relleno con camarones* (avocadoes stuffed with shrimp). We lean to the *sancocho* (thick vegetable soup) served only on Sundays, the *pabellón* (beef, beans, rice and plantains), and the *parrillada* (a mixed meat grill). Definitely try the arepas (corn rolls), *hallacas* (leaves stuffed with chicken, pork, beef, olives and onions), the yuca (potato-like manioc vegetable) and *crema de nata* (a sour cream-like spread). For dessert, sample the *flan* or the *cascos de guayaba* (guava fruit). No music on Sundays. Weekend reservations a must. Informal dress.

El Carrizo
Av Blandín
(La Castellana District)
Noon - 2:30 pm; 7 pm - 11 pm
Sundays: noon - 11 pm
☎ 32-9370
Inexpensive
El Carrizo's rustic log cabin simplicity and superb kitchen make it the favorite of several of our Venezuelan friends. Co-owner David Gomez, a delightful Portuguese-born epicure whose English is perfect, will be pleased to order for you and you are advised to take him up on the offer. He was formerly at the Lee Hamilton steak house and now is working hard to make El Carrizo a winner. His partner Mario is also a winner. David probably will suggest a steak, perhaps *punta*

trasera (tip: this steak often is part of a daily four-course luncheon special). Steaks usually come with two sauces (*guasacaca*), mild green and red hot. *Hallacas* serve as the vegetable for most dishes. Another recommended dish is *pollo deshuesado* (boned chicken). Say hello to David for us. You will invariably see him working the spotless kitchen. Informal dress.

Don Sancho
Av Pichincha (El Rosal)
Closed Sun.
☎ 952-1028
Moderate
A local favorite for over 30 years, typical Venezuelan cuts of beef, such as *punta trasera*, *churrasco* (sirloin) and *lomito* (tenderloin) are the staple here, along with Venezuelan cheeses and salads. You won't find anything very unusual or nouvelle on the menu here – just good, solid fare.

Tarzilandia
Final Av San Juan Bosco
10a Transversal Altamira
(Altamira District)
Noon - 11 pm
Closed Mon.
☎ 261-8419
Moderate
In a jungle-like outdoor setting, the Tarzilandia owners have created an outstanding eatery that specializes in steaks. Fantastic. Sample the pepper steak. Appropriately, stuffed animals, spears, and tortoise shells adorn the rear wall of this bi-level restaurant. Late evening breezes can be cool. Be sure to bring a sweater or jacket with you. Since the restaurant is 10 blocks from the main avenue, have your waiter arrange for a cab. Informal dress.

El Caney
Av Pichincha at
Av Casanova
(Chacaíto District)
Noon - 1 am (daily)
☎ 71-8754
Inexpensive

This award-winning restaurant features superb beef and a pepper and onion sauce (*guasacaca*), which complements all the meat dishes. Try the *parrillada mixta,* (a mixed grill), the *cordero* (lamb chops), or the *chuletas de cochino* (pork chops). For openers, the guacamole salad or the hearts of palm (palmito) are fine choices. El Caney is located at the border of the Chacaíto and the El Rosal Districts.

Los Pilones
Av Venezuela at Calle Pichincha
(El Rosal District)
☎ 718-8367
Inexpensive

A pretty, comfortable restaurant, Los Pilones focuses on steaks, soups, *pabellón* and stuffed avocados.

Occasionally, there is live music. The restaurant is conveniently located.

Posada Del Laurel
No. Pastor a Misericordia
(Parque Central District)
Noon - midnight
☎ 575-1135
Inexpensive

Small, loud, local and happening, Posada del Laurel is at the end of the park, walking away from the Hilton. The interior is shiny wood and glass. The local people pack the place for an evening drink and a hearty meal.

Italian

A major ethnic group in Caracas are the Italians. As they have done throughout the world, they have brought their great restaurant tradition with them. Here are the most authentic Italian restaurants in town.

La Dolce Vita
Av Juan Bosco
Edifico El Torbes
(Altamira District)
12 - 4 pm; 7 pm - midnight
☎ 261-5763
Expensive
An exciting atmosphere wrenches diners out of their seats as live music blares and the tiny dance floor lures. The choice is not easy – dance or eat, dance or eat? The food is excellent, with all kinds of pizza, and the specialty is *conejo cazador* (rabbit).

La Via Emilia
Av Orinoco
(Las Mercedes)
Mon. - Sat.
Noon - 3 pm; 7:30 - 11:30 pm
☎ 92-6904
Expensive
The very elegant Via Emilia is one of our more formal selections. Once a private home, candlelight creates an intimate ambience, as does the live music. The menu is primarily Italian. *Gnocchi en salsa de hongos* (gnocchi in mushroom sauce), and *penne a la crema* (penne in cream sauce) are both very good, as is the *trucha ahumada* (smoked trout). The dress code is on the formal side. Reservations are requested.

Rococó
Av San Felipe con 4a Transversal
(Altamira)
☎ 266-1851
Valet parking
Expensive
Eighteenth-century French rococo decor meets traditional Italian cuisine at this elegant restaurant in Altamira. Perfect for a special occasion, the limited menu varies with what was freshest at the market that morning. Breads and pastas are homemade. The beautiful setting is perfect for a celebratory champagne toast.

Il Padrino (the Godfather)
Teatro Altamira Boulevard
Plaza Altamira Sur
(Altamira District)
11:30 am - 2 am (daily)
☎ 263-3060
Moderate
In a straight steal from the Godfather, this huge restaurant features the names of the novel's major characters on each front step. The food is excellent, as proved by the masses of people, 400 at times, fighting the spaghetti blues. No fewer than three dozen antipasto variations are on the generous menu, which features fine pasta, veal, and chicken dishes. The veal scalloppine marsala is an outstanding value, as is the *saltimbocca a la romana*. For dessert, try the *fromaggi misti* (mixed cheeses). Party atmosphere nightly. Join in.

Il Vecchio Mulino
Av Francisco Solano & Los Jabillos
(Sabana Grande)
Noon - 3:30 pm; 7 pm - 12:30 (daily)
☎ 71-2695
Moderate

In consideration for the calorie-watchers of the world, this fresh and cheerful bistro notes the calorie content of its food next to the prices. Mama mia, what is happening to Italian restaurants! Nevertheless, the food is unusually good, regardless of calories. Waiters in brightly hued shirts and vests move briskly beneath the cathedral ceiling lined with light blue beams. The floral pattern is carried through on the chairs and benches, and you almost feel as though you're in a small town in Austria. But the fare is definitely Italian. Menu items we like include *saltimbocca, escalopas de ternera marsala* (veal scallopine) and the many pasta specialties. Jacket and tie at night. Violin music is a bonus.

A water mill in the back of a rear garden justifies the name, which means old mill in Italian.

Franco's
Av Francisco Solano at Av Los Jabillos
(Sabana Grande District)
Noon - 3 pm; 7 pm - midnight
☎ 762-0996
Moderate
This first-class restaurant, brilliantly conceived as a cloister-like luxury dining station, is rich in arched brick columns that blend into the brick ceiling, from which hang giant prosciuto hams and Chianti baskets.

The fettucini and cannelloni are fantastic, and the *zuppa de verdura* (vegetable soup) is a great opening. Occasional strolling musicians.

Stained glass windows, huge murals and subdued lighting create a special atmosphere.

Restaurant Da Emore
Centro Comercial Concresa
Noon - 3:30 pm; 7 pm - 11 pm
Closed Mon.s
☎ 979-3242
Flowers, candlelight and piano music are a few of the pleasures of an evening at the Restaurant da Emore. Not to be overlooked is the fine Italian menu comple-

mented by an excellent selection of cheeses and salads. The veal marsala is our top recommendation.

Il Caminetto
Av Principal (Las Mercedes)
☎ 92-1231
Closed Sun.
Valet parking
Expensive
Hostess Franca and Chef Vito make quite a pair. No false pretenses here, just solid Italian fare served in pleasant surroundings. Though a recent arrival to Las Mercedes, Il Caminetto has been a Caracas favorite for years.

Casa Vecchia
Av Mohedano (La Castellana)
☎ 267-1707
Parking
Moderate
The Marcuccis do their best to ensure that all their guests feel at home at this pleasant, neighborhood restaurant. Though the setting is nothing special, the homestyle cooking is far from ordinary. Along with the old standbys you'll find original recipes including risottos, seasonal mushrooms and homemade pastas, all served in generous portions. Its a great place to share a meal with friends and family.

Piccolo Mondo
Av La Trinidad
(Las Mercedes District)
Noon - 3 pm; 7 pm - midnight
☎ 91-2357
Moderate
Concentrating on its food and not its surroundings, Piccolo Mondo specializes in rigatoni and vermicelli

for appetizers, and saltimbocca for the main meal.
There are daily specials.

Il Foro Romano
Av Principal Bello Campo
☎ 263-7662
Dinner only
Expensive
Can you imagine working in a toga? Waiters at Il Foro
Romano do. The spirit of the old Roman Empire has
been aptly recreated here. Reminiscent of Caesar's Pal-
ace, the dining room is decorated with Roman statues
and lit with torches. By the way, the food is very good.

Steak Houses

Beef lovers have a meaty choice of either feasting in
Argentina-style steak houses, with small stoves (paril-
las) at your table and tangy sauces, or in a US-style
place with vegetables and fries. Here are what we
consider the best of Caracas' many steak houses.

Argentinian
Shorthorn Grill
Av Libertador (Near La Florida)
(El Bosque District)
Noon - midnight (daily)
☎ 731-0747
Moderate

*Typically Ar-
gentinean,
this was de-
signed to re-
semble a
ranch house
on the pam-
pas.*

Large, with stone archways, and bedecked with gaucho
paintings. Noted for fast service and superb beef. If you
are rushing to the theater, this is the place to dine. The two
best dishes are the *churrasco* (sirloin steak) and the *parrillada mixta Argentina* (mixed grill of beef, liver, sausage,
and kidneys) served on a small barbecue at your table.
You will like the *baby bife* (T-bone steak) and the *brochette
de lomito* (beef chunks en brochette). Tossed salads are
crisp and fresh. Informal.

La Estancia
Av Principal de La Castellana
(La Castellana District)
11 am - 1 am (daily)
☎ 261-2236
Moderate

Stop in at this quiet restaurant, where the ambience and food are both recommended. While there is a roof, the sides are open and the greenery and breezes contribute to the airy atmosphere. The *Churrasco Martín Fierro* and the T-bone steak are top recommendations. Before dinner, stop at La Tapera next door for cocktails around the piano bar. Informal.

Vistaaroyo
Venezuelan Steakhouse
Carretera Vieja La Guairita (Macaracuay)
☎ 986-1135
Parking
Expensive

The Llanos are to Venezuela what the pampas are to Argentina. If you can't experience the marvelous Venezuelan llanos (plains), at least you can sample one aspect of the llanero culture, grilled beef in a ranch-like setting, complete with cockfights, horses and country music. Rather than order from a menu, patrons tend to order by weight. Unless well-done is your preference, be sure to specify how you like your steak cooked. Fried yucca, typical cheeses and salads accompany the meal.

La Mansión
Av Tamanaco
(El Rosal District)
11:30 am - midnight (daily)
☎ 951-6636
Moderate

For garden dining as well as the best empanadas (meat pies) in Caracas, La Mansión is the place to dine. After the empanada appetizer, try the *punta trasera* or any of the chicken dishes. For dessert it's definitely the *panqueque de banana* (banana pancake). Informal.

North American-Style

These choices may provoke a bit of nostalgia.
Weekends
Av San Juan Bosco
(Altamira District)
Noon - 1:30 am
☎ 261-3839
Moderate
A huge tri-level eatery with excellent burgers and sandwiches reminiscent of home. While primarily a night spot, the food is tasty and the atmosphere excellent.

Lee Hamilton
Av San Felipe (corner of El Bosque)
(La Castellana District)
11 am - 11:30 pm
☎ 263-8429
Moderate
Begun by an American from Maryland, Lee Hamilton's is the best known American-style eatery in Caracas. Its popularity is justified. The filet mignon is tender and prime, served with garlic bread, baked potato, tossed salad and coffee. Reservations necessary on weekends.

Seafood

Dena-ona
Av Tamanaco #52, (El Rosal)
Noon - midnight (daily)
☎ 263-7739
Moderate
If seafood sets your palate tingling, plan a meal at this delightfully attractive restaurant, which serves no fewer

Choose any of the small dining rooms or ask for a table outside in the rear.

than two dozen house specialties. We particularly enjoy the trout (*trucha*) dishes and bass (*mero*) platters. The Spanish colonial setting adds to the appeal.

Rias Bajas
Edificio Artelito
(Los Palos Grandes)
Noon - 2 am (daily)
☎ 283-3580
Expensive

Turtle shells and ship replicas line the walls, giving the room a nautical air.

Lobster is the dish here and the *langosta al thermidor* and *langosta al whiskey* are both highly regarded by regulars, who relish the extensive Spanish-English menu. Owner-host Manual (Monolo) Cordero is likely to stop at your table to review the day's specialties. In addition to *langosta*, the shellfish casserole, *cazuela de mariscos*, is in demand, as is the *langostino al ajillo* (scampi). Here too is your source for exotic dishes such as squid and eel. Good solid seafare in comfortable surroundings. Tie and jacket.

Porlamar
Plaza Chacaíto
(Chacaíto District)
11 am - 1 am (daily)
☎ 32-1666
Moderate

Labeling itself "a corner of Margarita Island" (Venezuela's weekend retreat), this charming restaurant specializes in dishes such as *pargo habanero*, a seafood casserole topped with a cheese sauce, and *consomé de chipichipi* or *de guacuco*, clam soups that set Margaritans aflame. Other recommended dishes include *arroz a la marinera* and *paella Valenciana*. Straw baskets, shells and boat replicas, all from Margarita, cover the walls.

Boga Vante Marisqueria
Av Venezuela
(El Rosal District)
Noon - midnight
☎ 952-0146
Moderate
Resembling an old whaler's inn, this large restaurant is, in our opinion, probably the most attractive of the seafood restaurants in Caracas. The fare has won several gastronomic awards. You can't miss the large sail in front of the restaurant.

Brava Mar
Seafood
Av Principal, La Castellana
☎ 267-5941
Valet parking
Expensive
A favorite of politicians and executives, Brava Mar is one of just a few seafood restaurants in La Castellana. House specialties include *zarzuela de mariscos* (shellfish casserole), *hervido de mero* (sea bass soup) and grilled fish of all varieties.

Marisqueria Restaurant
Centro Ciudad Comercial Tamanaco
☎ 92-9034
Moderate
In a ship-like atmosphere, with the waiters in sailor outfits, the restaurant serves good fish meals.

Spanish

Many first-time visitors here think that Venezuelan food is typical Spanish or Mexican fare. By now you know that Venezuelan cuisine is distinctive and if you want Spanish food, you have to dine in a Spanish restaurant.

Casa Urrutia
Calle Madrid, corner of Calle Monterrey
☎ 993-9526
Closed Sun.
Valet parking
Expensive

Known for its male-only cooking clubs, Spain's Basque region is considered by many to be the home of that country's finest regional cuisine. Adolfo Urrutia brought that tradition to Caracas over 30 years ago when he opened his first restaurant in Sabana Grande. Adolfo Junior has since taken over and opened a second restaurant in Las Mercedes. Though he first tried new Basque cuisine, it didn't catch on and Adolfo went back to the tried and true tradition started by his father. Here and at the original Urrutia in Sabana Grande on Avenida Francisco Solano, corner of Los Manguitos (☎ 710-448), you'll enjoy hearty Basque cooking, including tongue in green sauce and a variety of seafood dishes.

El Lar del Jabugo
Spanish/Catalonian cuisine
Av Principal El Bosque
☎ 731-0329
Valet parking
Most expensive

Given his wide girth, it would seem almost contradictory to say that Angel Lozano, the chef and owner of El Lar del Jabugo, has spread himself too thin. Nor would it be true. Despite his second career as a popular television personality, Angel and his tireless assistant María have kept El Lar del Jabugo at the top of the list of Caracas' finest restaurants. Angel's penchant for using only the finest ingredients, and plenty of them, virtually guarantees that no one ever leaves hungry. Spanish cheeses and charcuterie complement a menu of classic Catalonian and Spanish cuisine.

El Hostal De La Castellana
Av Principal La Castellana
(La Castellana District)
Noon - midnight (daily)
☎ 33-3111
Moderate
The Spanish vibes here are almost overpowering – from the Don Quixote and Sancho Panza replicas outside the entrance to the colonial Spanish decor to the Flamenco music. Three formal dining rooms are on the upper level, where the armor and spears stare down at you from the walls. There is even a wishing well. For more informal dining, try the main level tavern, where the Flamenco music starts at 8:30. As for the food, you won't go wrong with the gazpacho, the *paella, trucha* (trout), or the *pierna del cordero Castellana* (leg of lamb).

Chocolate
Av Tamanaco
El Rosal District
Noon - midnight
☎ 951-7575
Moderate
Also following the pedigree of old Spain, Chocolate is on a busy street and is just as busy inside. There is live music, either a group or a duet of piano and singer, and a huge bar to rev up the festivities. Try *camerones al ajillo, cazuela de mariscos* or the *pargo Provencal.*

El Casario
C.C.C.T. Shopping Center
☎ 92-9034
Moderate
Not as blatant in its decor as the first three restaurants, El Casario specializes in Spanish food and not neces-

sarily a Spanish look. In the great shopping mall, El Casario is a fun place to eat because of its liveliness.

Cassandra
Hotel Eurobuilding
(Chuao)
☎ 959-1139
Expensive
An excellent Spanish restaurant in the Eurobuilding Hotel. The *caracoles y champignones en hojaldre gratinado* (escargot and mushrooms in a pastry shell au gratin) must be tried.

El Rocio
Av Venezuela
In the Venezuela Building
☎ 261-8218
Moderate
Despite its Andalusian name (El Rocio is the endpoint of an annual religious pilgrimage in Spain's southern province of Huelva), *paella Valenciana, bacalao a la Vizcaina* (cod prepared Biscayne style) and *cocido Madrileño* (a dish typical of Madrid) top the menu. Live Spanish music in the expansive dining room often leads to dancing.

Chinese

El Dragon Verde
Av Maturín (Cine Paris Building)
(Los Cedros District)
Noon - 3 pm; 6:30 pm - 11:30 pm (daily)
☎ 731-0428
Moderate
Never yet have we encountered a better Cantonese restaurant than the Green Dragon, an oasis for Asian diplomats here, as well as for North Americans. You enter past the bar with its imposing water-spouting

green dragon on your way to the upstairs dining area, where green Chinese lanterns hang from the ceiling. Menus are bilingual and the waiters are impeccably courteous and efficient, an appropriate complement to the food. Gracious dining indeed. Informal.

El Palmar
Plaza Lincoln
(Colinas de Bello Monte District)
Noon - midnight
☎ 751-4442
Moderate
Decorated in typical Chinese style, El Palmar has excellent food, particularly its lo mein and pork dishes.

Mee-Nam
Av Luis Roche
(near the Third Transversal)
Altamira District
Noon - 11:30 pm (daily)
☎ 261-0549
Moderate
Resembling a large pagoda, this brilliantly colored and decorated mini-palace even features a small bridge over a stream housing a fiery dragon of papier maché. The huge bilingual menu includes over 50 dishes and we recommend the sweet and sour shrimp, the roast pork (*cha sui ding*) with almonds and vegetables and the boneless duck.

Mr. Chow
Av Rio de Janeiro
(Las Mercedes District)
Noon - midnight
☎ 752-6335
Inexpensive
Busy and active, Mr. Chow is good for a faster, less complicated Chinese meal. The food is fine, and Mr.

Chow is a good quick stop in the middle of a touring day.

Korean

Restaurant Seoul
Calle El Cristo
(Sabana Grande District)
Noon - 11:30 pm
☎ 762-3222
Inexpensive
A relatively small restaurant, Seoul is nonetheless a good place for dinner. The menu is both Korean and Spanish, obviously because many Koreans come here, which is a good sign about the food. Dishes are *tang soo yook* (meat in sweet and sour sauce), *yook ge jang* (spicy soup), *mas ji bog um* (octopus), and *saeng sun gui* (baked fish). All are safe and delicious bets.

Swiss-Bavarian

La Petite Swiss
Calle La Trinidad (Las Mercedes District)
Noon - midnight, noon - 7 pm on Sundays
☎ 993-2749
Moderate
An attempted recreation of Switzerland, with a chalet, flags of the Swiss regions, and checkered cloths. Fondue is, of course, the main delight, with cheeses and potatoes and other Swiss delicacies abounding.

El Chalet
Hotel Crillon
Av Libertador (Corner Las Acacias)
(Sabana Grande District)
☎ 761-4411
Moderate

For a touch of Switzerland in Caracas, head for the main floor of the Hotel Crillon, where you can taste Switzerland in an authentic setting.

German

El Rincon de Bavaria
Av Gamboa (corner Panteón)
(San Bernardino District)
12:30 - 3 pm; 7 pm - 9 pm
Sundays 12:30 - 4 pm
☎ 51-8562
Moderate
This is a long-time favorite of ours, and one of the best restaurants in the San Bernadino area.

Peruvian

El Tizon
Centro Comercial Bello Campo
(Bello Campo District)
Noon - 3 pm; 7 pm - 11:30 pm
☎ 31-6715
Inexpensive
Next door to El Sarao, one of our featured night spots, this small restaurant specializes in both Peruvian and Mexican food. Stick to the Peruvian platters. Specialties include *ceviche* (marinated fish) and *anticuchos de corazón* (heart). Pisco sour, the popular Peruvian drink is a must. A touch of Lima, in Caracas.

Arabian

Kibbe Steak
Calle Madrid
(Las Mercedes District)
Noon - midnight
☎ 993-5818
Inexpensive

With cous-cous at the top of the sand dune, Kibbe has all kinds of Arabic dishes: falafel, hummis, and others. Take-out is possible. The food is excellent.

Tex-Mex

Crystal Ranch
Av Principal de las Mercedes
☎ 91-1282
Moderate
A bilingual menu, Tex-Mex favorites, and Old West decor make the Crystal Ranch as appropriate to Texas as it may not seem to be to Caracas. Busy and lively, it always feels like a party here. The menu features both Venezuelan and American cuts of beef, ranging from T-bones to *lomito, churrasco* and hamburgers.

Outdoor Cafés

These are perfect meeting places.

Informal and open all day and evening, these cafés are perfect for a restful break during sightseeing or shopping. Service is leisurely and the menu ranges from espresso to beer to cocktails, from ice cream to double hamburgers.

The Forum
Edificio Centro Capriles
Plaza Venezuela
On the ground floor of this modern office building is the Forum, which has good food and drink at modest prices and as a bonus offers live music in the late afternoon and evening. The place grooves between 5 and 7 most evenings as the young office singles gather en masse. Shoeshine boys are at the ready here.

Two other splendidly slow cafés where you can relax with a rum cocktail or espresso are **Papagallo**, Centro Comercial Chacaíto, Chacaíto District, and the **Café Piccolo**, Calle Real de Sabana Grande near Los Jabillos,

Sabana Grande District. The Piccolo's impromptu music keeps the place jammed.

There are other outdoor cafés spread all over the city.

Vegetarian

El Buffet Vegetarian
Av Los Jardines #4
(La Florida District)
Mon. - Fri., 11 am - 2 pm
☎ 74-7512, 74-7490
Inexpensive

A long time favorite among Caraqueños longing for macrobiotic food and other dairy dishes. You will enjoy eating here. Particularly recommended for lunch or if you happen to be in the La Florida area.

For healthy food fans.

Fast Food

The **Cada** supermarket chain, with branches throughout Venezuela, features fast food outlets attached to each market. You can get a snack or a full meal.

From the US are **Burger King, McDonald's, Dunkin Donuts, Kentucky Fried Chicken, Domino's Pizza** and **Pizza Hut**. Local chains include **Tropiburger, Pizza King, and Arturos**. The **Plaza Broadway** at the end of Sabana Grande (nearest to the Chacaíto) is a complex featuring **Tropiburger** (hamburgers), **Pizza King** (pizza), **Lung Fung** (Chinese), and **La Alemanita** (hotdogs and sausages). Kids love it!

Dessert

For dessert one of our favorite ice cream parlors anywhere is **Tutti Frutti** at the corner of Calles Madrid and Veracruz in Las Mercedes. Don't come alone; servings are generous, with plenty of toppings. You can definitely order one dessert to share and no one will feel slighted.

Sunup To Sundown

Climate is a blessing in Caracas; its perennial autumn weather is a boost for any sightseeing. Because of this, just walking is an option. And old Caracas should be walked, so you can soak up its past.

A Stroll Through Old Caracas

The city's historical center since colonial days has been El Silencio, a wonderful name. Within an hour's time you'll be able to cover this 10-block area of Caracas' earliest history.

Plaza Bolívar

Originally called Plaza de Armas, Plaza Bolívar is the site of Caracas' birth over 400 years ago. This is the natural starting point for any walk in El Silencio. It is a tranquil one-square-block area surrounded by the **Cathedral of Caracas**, the **City Hall** and the **Congress building**.

Plaza de Armas was the original blueprinted center of the new city, the cornerstone of Diego de Losada's vision. Today, busy Caraqueños and shoeshine boys ply the Plaza.

As the monumental heart of the city, Plaza Bolívar, then still "de Armas," was at the heated center of the independence fight. And, after independence, this was the spot where the Constitution was read aloud. But it was still not until 1883 that this atavistic square was officially devoted to Bolívar.

It was actually under President Guzmán Blanco, serving in the 1860's, that the Plaza was made into what you see today. The ironwork, fountains, lampposts, bandstand and equestrian statue of Bolívar were all his doing.

On that statue of Bolívar riding high are several inscriptions. At the front it says, "Libertador de Venezuela, Nueva Granada, Ecuador y Peru y Fundador de Bolivia." On one side, the inscription reads, "Born in Caracas 24 July 1783 died Santa Marta 17 December 1830. Remains transferred to Caracas 17 December 1842." On the other side: "The nation in honoring its Liberator erected this monument in 1874."

It is a touching sight if you are able to transpose yourself into a Venezuelan frame of mind. This is their great man, their founding father.

The plaza is crowded most afternoons and there are Thurs. evening concerts. The **Lectura Salón**, behind the statue, exhibits the works of young Venezuelan artists.

Leaving the Salón, on your left is the famous **Cathedral of Caracas**, which was completed in 1595, later destroyed by an earthquake and, of course, reconstructed. The Cathedral houses famous art works, gold altars, chandeliers and beautiful stained glass windows.

The yellow building facing the plaza is the **City Hall (Concejo Municipal)**, which contains historical paintings and documents of the independence war.

El Museo Criollo Raul Santana

Inside City Hall, this museum has miniature representations of colonial and pre-colonial implements, furniture and wood art. Scenes of old Venezuela are recreated and there are enormous blow-ups of Caracas street scenes circa 1950.

To reach the museum, enter the City Hall at the side, and walk up a narrow and twisty wooden stairway. Open Tues. through Fri., 9 am - 11:30 am and 2:30 pm - 4:30 pm. Sat. and Sun., 10:30 am - 4 pm. It is free.

La Casa Natal

*In 1813,
Bolívar was
given his title
of El Libertador
in the chapel.*

As you leave the City Hall from its main entrance, head east (right) one block to Calle Traposos, a narrow cobblestoned street that is closed to traffic. On this block is La Casa Natal, birthplace of Bolívar – not the original house of his birth but a recreation. In the front room are a series of paintings by Tito Salas depicting the landing of Columbus, the rape of the Indians and the Bolívar-led uprisings. The family chapel and the bedroom are near-authentic versions of the original.

Open 9 am - noon and 2:30 pm - 5;30 pm, Tues. through Sun.

El Museo Bolivariano

On the same street with the Casa Natal, the museum is a pink-hued building that houses revolutionary memorabilia, documents, rifles, swords, military uniforms and battle paintings. You will come away with a better understanding of the era in which Bolívar lived by browsing through the museum.

Museum hours are: Tues. - Sun., 9 am - noon and 2:30 pm - 5:30 pm.

More of El Silencio

From the museum walk back to the Plaza and just beyond the City Hall is the gleaming white **Capitol Building (El Capitolio)** with its outstanding gold dome. In the rear is a magnificent fountain in a garden setting.

Around the corner is the **National Library (Biblioteca Nacional)**, which houses volumes from the 15th century. Heading a block south you come to the famous San Francisco Church, completed in the 16th century with an exquisitely etched wooden altar.

At this point you have two choices. Either return north for five blocks uphill to the Panteón Nacional, where

Bolívar and other leaders are interred, or continue south three more blocks to the Centro Simón Bolívar, the twin 32-story office towers that are the commercial center of downtown Caracas. Underground passageways lined with shops and restaurants connect the two buildings.

The Pantheon, set at the end of a narrow cobblestoned street, was built in 1874 by Guzmán Blanco, the same president that decorated Plaza Bolívar. In some ways the interior marble designs resemble those of the Jefferson Memorial in Washington, DC. Open Tues. to Sun., 9 am - noon and 3 pm - 5 pm.

Caracas by Cable Car (Teleférico)

There may be a more spectacular sight in this world than gliding into Caracas from the 7,000-foot Mount Avila peak via cable car, but we haven't come across it yet. Particularly at night. However, this is getting ahead of the story. After all, we must first get you up to Mount Avila before we can bring you down. Fortunately, that's simple.

The cable car ride takes you into the "lungs of Caracas" – the surrounding mountains that give the city its majestic air. From the pit of the city, it is easy to spot Mt. Avila, because of the hotel that sits upon it. It is to this peak that the cable car will take you. Allow a full day for the trip.

The whole mountainous region was declared a National Park, which extends down to the Caribbean as well. There are 160 miles of hiking trails in the park.

The terminal is located in the Mariperez District of Caracas, on its north side. The cable cars are large and offer ample visibility for photos. The ride is 15 minutes, even allowing for a stop or two en route, and is spectacular; the best views are from the rear of the car. The city recedes, and the vegetation changes.

Although the sun will be just as strong, you'll feel the change in temperature as you rise.

Once on top of the mountain there are many things to do. First, you can just walk aimlessly. As dusk approaches, it is a sort of lover's lane, and many couples come here. There is also an **ice skating rink**, many small shops selling souvenirs, a coffee shop and several stalls of food vendors, particularly men selling strawberries and cream.

The cable car ride also descends to the Caribbean side, taking you down into the beach town of Macuto and highlighting the vast panorama of the Caribbean. At this writing it is out of service – not for good, but with no definite date of reopening.

Hiking in the park is recommended. There are many trails twisting through the mountains. You'll notice how the terrain and vegetation changes as you move along. If feeling strong, you can hike up the mountain. But you must feel confident in your strength because, not only is it long and arduous, but for the first 3,000 or so feet there is no shade. For hiking around on top you need a pass, which can be obtained from the Parques Nacionales (National Park Institute), located next to the parking lot of Parque del Este. Overnights are also possible.

Unfortunately, when we visited Caracas in the Winter of 1997 to update this edition, the cable car was not running. Happily, it had been purchased by an Italian company, which was planning to make repairs and open a new hotel and casino on Mt. Avila sometime before the year 2000.

The Best Museums

Museo Del Arte Colonial
Quinta de Anauco
(San Bernadino District)
The museum is actually in an old and famous colonial house with particular significance for Venezuelans. Called the Quinta de Anauco, it was originally built in 1797 by a Spanish captain. In 1821, when loyalists were fleeing the city, Bolívar's friend, the Marques del Toro, began renting it. He eventually bought it, at Bolívar's urging.

In 1861 the Anauco was purchased by the Eraso family, and almost 100 years later given to the city of Caracas. In 1961, it became the Colonial Art Museum, replacing the older one and getting much of the other museum's treasures. In what were the slaves' quarters is now the Carlos Manuel Moller Library, specializing in colonial art and history.

The rest of the house is a reasonable representation of its original design and style. The furniture is obviously colonial, and the house is adorned with art from the period. The kitchen is worth looking at, and the bathroom has a sunken rectangular bathtub which was fed by a cold water stream that flowed through a channel in the bathroom floor. The gardens around the house are nice for strolling, with many tropical plants and orchids (the national flower).

Bolívar was a frequent visitor to this house, which he loved, and actually spent his last night in Caracas here.

Open Tues. - Sat., 8:30 am - 11:30 am; 2 pm - 4:30 pm. There are usually free concerts at 11 am on Sun.s.

Museo De Bellas Artes
Los Caobos Park
(El Conde District)
Located near the Caracas Hilton Hotel, in Los Caobos Park, the Fine Arts Museum features varying exhibits of Venezuelan artists, representing all eras, and displays major collections of Egyptian art, Latin American art, Cubism, international sculpture and a large and fine collection of Chinese art.

Open Tues. - Fri., 9 am - 5 pm; weekends, 10 am - 5 pm.

Museo De Ciencias Naturales
Los Caobos Park
(El Conde District)
Dedicated to the natural sciences, the museum has exhibits of paleontology, archaeology and taxonomy. Finds from Venezuela, the rest of Latin America and

The second floor is devoted to the tribes of the Amazon. Don't miss it.

Africa are exhibited, as well as African animals and Venezuelan birds.

Open Tues. - Sun., 9 am - 4:45 pm.

Galería De Arte Nacional
Plaza Morelos
Dedicated to preserving the history of Venezuelan art, the National Art Gallery has many rooms devoted to native artists and sculptors from throughout Venezuelan history. There are permanent shows of contemporary art. Guided tours are available.

Open Tues. - Fri., 9 am - 5 pm; Sat. and Sun., 10 am - 5 pm.

Museo De Arte Contemporáneo De Caracas Sofia Imber
Parque Central - East
Edificio Mohedano, Sótano 1
Founded in 1973, the museum is home to a growing collection of works by famous international artists, including Picasso, Botero, Chagall, and Matisse. Wall sculptures by Jesus Soto, a free-hanging rope sculpture by Gego that spans all three floors of the museum, and sculptures by Alejandro Otero and Francisco Narvaez form an integral part of the museum's architecture and landscape. Temporary exhibits are featured in the museum's eastern and western annexes.

Works by local artists are offered for sale at the museum's artisan shop. A poster and frame shop and a mini-mall with a restaurant, boutiques and artshops form part of the museum complex.

Open Tues. - Sun., 10 am - 6 pm.

Museo Arturo Michelena
Esquina Urapal
(La Pastora)
Probably Venezuela's most internationally famous artist, Arturo Michelena was born in Valencia and trained

in Paris. He was the student and prodigy of Juan Paul Laurens, and was widely appreciated in Europe as well as in his own country. He died at 35, but not without bringing much acclaim to himself and his country.

Little of his more important work is actually in the museum, although many of his sketches are. Much of his work is in the National Gallery.

The museum is closed on Mon. and Fri., and open from 9 am - noon and 3 pm - 5 pm on the remaining days.

Museo De Los Niños
Parque Central
Between the Catuche & Tacagua Buildings
☎ 572-4112
Learning is lots of fun at this marvelous hands-on museum, which is spread out over five levels. Kids of all ages explore the physical sciences, biology, the workings of modern communications, and the importance of ecology and the conservation of scarce natural resources.

Open 9 am - noon, 2 pm - 5 pm, Wed. through Sun.

Parks & Monuments

El Paseo De Los Proceres
(Av de Los Proceres)

As is true throughout much of South America, the famous Revolutionary War Battles of the early 19th century are marked in Caracas by monuments, memorials, and designations of streets and plazas. However, Caracas is unusual in one respect. Most of the monuments are to be found on one avenue, called the Avenue of the Leaders (Avenida de los Proceres), located in a lovely park (Proceres Park). Fountains, benches, and flowers line the main walk as you approach the monuments, which are in the form of huge concrete slabs, each with a battle noted on it. Statues in front of the slabs are of famous Revolutionary War generals who fought under Bolívar. Looking beyond the monument you will see grandstands, used for reviewing military parades. At the far end of the park is a military officer's club, situated on 20 acres, complete with its own theater and pool. You can walk the grounds for a small fee.

Parque Del Este

There is a planetarium (Planetario Humboldt) on the grounds, which is free. Special shows take place on weekends for about $1.

Faintly resembling New York's Central Park, Parque del Este is great for a day's outing. The city's largest park, it has basketball and volleyball courts, a small zoo and an aviary, a planetarium and lots of walking paths and picnic areas. The park is crowded on the weekends. As in any public park, all classes of Caraqueños share its relaxing atmosphere.

Come for the day and take the metro, which has a stop marked Parque del Este that lets you out at its entrance. It costs 10¢ to enter the park, open from 5 am to 5 pm Tues. through Sun.

Next to the park is the **Museo del Transporte** (Museum of Transportation). Its hours are: Tues. - Sun., 9 am - noon, 3 pm - 5:30 pm; closed Mon.

Botanical Gardens
Universidad Central de Venezuela

The Botanical Gardens are home to hundreds of species of palm trees, cacti and tropical plants, all well cared for and identified by name. It is a great respite from the city; you'll feel as if you've been transported to a tropical paradise as you wander its pathways.

Getting here is easy. From the Plaza Venezuela follow the signs for the Autopista Francisco Fajardo, then cross the access road into the university. The gardens will be immediately to your right. The park is open from 8:30 am to 5 pm daily.

Parque Los Caobos
Plaza Morelos (opposite the Caracas Hilton)
Open Tues. - Sun.
Formerly a coffee plantation, wide paved pathways make this shady park a favorite with cyclists, joggers and skateboarders. The park gets its name from the tall mahogany trees (*caobos*) planted here to protect the young coffee plants.

El Pinar Zoo
(Plaza El Pinar, El Paraiso District)
Featuring a children's zoo, where kids can touch small goats and other domestic animals, El Pinar is fun for a family outing.
Open 9 am - 6 pm daily (closed Mon.).

University of Caracas
Called University City, the 400-acre Caracas University is internationally known. What gives the university its international reputation is its art and architecture. The design is not a rehash of classical academic conventions – Gothic towers, ivy-covered dorms – but a contemporary amalgam of buildings and art works. There are 49 murals, 10 sculptures, four frescoes, and four works in stained glass. All are integral components of the campus, not just exhibits.

The campus is also a center for sports events and there is a botanical garden on the premises.

The campus can be reached by taxi, of course, metro, and public transportation. It is located south of the Plaza Venezuela.

Parque Zoologico De Caricuao
Caricuao
☎ 431-9166
The natural habitats of giraffes, elephants, rhinoceros, deer and many other animals have been recreated in the hills outside Caracas at the Parque Zoológico do

Caricuao. Peacocks and cuacamayas seem to take infinite pleasure in showing off their plumage.

Flamingos and other birds add their charms to the park's lakes and ponds, while all kinds of snakes bask in the sun in their private garden. There's also a petting zoo for kids with a variety of goats, ducks and other small animals. On the weekends complimentary trains offer a complete tour of the park.

You can take the metro to get there or, if you're driving, take the Autopista Francisco Fajardo west and follow the signs to Caricuao. Once in Caricuao, follow the signs to the park.

Open Tues. through Sun., 9 am to 4:30 pm. There is a small admission fee.

Carnival

If you are lucky enough to be in Venezuela for the five days before Ash Wed., you are in for a festive treat. Each city has its own way of celebrating, with daytime costumes and parades.

In Caracas, although celebrations are not in the league of those in Rio de Janeiro, we enjoyed the costumes of the children marching gaily along the Sabana Grande. They fling confetti in every direction, and the atmosphere is ecstatic.

Flea Market

If it is your thing to spend hours intimately stalking silver items, used clothing and exotic foods, then the *Mercado Libre de Chacao*, off Avenida Francisco de Miranda, is the place. On Thurs. mornings from 8:30 am to 1 pm and all day Sat. the streets are lined with booths selling exotica as well as fine junk.

Sporting Life

Venezuelans revel in sports. Whether it is the ponies, *beisbol* (baseball), *futbol* (soccer), or bull fighting, Caraqueños flock to the arenas. There is also good golf. Boxing is big, and bowling, skating, basketball and swimming are other popular activities.

Horseracing – El Hipódromo La Rinconada

Located in the scenic suburb of El Valle a 20-minute ($5) taxi ride from the center of the city, the racetrack is open Saturdays and Sundays all year round. The track holds 48,000 spectators, and has a 1 pm post time.

Head to Section "B" for the best views.

Venezuela was made most famous in the horseracing world when a homegrown horse won the Kentucky Derby in 1971. The horse, Cañonero II, gave Venezuela international respect and admiration.

There is a Sun.-only competition that takes place all over the country, and hence can be entered from home. Called the "cinco y seis" (five and six), the competition involves selecting winners of five of the last six races.

Betting places open all over town at 11:30 am on Sun.

Boxing – Poliedro Stadium

Venezuela boasts some of the world's finest boxers, and a great fighting ring that was inaugurated in 1974 with the Foreman-Norton championship fight. Located near the racetrack, matches are usually held on Sat. nights. Prices depend on the quality of the fight. Check *The Daily Journal* for schedules.

Bull Fighting – Plaza de Toros – Nuevo Circo

Bull fighting is held in this stadium in the El Silencio district on Avenida San Agustín del Norte. Prices are usually about $2.50 for bleachers and $3 for shaded seats. When fighters from Mexico and Spain are in town, prices are higher. Check the newspaper for schedules. The season runs from November to March. Fights are held Sun. afternoons.

Baseball — Estadio Universitario

There are many Venezuelans in American baseball, and some come back to play here in the winter, so the quality is high.

Between October and February is the Venezuelan baseball season. The sport is followed seriously and intensely, some people saying it is Venezuela's major sport.

The best ball is played at the University Stadium, and games are at night, except on Sun., when play is in the afternoons. No games are played on Monday. A reserved seat is about $5.

Soccer

Soccer is also played at University Stadium. The soccer season is from December to March; and the most popular games are Sat. nights. Venezuelans are not as crazed about this sport as Brazilians and Argentineans, but it is still popular. Tickets run from $2 - $4.

Participant Sports

For participants instead of spectators, there are several sports that are accessible. The easiest and most popular is **basketball**, with courts all over the city, and great games going on in Parque del Este. **Volleyball** is also popular, and is played in Parque del Este too.

Ice skating is not unknown to Venezuela. Caracas's newest skating rink is at the Ice Center on the Plaza Venezuela. There is more skating at the Mucubaji rink (☎ 54-3557), located in the Parque Central. The rink is open Mon. – Fri., 3:30 pm - 10 pm and weekends from 10 am - 11 pm. The cost is about $1 for 90 minutes of skating and about 75¢ for skates.

There is also skating on top of Mt. Avila at the Pista de Hielo, as mentioned before.

Golf

There are four first-class 18-hole golf courses in Caracas, each attached to a private club that admits guests from the better hotels – usually on weekdays only.

Weekends are jammed and visitors are not allowed.

The clubs are: Country Club, Lagunita Golf Club, Valle Arriba Golf Club and Carabelleda Golf Club. The first three are within city limits and can be easily reached. The Carabelleda is near the beach. You can rent equipment. Greens fees are about $10 and a caddie is about $5. Make arrangements through your hotel.

Tours & Excursions

The Audubon Society of Venezuela
Centro Comercial Paseo Las Mercedes
Sector La Cuadra
☎ 993-2525
Mon. - Fri., 9 am - 12:30 pm; 2:30 pm - 6 pm
If you'd like to learn more about Venezuelan wildlife while visiting Caracas, stop by the Audubon Tienda in the Centro Comercial Paseo Las Mercedes. You may be able to participate in one of the nature talks, courses or excursions offered by The Audubon Society of Venezuela. Proceeds go to the funding of conservation projects.

Colonia Tovar

In 1843 a band of 350 immigrants from Kaiserstuhl, a farming community in Germany's Black Forest, landed on Venezuela's Caribbean shore. Finding that area too warm, the elders decided their band should push on into the mountains. They settled in a forest within the coastal sierra, which they soon cleared, 41 miles west of Caracas high in the state of Aragua. Relatives and friends joined them over the years. Industrious and shrewd, these Bavarians built a self-sustaining, largely agricultural community that was accessible (until 1955) only by donkey.

Because of its inaccessibility, the town was shielded from Venezuelan influences and thus retained its century-old southern German village traditions in dress and food.

Today the chalet-style homes, restaurants, and shops are home to a population of 7,000 residents. A steady stream of visitors drives up the 6,000-foot elevation, passing a number of charming towns along the way, each with its own open-air fruit market.

To get here, either rent a car and take the CL4 from Caracas or go via an organized tour. Entering town, you will know you have reached Colonia Tovar by the archway leading into the huge multi-colored vase that stands there as a symbol of the town's only industry, a ceramic factory. The road peaks and then edges down toward a church, a hotel and restaurant in the village center. Even if you're not hungry, stop in at the hotel, appropriately named **Selva Negra** (Black Forest) for at least a stein of excellent German beer. The sauerbraten will set your appetite aflame. A hearty three-course lunch is about $5. After that respite, stroll along the main street of Avenida Bolívar; stop in at the local museum, which visually traces the town's history; the lovely black and white church (marred by a modern exterior clock); and visit the shopping arcade. By the way, as you walk around, note the fair skin and blond hair of the residents which contrasts markedly with most Venezuelans. Yes, they speak Spanish, if you're wondering.

Stop at El Junquito, virtually hiding in the Humboldt Valley. If it weren't for the palm trees, you'd swear you were in Austria. This is one place you'll want to photograph.

Other German restaurants, in addition to Selva Negra, are **Café Edelweiss**, serving the best German sausage (wurst) in town, located behind the church; and the **Kaiserstuhl**, facing the church, which is justly celebrated for its homemade strawberry tarts. The Kaiserstuhl also has a few rooms for rent. If you have a second meal in town, try **El Molino** or **La Baliesta**.

Most shops here seem to specialize in typical tourist souvenirs but one, **Casa Benítez** located above the Café Muhstall, has an interesting display of cuckoo clocks

and beer mugs that we liked. Still, homemade pre-
serves – blackberry, strawberry, and peach – are your
best buys.

Staying Overnight

If you want, stay till morning at the Selva Negra, the
Hotel Alta Baviera or at any of several guest houses.
The 36-room **Selva Negra** (☎ 51415) charges $30 for a
double, with private bath and meals. A rustic cabin for
two is moderate. Owner Wolfgang Gutmann speaks
English. Prices at the **Alta Baviera** (☎ 51333) and the
14-room **Hotel Freiburg** (☎ 51313) on Calle Bolívar are
comparable. Guest houses run less but you might
have to share the bath. For after-dark entertainment,
there is one cinema (with US films... sometimes) and
one dance club, the basement-level **Bodegón de la
Bruja** (☎ 51154) on the main street.

Los Roques

If you think that for every pristine stretch of beach in the Caribbean there's got to be a hotel lurking somewhere nearby, Los Roques will prove you thankfully wrong. This archipelago of 200 small cays and islets, coral reefs and sand bars is one of the last vestiges in the Caribbean where there will never be a high-rise hotel, five-star resort, or time-share condominium complex. Not only are none of the tiny islands which make up Los Roques large enough to hold a resort, but Los Roques was declared a National Park in 1972.

While you won't find free-form swimming pools with swim-up bars, duty-free shopping, gourmet restaurants or glitzy casinos, you will find terrific snorkeling, diving and bonefishing. Bring your field glasses too for birdwatching. Within its beautiful turquoise seas and unspoiled landscapes, Los Roques harbors all of the ecosystems of tropical marine and coastal zones, including mangroves, sandy beaches, coral reefs, saltwater lagoons, saltgrass marshes and rocky peaks. Los Roques is one of the few archipelagos in the world with atolls of coral, rather than volcanic, origin.

Nearly 1,000 years ago several of the larger islands were inhabited by Indians from the mainland. Later, during the colonial period, the islands were frequented by pirates and explorers, though none set up permanent residence there. More recently, the main island of Gran Roque was settled by fishermen from Margarita, who originally came to fish lobster between November and May. With the advent of tourism in the late '80s and early '90s, many took up year-round residence and turned their homes into small guest houses or posadas. Nowadays the 150 families who live in the village of

Gran Roque depend primarily on tourism for their livelihood.

Overview

The dazzling turquoise waters and pristine cays of Los Roques occupy 869 square miles of the Caribbean, an area larger than that of the British and American Virgin Islands combined. Located just under 90 miles north of Caracas, the entire archipelago is roughly 15 miles wide by 1¾ miles long. In order to preserve and protect the park a decree was issued in 1990, which divided the park into different zones, restricting public access to all but a few of the cays.

The decree designated the northeast corner of the archipelago, the area around Gran Roque, for recreational use. Access by the general public is limited to Gran Roque, Madrizquí, Pirata, Nordisquí and the three Francisquises. To help control development, building is permitted only on Gran Roque, Madrizquí, and Rasquí. and has been limited to current landowners.

To preserve the park's vital ecosystems, the decree also established restricted zones. These include areas of mangroves, reefs and prairies of sea grasses that serve as areas of refuge and the spawning grounds for much of the wildlife in Los Roques. While some areas are especially important for the reproduction of sea turtles and birdlife, others are dedicated to scientific research. There's a marine biology station on Dos Mosquises, one of the southernmost cays.

Certain cays have archaeological interest and are part of the arqueopalenontológico zone. These include Cayo Sal, Dos Mosquises, Cayo de Agua, Bequeré, Noronquí del Mundo, Los Canquises, Crasquí and Gran Roque.

Los Roques
National Park

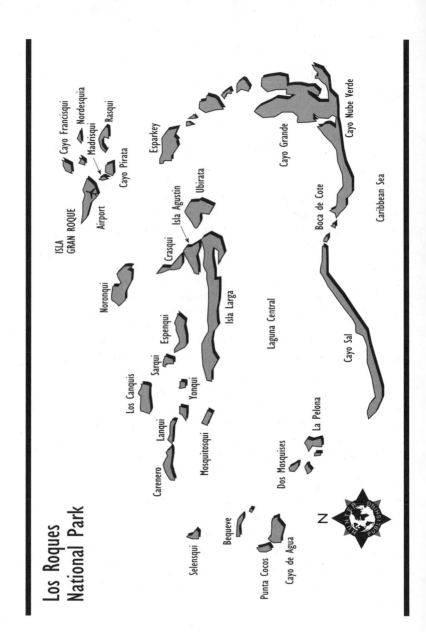

ISLA
GRAN ROQUE

Cayo Francisqui
Nordesquia
Madrisqui
Rasqui
Cayo Pirata

Airport

Esparkey

Ubirata

Isla Agustin

Crasqui

Noronqui

Isla Larga

Cayo Grande

Cayo Nube Verde

Boca de Cote

Caribbean Sea

Espenqui

Sarqui

Laguna Central

Los Canquis

Yonqui

Cayo Sal

Lanqui

Carenero

Mosquitosqui

La Pelona

Dos Mosquises

Selensqui

Bequeve

Punta Cocos
Cayo de Agua

N

Divers and snorkelers who venture beyond the recreational zone will appreciate the efforts made to preserve Los Roques' vital ecosystems. The archipelago's ideal combination of mangroves and abundant sea grasses create a nutrient-rich nursing ground for the many different species of marine life living amidst the coral reefs. Native to Los Roques is a variety of conch known locally as the botuto. In fact, Los Roques is one of the few areas in the Caribbean where conch still maintain a viable population.

Overall, Los Roques underwater landscapes are not unlike those found throughout the Caribbean, with one important difference. The archipelago is still relatively unknown to recreational divers. With the possible exception of the recreation zone, brain, elkhorn and staghorn corals, as well as bushy soft corals and seafans remain virtually undisturbed in many areas. Growing among them are colorful varieties of sponges, including barrel, tube and pillow sponges as well as fire sponges.

The variety of marine life seems endless. Most common are fireworms, feather dusters, squid, octopus, the West Indian top shell, spiny lobster, coral crabs, land crabs, banded coral shrimp, long-spined black urchins, sea cucumbers, sea eggs, and sand dollars. Sea turtles, including loggerheads, are also quite common. And, of course, virtually all species of fish native to the Caribbean are to be found swimming amidst the reefs, including yellowtail damselfish, parrotfish, doctorfish, spotted moray eels, angelfish, porcupine fish, barracuda, and flounder.

In sharp contrast to this lush marinescape, the cays are dry and barren. The landscape is dominated by blinding white sand, broken only by patches of cactus and scrubby undergrowth. The few animals that can survive such harshness include iguanas, black lizards and salamanders. Birds, on the other hand, thrive in Los

Roques. Common to the area are white and red coro coros, ruby topaz, great blue herons, reddish egrets, a few varieties of boobies, common ground doves, hummingbirds, sooty terns and yellow warblers. Not surprisingly, several different types of gulls make their home in Los Roques, as do pelicans. Flamingos inhabit Los Canquises on the north-central edge of the lagoon, where the sand has a pinkish hue.

Making Arrangements

Though daytrips are fine, an overnight stay is best.

Several domestic airlines fly to Los Roques with daily departures out of Margarita, Maiquetía, and Puerto La Cruz. Flying time from Caracas is around 30 minutes, while the flight from Margarita is just under an hour.

The most popular and least complicated way to visit Los Roques is with an all-inclusive package arranged through one of the airlines or with a tour operator. One- and two-night packages are standard and generally include round-trip airfare, accommodations, meals, and excursions to the islands aboard either a catamaran or *peñero*, a small launch. Lunch, snorkeling equipment, and beach games are usually included in the excursion.

Most airlines also offer daytrips that include round-trip airfare, a short tour of the islands around Gran Roque aboard a catamaran or yacht, snorkeling, a picnic lunch on one of the cays, and a few hours on the beach before returning. Daytrips generally cost around $100 US and leave early in the morning, returning in plenty of time for dinner. These excursions are fine if you would not have the time to see Los Roques otherwise, or if you can't do without luxurious accommodations and cosmopolitan restaurants and nightclubs. But if you do have the time, we urge you to spend at least two days and one night in Los Roques, if not longer.

Al⋯ own flight and accom-
m⋯ up trips to the islands
on⋯ with a package. Pack-
ag⋯ enerally, you won't do
bet⋯ even fare worse. Since
foo⋯ rom the mainland, it's
bes⋯ Otherwise, there may
be ⋯ If you do make your
ow⋯ you arrive, you may
be ⋯ dollars are generally
pref⋯ ements through **Log-
gag**⋯ s from the Avensa
coun⋯ at Maiquetía, or with
the a⋯ most of the year, you
can ⋯ or two days notice.
How⋯ ng high season, Au-
gust ⋯ ed to make arrange-
ment⋯ will have to pay an
admi⋯ US) for entry to the
Natio⋯

The f⋯ es to Los Roques:

Línea⋯

In Ca⋯ rande, Edf. Gran
Saban⋯ arrangements at
their ⋯ t. ☎ (02) 761-6231,
761-62⋯ 4.

In Ma⋯ antiago Mariño in
the Vis⋯ r. ☎ (095) 63-2211,
63-030⋯

The la⋯ service to Los Roques, ⋯ s. Packages range
from a ⋯ archipelago to customized
trips aboard the *Antares III* for fishing enthusiasts and
divers. The standard package features two days and
one night with meals and lodging in an Aerotuy
posada, and daytrips to the cays aboard an Aerotuy

catamaran or in a *peñero* arranged by your posada. Aerotuy will also make arrangements for sports fishing or scuba diving tours for PADI or NAUI certified divers.

Located on the beach in Gran Roque, the 11-room **Vistalmar** and the three room **Posada El Muelle** are the most luxurious of the Aerotuy posadas. All rooms feature a private bath with hot and cold water. Their shared waterfront terrace is the perfect vantage point for winding down and taking in the sunset after a day on the water. Traditional accommodations are offered by the two-room **Posada Natura Viva,** the three-room **Posada Las Palmeras** and the three-room **Posada Macabi Lodge**. All three are located in the village and feature rooms with cold water only.

Aerotuy offers a complete range of accommodations and activities on Los Roques.

Aerotuy also offers daytrips from Margarita or Caracas. After an early morning flight to Gran Roque, you'll immediately board an Aerotuy catamaran and spend the morning touring the cays with some time for snorkeling. Then you'll head to the Aerotuy camp on Francisquí en Medio, where you'll enjoy a gourmet lunch and spend the afternoon on the beach before returning to Gran Roque to catch the afternoon flight to Caracas or Margarita.

An unforgettable way to visit Los Roques is an overnight cruise aboard Aerotuy's 76' trawler the *Antares III*. It's perfect for divers and sports fishermen. You'll visit some of Los Roques' less frequented sites in modern comfort. Each of its five double and one quadruple cabins has a private bath and is air-conditioned. There's plenty of room on deck for socializing along with a small library of books on marine life, stereo equipment and a TV/VCR. The basic package includes meals, snorkeling equipment and beach chairs. Equipment rentals for diving and fishing can be arranged.

AeroEjecutivo
☎ (02) 91-7942, 91-9286
Fax (02)953-8181
AeroEjecutivo, one of Venezuela's newest domestic airlines, offers both daytrips and overnight packages to Los Roques. You'll tour the cays by peñero with a few stops for snorkeling and swimming in the morning. A homestyle picnic lunch is served at the Aeroejecutivo camp on Francisquí Abajo where you'll spend a couple of hours before heading back to Gran Roque. Mask, snorkel and fins are provided, as are beach umbrellas and chairs.

Accommodations are at two typical posadas. The **Posada Loromar**, which doubles as AeroEjecutivo headquarters on Los Roques, offers one double and one triple room with a shared bath. There's room for one more on the couch in the living area. Dining is al fresco on the waterfront terrace. A new posada was being built next door at the time of our visit. The **Posada Terramar** has room for nine in three triples with shared bath. Expect a 10% surcharge if you pay by credit card.

Rutaca
Caracas:
At the airport in Maiquetía: ☎ (031) 524765 or 521441.
Fax (085) 24010 or 25955
Margarita: ☎ (095) 691447, 691345
Puerto la Cruz: ☎ (081) 768914, 767090
Rutaca also flies to Los Roques and offers daytrips aboard their own catamaran. You'll have to arrange your own accommodations if you'd like to stay overnight.

Independent Posadas

If you've made your own flight arrangements, contact the following agencies or posadas to book accommodations. They will usually organize daytrips to the cays as well. Meals are usually included in the price.

Roques Air, Land & Sea
☎ (02) 952-1840, 952-6210, 952-1806
Fax (02) 952-5823
Roques Air, Land & Sea offers two levels of accommodations in the seven posadas it operates on Gran Roque. "Superior" accommodations include a room with private bath (cold water) and a ceiling fan or air-conditioning in one of its five posadas, 30 rooms in all, on Calle Las Flores. Located two blocks from the beach, the posadas share a restaurant, La Escafandra, which is a combination *tasca*, bar, and discotheque. Outdoor candlelit dining in the evenings. The staff speaks English and Italian. More basic or "roquero"-style lodgings are available in the other posadas, which have shared baths and homestyle cooking.

All-inclusive packages from Maiquetía feature roundtrip flight, welcome cocktail, all meals and national beverages and excursions to the cays aboard the catamarans *Fiesta* and *Tocorón,* including snorkeling equipment and beach games. Payment can be made in cash (US dollars) or Visa/MasterCard with 10% surcharge.

Posadas Bahia de Coral
Caracas: ☎ (02) 975-0237, 975-0906
Gran Roque: ☎/fax (5814) 285-471, 975-0355
Posadas Bahia de Coral operate three modern posadas, 12 rooms in all, on the Plaza Bolívar. Rooms with private or shared bath are available. Packages include all meals and beverages, sailing excursions, and snorkeling equipment. Bone fishing and diving with Sesto Continente as well as overnight sailing trips can be arranged. Air transportation can be included in the package as well.

Posadas Turísticas Chez Judith
Caracas: ☎ (02) 213660
☎/fax (02) 217260
Chez Judith offers superior (private bath) or basic (shared bath) accommodations in the two posadas it operates on Gran Roque. The standard plan features breakfast and dinner at your posada with a guided excursion including lunch during the day. A VIP plan with a multilingual guide includes beach chairs, umbrellas, snorkeling and bonefishing equipment, along with a three-course dinner, with wine and a cocktail. For those on a tight budget, the basic plan features accomodations in posadas "roqueñas" (basic rooms and shared bath) with breakfast and dinner. Daytrips are additional.

Reservations must be made in writing in advance and require a 50% bank deposit. The remainder must be paid 72 hours prior to departure. Payment in US dollars. Air transportation can also be arranged.

Posada Bora La Mar
☎ (014) 25-7814
Caracas: ☎ (02) 2385408, fax (02) 238-5408.
This beachfront posada is owned by Marta Agusti, a native of Cataluña. Its four rooms all have private baths. Breakfast and dinner are included. Picnic lunch is available upon request. The outdoor restaurant is open to the public from 7:30 am to 9 pm. Payment is by cash or certified check only (US dollars or bolívares) and reservations require a deposit in their bank account.

What to Bring

Plan on packing light since luggage space is limited on the flights to Los Roques. All you will really need is plenty of sunblock, a bathing suit and towel, shorts and

T-shirts (no need to dress up), sunglasses, a hat, sandals and your passport.

Exploring the Cays

Chances are that after breakfast at your posada you'll board a catamaran or a peñero and set off on a tour of the cays closest to Gran Roque: Madrizquí, Pirata, Nordisquí and the three Francisquises. Unless you've made special arrangements, you'll follow a standard itinerary: visit one or two of the nearby cays in the morning, possibly with a stop at **La Piscina** for a guided snorkel tour, and then head to your final destination where you'll have lunch and spend the afternoon, swimming, sunning, or playing beach games until around 3 pm. If you're with Aerotuy or AeroEjecutivo, you'll be at their camps on Francisquí en Medio and Francisquí Abajo. Then it's back to Gran Roque in time to shower and catch the afternoon flight back to Caracas.

One of the cays you're likely to visit is Madrizquí. Directly southeast of Gran Roque, it's the cay you see when you're standing on the shoreline in front of the Posada Loromar or on the landing strip at the airport. The vacation home of Venezuela's wealthiest and most powerful family, the Cisneros, as well as the President's houses are here. There are also fishing shacks which belong to fishermen from Margarita who come to fish lobster from November to May. In former days the fishermen fished conch, of the local variety known as *botuto*. Now, however, as in all of the Caribbean, conch fishing is prohibited by law. If you walk west along the beach on Madrizquí you'll come to a patch of conch shells which have washed up on the shore. Some are covered with coral and blackened by the sun. Isla Fernando, one of the smallest of the cays, was formed entirely of conch shells.

Exploring on Your Own

If beaching it is your primary reason for visiting Los Roques, the standard itinerary should be sufficient. However, the best of Los Roques lies outside the recreational zone. To truly experience Los Roques, you've got to break away from the crowds of daytrippers and overnight tourists and spend at least a day sailing around the archipelago aboard a chartered boat.

A chartered sailboat is the best way to explore Los Roques.

Consider combining an overnight package and its visits to the nearby cays with an overnight on a chartered yacht. Or, if your budget allows, forego the overnight package altogether and give yourself at least a few days (an entire week would be best) to visit the outlying cays. This is really the only option for serious divers. Charter companies serving Los Roques include **New Life Charters** (☎/fax 5814-953195) and **Alpi Tours** (toll-free US, ☎ 1-800/506-2308, ext. 2574; in Venezuela, ☎ 582-283-1433 or 283-1966; fax 285-6067). Most charter companies require a deposit and payment in cash or by certified check.

The *Kaya*, a 47' sailboat with two private cabins and bath, is available for private charters. Meals and open bar are included in the rate. Arrangements can be made for scuba diving and fishing equipment. Contact Captain Giuseppe Legori (English, French, Italian and Spanish, ☎ 5814-258475 or fax 285471).

Also available for private charter, *Guaicamar* is a 76' classic yacht with air-conditioned cabins and bath. Again, meals and open bar are included in the rate and arrangements can be made for scuba, snorkeling and fishing equipment. Contact Kathi Arcil in Caracas (☎ 582-235-2222).

Ask your captain to make arrangements for a visit to the **Marine Biological Station** managed by the Fundación Científica Los Roques. It is on the tiny island of Dos Mosquíses Sur at the southwestern edge of the

Laguna Central. The station raises sea turtles and other endangered species which are released into the wilds of the archipelago. Visitors who make arrangements ahead of time are welcome on weekends and public holidays. Contact the foundation's Caracas office in Quinta Machado, Avenida El Estanque, corner of Transversal B, Caracas Country Club (☎ 261-3461).

Diving in Los Roques

If you'd like to dive in Los Roques, contact **Dive Center Sesto Continente Los Roques** at their office in Caracas on Avenida Los Jardines, Residencia Los Girasoles in La Florida (☎/fax 582-743873 and 749080).

Because they are still relatively unknown, dive sites in Los Roques tend to be more pristine than those in other areas of the Caribbean. However, there is one important caveat. Diving in Los Roques is best reserved for experienced divers. Deep dives and strong currents, combined with less supervision than is standard at other Caribbean destinations catering to beginning and holiday divers, make conditions less than ideal for the uninitiated. To make the most of your dive, you should dive with someone who has first-hand knowledge of the sites where you are planning to dive.

The best diving in Los Roques is in the waters along the south side of **Cayo Sal,** the 2½-mile strip of land running along the southern edge of the archipelago. In fact, it is the first piece of land you'll see when flying to Los Roques. Because it is on the outer edge of the archipelago, currents tend to be quite strong. The reef crests at 60 feet, where you will find brain, fire, staghorn and elkhorn corals as well as white, green and purple sponges. A vertical wall drops 300 feet to a sandy bottom where a 30° slope continues as far downward as 1,000 feet. Large fish, including sharks, frequent the deep waters.

The highlight of diving Cayo Sal are two caves. One is at 130 feet on the west side, while somewhere along the center of the cay a long tunnel leads to the second one. Both caves are full of corals.

Cayo de Agua, the most westerly of the cays, and **Dos Mosquises** and **La Pelona** nearby, offer great diving and snorkeling. Since they are a four- to five-hour trip from Gran Roque by boat, you should plan on an overnight stay. On the northeast side of Cayo de Agua there is a drop down to about 1,300 feet. Lots of coral and fish in relatively shallow waters make the area between the Dos Mosquises terrific for snorkeling. The Fundación Científica is on the east side of Dos Mosquises.

A Special Trip: Isla Las Aves

For a real adventure, charter a yacht and set sail for Isla Las Aves, an uninhabited island to the west, midway between Los Roques and Bonaire. This unspoiled paradise of virgin reefs and turquoise seas is like Los Roques 20 years ago before they were inhabited. It's a four- to five-hour trip from Gran Roque. To make the most of it you should plan on spending four to five days there. Because the island is uninhabited, you'll need to bring supplies for the entire time you plan to be away, plus enough for an extra day or two, just in case.

A Stroll Around Gran Roque

Be sure to take some time to wander around Gran Roque, either in the morning before breakfast or in the afternoon after you return from a tour of the cays.

Until around 1992 there were no posadas or lodgings on Gran Roque. The island's only inhabitants were the seasonal fishermen and their families, most of whom came from Margarita when lobster was in season. Once commercial airlines began to provide service to Los Roques, tourism became an additional source of income and many of the fishermen converted their homes to posadas or small guest houses.

Between the airstrip on the eastern side of the island and the beach on the western edge, is the village of Gran Roque. At its center is the requisite Plaza Bolívar. A small bust of El Libertador replaces the equestrian statue common to most larger towns and cities. You won't find any cars here, just a few dusty dirt roads branching out from the plaza. Everything is within a short walk of everything else.

Small one- and two-story homes, colorfully painted in pastels, line the narrow streets and surround the plaza. Several, if not the majority, are posadas. Residents shop in the commissary, which stocks goods from the mainland. Fresh water is brought in by tanker every two weeks or so. Television is conspicuously absent. The **Nueva Cadiz Bar** and the **Pizza Plaza Pub**, as well as the **Luna Blu**, a small souvenir shop that features handpainted T-shirts, are located on the Plaza.

The beach on the western side of Gran Roque is a lovely vantage point for watching the sun set as the locals secure their launches for the night.

On the western side of the hill on the back of the island, a path leads to the lighthouse. The lighthouse was constructed during colonial times by Dutch settlers who had come to Gran Roque to farm salt. They were given permission to settle here on the condition that they built a **lighthouse**. The top of the hill offers a panoramic view of Gran Roque as well as the neighboring cays and as far away as Cayo Sal and Dos Mosquises.

The **lagoons** on the northeastern edge of the island are a popular feeding ground for birds. As many as 80 different types of seabirds live in Los Roques, either

year-round or during the winter months. Though practically bone dry in the summer, the lagoons fill up with
water during the "rainy" winter months. The view of
the lagoons from the top of the hill is especially lovely
in the early morning when the birds are arriving to
feed.

Caracas After Dark

Caracas is very much a town for night people. This is no place for a hot Ovaltine and early-to-bed routine. The restaurants, nightclubs and sidewalk cafes remain open late, often well into the early morning hours. The reason is simple. Caraqueños still maintain the centuries-old tradition of the midday break, which usually extends from noon to 2 or even 3 pm.

Office workers finish work about 7 pm, head home for a drink, shower, change clothes, and head out for a 9 pm dinner. To ready yourself for this style, we recommend an afternoon nap.

We have listed theaters, cinemas, opera houses, concert halls and nightclubs. We have nine categories of clubs, ranging from singles spots to jumping mariachi places, from strip joints to cocktail lounges.

Theater

A ramp over the highway connects the theater with the Hilton.

We start sedately with theater; and in Caracas that means the **Teatro Teresa Carreño**, a modern cultural complex similar to New York's Lincoln Center. It is the hub of cultural events for the city. Rotating with opera, plays, music and dance, the Teresa Carreño is a great place to experience Caracas and its own culture as well as how it plugs into international culture.

Teresa Carreño was a pianist, and the statues of her and Vincente Emilio Sojo outside the entrance pay homage to two of Venezuela's cultural heroes. I saw Bellini's *Norma* here and it was first rate.

There are no bad seats in the Teatro Teresa Carreño, and with $15 orchestra seats you can't go wrong. The theater is across from the Caracas Hilton Hotel.

In the El Silencio district is the **Teatro Municipal**, the center of activity before Teresa Carreño. Working on a slightly less active schedule and losing many of its customers to Teresa Carreño, the municipal theater still is host to visiting operas, ballets, symphonies and theater groups.

Both theaters have schedules listed in *The Daily Journal.*

English-language theater can be seen occasionally at the **Caracas Playhouse**, Calle Chivacoa in San Román near Las Mercedes. Plays as various as *Sleuth, Waiting for Godot, Fiddler on the Roof,* and *Prisoner of Second Avenue* can be seen. Performances are in a 400-seat theater, with shows usually on the weekends. Check *The Daily Journal.*

Cinema

Movie buffs will not have to miss a single US release, since film houses here stay current and so far have resisted dubbing (except for children's films). *The Daily Journal* has complete listings, reviews and times. Films are rated by age groupings, and admission restrictions are enforced.

Nightclubs

If you have come to Caracas for a rest, skip this section because Caraqueños love to dance, loudly and with vigor. As is common throughout Latin America, most clubs have a couples-only policy. We have noted the exceptions. Minimum drinking age is 18 unless otherwise noted. We have surveyed intimate cocktail lounges, singles places, student hangouts, gay bars, and clubs where entertainment is the draw.

Clubs with Music

Pal's Club
Centro Comercial
Centro Ciudad Comercial Tamanaco
Level C-1
☎ 9599-3274
Open 8 pm, Tues. - Sun.

A private club, dress here tends to be more formal. Men may need a jacket to get in.

Pal's Club is the most recent rendition of a place whose name and decor are always in synch with the latest trends in the club scene. This private club is always in vogue and you should dress accordingly. It was formerly the Paladium, and City Hall before that.

El Sarao
Centro Comercial Bello Campo
Basement Level
☎ 267-4581
Parking

A fashionable crowd gathers to *rumbiar* (to party) at El Sarao. It has all the right ingredients: rum, non-stop salsa and a large dance floor. Music is often provided by a live orchestra. The dress code, jacket for men and appropriate attire for women, is enforced.

Barrock
4a Transversal between
4a Av and Av San Felipe
(Altamira)
☎ 266-7841
Valet parking

This is definitely the most unusual of Caracas' night spots. The decor has been carefully crafted to look as if it's been there since the 18th century. Heavy furnishings and imposing draperies combine with peeling wallpaper and cracks in the plaster to create an air of decadence. You have your choice of several different settings, including a smoking lounge, semi-private sitting rooms, a billiard area, and a piano bar.

Moma
Av Principal de la Castellana
☎ 263-0453
Closed Sun. through Wed.
Parking
One of the hottest clubs in Caracas, Moma is the gathering place for the younger members of the city's idle rich. There's a large dance floor downstairs and pool tables on the upper level.

Magic
Calle Madrid
(Las Mercedes)
☎ 993-6829
Closed Sun.

Live music is often on tap at Magic, another of the more popular spots in town. A favorite with singles, the large dance floor is surrounded by comfortable couchettes and tables. You can't miss the waterfall at the entrance. No cover charge.

Cafe L'Attico
Av Luis Roches
(Altamira)
☎ 261-2819
Very European in style, L'Attico has video discs that shake the place and make it hop. There are pop posters lining the walls and a large bar in the center of the dance floor. Food and drinks are served. There is a Sun. brunch and occasionally Ladies Nights, where second drinks are free. This is a good place to meet single guys and gals.

Another place where singles are admitted.

A portrait of Winston Churchill stares at you from the bar.

Madison Pub

Av Principal Bello Campo
Open Mon. - Sun., 8 pm
☎ 263-7662

The elegantly furnished Madison's Pub is a perfect choice if you are looking for a more refined atmosphere. Guests settle into upholstered couches and Windsor chairs to chat and listen to live piano music. Frequented by a chic crowd.

La Cantina

Calle Madrid, between Veracruz and Caroní
(Las Mercedes)
☎ 993-5548

The crowd outside La Cantina reminds us of clubs in Manhattan where everyone hopes they look hip enough to be allowed in by the bouncers guarding the entrance. Inside, Colombian music dominates. Cumbias, vallenatos and salsa grace the dance floor.

Hipocampo

Centro Comercial Chacaíto
No. 215 (Chacaíto District)
Open 10 pm - 5 am (nightly)
☎ 952-0882

Live music that staggers Latin, French, English and American tunes. The dance orchestra is of the old jazz sort and fun to watch. The Salani brothers – Renato and Julio – lead the main combo but there are alternating combos for rock and Latin music.

Liverpool

Av Principal de Las Mercedes (corner of Calle Londres)
(Las Mercedes)
Open 4 pm onward
☎ 993-6165

Liverpool is another club featuring live music. Dress is on the formal side.

90 Grados
Centro Ciudad Comercial Tamanaco
1a Etapa, Level C-2
9 pm - 4 am
Parking
☎ 959-0441
If you really want to dance, this is the place. The rhythms will really get you moving. Dress appropriately, as how you look on the outside may be your ticket inside.

Le Club
Centro Comercial Chacaíto
(Downstairs)
9 pm - 3 am (closed Mon.s)
☎ 951-2084
The oldest and still considered the most exclusive private club in Caracas, its decor goes back to the '70s when Venezuela was oil rich and the most prosperous country in Latin America. Nowadays it's becoming a bit run down – though still worth trying to get an invitation.

Croco's Club
Av Venezuela
(El Rosal)
Open every night till 5 am
☎ 951-4703
Croco's is another very popular private club. Despite the ivory bar, dress here is less formal than at some of our other selections.

If you're looking for an all-American sports bar, complete with large-screen TV, head next door.

Club M-LXXX
Av Francisco Miranda
Centro Lido
☎ 953-6614
Parking

A favorite of well-to-do university students, Club M-LXXX features hard-driving music and a huge dance floor in a Grecian setting. There's often live music.

Weekends
Av San Juan Bosco at 2nd Transversal (Altamira)
12 noon - 1:30 am
☎ 261-4863

A good place for a sandwich any time of day.

Although not a place to dance, this is a premiere night spot. Very hip, with three levels of intertwining booths and tables, bars and videos. There's a huge video screen in the center of the bar and little video screens scattered throughout, along with several pool tables. The fancy bar is both technologically advanced and chic. Weekends are a magnet for singles and couples. Even if it is for an hour, you owe it to yourself to stop by. There is often live music.

Couples only.

The Flower
Av Principal La Castellana
Plaza La Castellana
6 pm - 3 am
☎ 393-3013

You've heard of hearts and flowers. In this disco-theque it's music and flowers. You have a choice between hard rock (lower level) and Latin and pop (upper level), but whatever you choose, the petals will follow you. With a flower-shaped bar, flowered walls, flowered vests on the waiters, you wonder for a moment if you've wandered into a hothouse. Flower nuts will dig it. As for the rest of you, come in and smell your way around.

Xanadu
Av Blandín, Plaza La Castellana
(La Castellana)
Open Mon. - Sat.
☎ 263-0415
Formerly La Jungla, Xanadu, in our eyes, is an improvement over its predecessor. Patrons here dance and listen to both live and disco music in very nicely decorated and comfortable surroundings. A jacket is required for men.

Brooklyn
Av Tamanaco 36
(El Rosal)
☎ 952-2511
Closed Mon.
It's not the East River, but you do cross a bridge to get there. A replica of the Brooklyn Bridge is at the entrance to this popular dance club characterized by contrasts. Live bands alternate with Techno-house and, though it has an east coast name, the food is Tex-Mex. Eclectic decor includes *Gone with the Wind* posters, ice cream parlour booths and video screens. There are several large pool tables as well.

Doors
Calle Madrid
☎ 91-2022
Closed Mon.
If heavy metal, female mud wrestling and vaseline wars are your thing, then check this club out. Otherwise, don't waste your time. However, some good local bands do perform here from time to time.

Mariachi Clubs

There are a couple of good mariachi clubs here that serve up authentic Mexican music and food. You should try one. The music is loud and boisterous and you will find yourself joining in the festivities. Lots of fun.

Las Trompetas De Mexico
Av Venezuela
(El Rosal District)
7 pm - 5 am
☎ 951-7986

The margaritas are strictly first-class here.

Loud, sprawling and jumping, Las Trompetas is a touch of Mexico in Caracas. Patrons throng the place night after night, eager to clap and sing along with the strolling sombrero- and serape-clad mariachi musicians who start at 9 nightly. The Mexican atmosphere extends to the food and you should sample the tacos, tamales, and enchiladas. Sip a cocktail. A long passageway extends from the street, leading into the large ranch-like main room, complete with wall decor of saddles, bows and arrows, and sombreros.

Píano Bars

La Ronda
Caracas Hilton
(El Conde District)
Subdued and blue-lighted, La Ronda is for the overworked person who wants to be lulled. Along with the drinks are excellent snacks. No cover or minimum.

Barba Roja
Av Tamanaco
(El Rosal District)
9 pm - 4 am
☎ 951-6069
This is a popular, crowded stop for Caraqueños.

Cocktail Lounges & Pubs

Juan Sebastian Bar
Av Venezuela
(El Rosal District)
11 am - 4:30 pm; (closed Sun.)
☎ 951-0595
With a jazz trio, Juan Sebastian is slightly more active than the other pubs mentioned because of the music. Also with a regular clientele, the pub has a good onion soup. Singles admitted.

Dallas Texas Café
Av Principal de las Mercedes
An all-American sports bar complete with big screen TV and everything that goes with it. This is the place to be on Sun. afternoons and Mon. nights during football season. You can watch NBA games here too.

Greenwich
1a Av Ed. Marvin
(Altamira)
☎ 267-1760
Valet parking
This tiny English-style pub gets crowded very quickly. Unless you arrive early in the evening, you'll have to stand with everyone else. Occasionally there is live music. It adds to the crowd and the noise, but little else. Greenwich is a popular pick-up joint.

Stage
Av Luis Roche
between the First and Second Transversales
(Altamira)
☎ 285-7172
This jazz club on the second level of the Safari Cafe had just opened when we were last in Caracas in January of 1997.

A Note for Singles

Single women are not viewed favorably in Caracas, a product of ages-old Spanish culture. Although Caracas is way ahead of other Latin American countries in accepting the autonomy of women, going out at night on your own can still be a tense thing. It's not worth getting heated up over. This is their culture and, as a visitor, you don't need to clash with it.

There is a weekly singles gathering at the Hotel Continental Altamira every Thursday. It takes place at the bar on the main floor. Look for the ad in the Thursday *Daily Journal.*

Cervecerías

There are hundreds of these establishments throughout Caracas. Loosely translated as "beer halls," cervecerías do not resemble what you might find in downtown Munich. It is difficult to generalize since some are earthy, others elaborate, some noisy and crowded. All are great fun.

Salas de Bingo

Within the last five years, a new form of entertainment has sprung up all over Caracas. Known as Salas del Bingo or simply Bingos, they have little to do with bingo as we know it. Instead, they are a Las Vegas-style alternative to the Video Arcade. Electronic slot machines and video poker, blackjack and the like are the gamblers alternative to pinball.

Caracas Shopping

Shopping centers, called "Centros Comerciales," dot the city, filling it with the bustle of the consumer. The range is as wide as in the US, with high-priced international goods, department stores like Macy's and local stores that are more ragtag.

Boutiques freckle the city, and have excellent clothes. Both men and women can order custom-made clothing and have it ready within a few days. Sales personnel may be more attentive than you're accustomed to. Many will insist on accompanying you while you browse. Occasionally, a proprietor might even approach you while you're window shopping.

Stores open at 9 am and close at 7 pm, including Saturdays. They are often closed from noon until 3 pm for midday break.

Most shops are open on Sat.

Where to Shop

To simplify your search, we have concentrated on the key shopping areas: **Avenida Lincoln**, the main thoroughfare in La Sabana Grande district; the **Centro Comercial Chacaíto**, an important shopping center – virtually an extension of the eastern end of the Sabana Grande district. The Broadway Cinema on Avenida Lincoln is an approximate demarcation point between Sabana Grande and the Chacaíto shopping center. The third shopping point is the tri-level **Concresa**, largest in Caracas, in Prado del Este.

The fourth is the **Paseo Las Mercedes**, part of an attractive shopping complex that includes the Paseo Las Mercedes Hotel in Las Mercedes.

Near La Carlota Airport is **Centro Ciudad Comercial Tamanaco** (usually called C.C.C.T.), newest of the shopping centers and probably the best. The new Eurobuilding, a five-star hotel, is located almost within walking distance.

La Sabana Grande

The Metro has a stop at each end of La Sabana Grande.

Along a one-mile stretch of Avenida Lincoln (also called Calle Sabana Grande) there are hundreds of shops offering clothing, shoes, toys, jewelry, native crafts and gifts. There is an almost infinite variety. You can stroll through here for two days and still not visit all the shops of interest.

Centro Comercial Chacaíto

This elegant tri-level shopping center specializes in high fashion boutiques where you will find outlets for Pierre Cardin, Yves St. Laurent, Charles Jourdan, and Gucci. But even if you're not looking for a Pucci, the center deserves some of your browsing time.

Concresa

There are five cinemas in this complex.

On a par with the Chacaíto Center, this tri-level structure features high fashion outlets such as Charles Jourdan, Carnaby, King's Row and Biki Bou. Located south of the Tamanaco Hotel in Prado del Este.

Paseo Las Mercedes

This large and elegant tri-level shopping center houses fine restaurants (Il Romanaccio), popular shops and "La Cuadra," an area on the main level that is a replica of colonial Caracas, from its cobblestone streets to its shops.

Centro Ciudad Comercial Tamanaco

Probably the most modern of the shopping centers, C.C.C.T. is home to branches of many fine chain stores. The Marisqueria Restaurant is here, and the shopping center is usually crowded even at night when the stores are closed. The C.C.C.T. Hotel is also here.

Sizes (Tamaños)

Sizes are different here than in North America. Just to be safe, we recommend that you try on everything first. The comparison chart on page 13 will give you a good start.

What to Buy

Without question, shoes provide the best value – low price coupled with fine quality. Fine shoes line the windows of many shops at half, and more, off the price you'd pay in the United States. Also, leather, toys, gold and handicrafts stand out as items to concentrate on.

Shoes

Shoes are a great buy. There are rows of shoe stores on Avenida Lincoln in Sabana Grande and many in the C.C.C.T. and Chacaíto shopping centers. Venezuela has its own shoe industry and is not merely an importer of European and American designs. All styles have one thing in common – they are sold at great discounts. Here is a brief list of stores.

Charles Jourdan
Centro Ciudad Comercial Tamanaco
☎ 925-405
A huge outlet, with a myriad of choices, both international and domestic.

Nardi
Centro Ciudad Comercial Tamanaco
Main floor
☎ 915-849
Specializing in women's shoes, with prices starting at about $20 and reaching much higher. Men's shoes too. Bags for ladies in elegant designs.

Trevis
Centro Comercial Chacaíto
☎ 729-851
Ladies' and men's shoes are bargains here.

Matignon
Centro Ciudad Comercial Tamanaco
☎ 959-3113
Another fine outlet for high fashion ladies' shoes. They have the exclusive on Christian Dior.

Calzador Tulio
Centro Comercial Chacaíto
☎ 952-0920
Centro Ciudad Comercial Tamanaco
☎ 959-0564

Leather shoes are an incredible bargain.

This store carries a small selection of high quality shoes. The store will order your size, which will take a few days, if they do not carry it. The fabrics for the shoes are imported but they are made in Venezuela.

Beltrami
1) Centro Ciudad Comercial Tamanaco
☎ 959-2545
2) Calle El Recreo, The Rupi Building
(Sabana Grande)
3) Centro Comercial Paseo Las Mercedes
Beltrami is another fine choice for designer footware.

Leather

Fascinación
Centro Ciudad Comercial Tamanaco
☎ 261-9022, 261-7998
With fantastic leather goods, ranging from clothes to bras and other accessories, this is a good start for the beginning foray into Venezuela's shopping world.

Ferradini
Centro Ciudad Comercial Tamanaco
☎ 969-1010
Near Fascinación. We consider these two shops the best for leather items.

Cesare Farima nearby (☎ 959-1579) is another fine option.

Boutiques

The boutique is as common to Caracas as to Paris. Yet, wonderfully, the prices seem garage sale by comparison. The shops mentioned stress sportswear, usually imported from France, Italy, Spain and the US. The boutiques we have listed are centered around the C.C.C.T. and Paseo Las Mercedes shopping centers and the Sabana Grande, but shops are all over the city.

These attractive shops draw an upscale clientele.

People
1) Centro Comercial
2) Paseo Las Mercedes, Local N1A2
☎ 918-742
One of my favorites. Trendy items.

Aqualady
Paseo Las Mercedes
☎ 923-108
Racks and racks of super items.

Sylvia S. Denis
Centro Ciudad Comercial Tamanaco
☎ 918-163
For that special outfit.

Maria Pia
Nivel C-1
Centro Ciudad Comercial Tamanaco
☎ 959-1240
Emphasis on Italian imports.

Tokyu
(Next to Cada Supermarket)
Centro Ciudad Comercial Tamanaco
☎ 928-691
Wide selection. Friendly sales staff.

Rori 2000
C.C.C.T., downstairs
☎ 261-6938, 261-5914
Futuristic in decor and merchandise.

King's Road Beat Time
Centro Comercial Chacaíto
Main Level
Super chic and alive, this high-priced bi-level boutique prides itself on a clientele that includes the daughters of Caracas' wealthiest families.

Nosotras Boutique
Av Lincoln and Pasaje Recreo
(Sabana Grande District)
Nosotras Boutique highlights Venezuelan designs instead of the international look, and for this reason is special.

Rachel's Boutique
Calle Unión (Off Av Lincoln)
(Sabana Grande District)
French and Italian imports are king here and are attractively showcased by Rachel, who offers a selection of versatile costume jewelry as accessories for her nylon dresses and pants suits. Nice shop, a half-block off Avenida Lincoln.

Chopper
Av Lincoln
(Sabana Grande District)
Good location, fine quality and selection.

Angelo Modas
Av Lincoln
(Sabana Grande District)
The wildest styles are always in Angelo Modas, and for this reason he is most popular with the younger crowd.

And for Men...

L'Incontro
Centro Ciudad Comercial Tamanaco
☎ 959-7577
A fine choice for those whose taste runs to European-style designer men's wear.

Vogue
1) Centro Comercial Chacaíto
2) Av Lincoln, Sabana Grande
3) C.C.C.T.
For a large and varied selection of both handmade shoes and custom suits, Vogue's three branches have it.

O'Leary
Av Lincoln (edificio Don Victor)
(Sabana Grande District)
With French, Italian, Spanish and West German imports. O'Leary has suits, shoes, ties and socks at prices from moderate to high by Venezuelan standards.

Phil Davis
Av Lincoln
(Sabana Grande District)
This store sells all men's clothing, including Venezuelan-made Givenchy suits and first-rate Italian shirts. There are other branches in Caracas.

Georges
1) Av Lincoln
2) Av La Mercedes
3) C.C.C.T.

With two other shops, one in the Macuto Sheraton, this was the original men's boutique in Caracas, and still carries weight. Arnold bought a pair of swim trunks here during his last visit, and drove the ladies wild (so he says).

Carnaby

Four outlets: one in the Centro Comercial Chacaíto, another in the Concresa Shopping Center a third at Calle Real de Sabana Grande, and another at C.C.C.T.

Antique Shops

ACD Antiguedades
Hotel Tamanaco
(Shop 23 – Main Floor)
☎ 909-8227

There is an incredible selection of fine items here. Prices are high.

The owner and director of ACD Antiguedades is a member of LAPADA, the London and Provincial Antique Dealers' Association, and has spent over two decades gathering antiques, especially in Europe and the Orient. Harmoniously displayed at the Tamanaco branch are a wealth of objets d'art which she has culled from widely varying cultures.

Notable among the American antiques is the collection of pre-Columbian stone heads from the Tumaco-La Tolita civilization of northwest South America. There are wood and ivory sculptures from west and central Africa.

A Chinese embroidered silk panel from the Ching Dynasty covers one of the walls. Also from China are selected examples of cloisonné, blue and white porcelains, jades, and an extensive collection of snuff bottles – beautifully worked in jade, porcelain and many other materials. Japanese woodcuts, ivories and porcelains are among the antiques from other parts of Asia.

ACD Antiguedades is open Tues. through Sat., from 10 am to 7 pm, with a midday break for lunch. The shop changes part of its exhibit every month, making it a rewarding place for browsing at any time.

Manuel Herrera
Case De Antiguedades
Calle Paris
(Las Mercedes)
While the once abundant colonial and pre-colonial antiques are largely depleted, by careful browsing you can still come up with an occasional nugget amidst the dross. One place to look is Manuel Herrera's, a ramshackle store that is almost impossible to find because there is no sign and no street number. Look for the Red Cross Hospital on Avenida Andrés Bello. The shop is behind the hospital and the only designation is a faded sign that reads: "Cervecería a Paradero," which tells you only that a brewery once existed there. Bargaining is in here. We are partial to the old brass buried under the debris. The hours are 8 am - 6:30 pm.

A. E. Limes
Calle Girasol
(Prados del Este)
This fine shop features reproductions of Spanish colonial furniture and accessories. There are also genuine antiques.

Galeria Prestige
Av Principal
La Florida
☎ 784-365
Paintings by classical Venezuelan masters; a fine selection of European furniture and silver; and one of the most famous Bacarat lamp collections in the city are a few of the treasures you'll find here.

Boris y Samuel (B y S)
Av Luis Roche
Edificio Helena, Loca 1
(Altamira)
☎ 284-5009

This Colombian company enjoys a world-wide reputation. You can shop with confidence.

Among the most knowledgeable and respected antique dealers in the city, Boris y Samuel have just opened up shop in their new location in Altamira. If you don't find what you're looking for here, they'll send you to the main shop in Los Chorros. B y S is patronized by Caracas' most well-heeled residents.

Pre-Columbian Artifacts

Galeria Cano
Paseo Las Mercedes
Mezzanine No. 110
☎ 917-324

You will find excavated relics, some 1,000 years old. Prices start at $50. With its main office in Bogotá, Galería Cano is a special place, well worth visiting.

Típico Shops (Handicrafts)

Handicraft shops, also known as típico shops, are the stores that sell the wide gamut of goods falling under the title "ornaments," from jewelry, folk art, and toys, to wood pieces.

Típico
Hotel Tamanaco
☎ 911-413

A fine assortment of paintings, handmade rugs, pottery and pillow covers, as well as handprinted T-shirts, hostess outfits and handbags. Unusual Indian items, ceramics and novelties are on sale too. Great for browsing.

Tipicalia Hilton
Caracas Hilton
This large shop in the Hilton Hotel is a good place to browse for an unusual gift.

El Taller de La Esquina
Centro Comercial
Paseo Las Mercedes
☎ 926-308
You'll find lovely handcrafted gifts and artwork.

Rocio
Plaza Bolívar
An interesting open-air place to browse. They even sell musical instruments.

Artesanías Venezolanas
Gran Av Sabana Grande
Palacio de Las Industrias
(Sabana Grande District)
Offering a wide selection of gifts, this store has paper maché, hammocks, blankets, wood sculptures, etched ceramic pieces, rag dolls, ash trays and jewelry.

Casa De Las Artesanías
Pasaje El Recreo
(Sabana Grande District)
Operated by the government, this shop sells off-beat items from all over the country, and at the same time serves as an exhibition site for national handicrafts. Selections are limited but you can find first-rate hand-made rugs and pillow covers, as well as more common items.

El Artesano
Av Mirador (near Cine Paris)
(La Florida District)

Off the beaten track, this típico shop has handicrafts from other Latin American countries as well as Venezuela. Llama rugs and ceramic bulls from Peru, and belts and ponchos from Guatemala and Costa Rica are all available.

Venezuelan Art

Salón Lectura
Plaza Bolívar
(El Silencio District)
Probably stocking the best values in Caracas, Salón Lectura is run by the government and is an art gallery that showcases undiscovered talent. Exhibitions usually feature one artist.

Galería Odalys
Centro Comercial Concresa, Ground Floor
☎ 979-5942
A terrific place for budding art collectors to start. Venezuelan artists are featured.

d'atelier
Caracas Hilton
☎ 503-4307
You're certain to find a lovely gift among original enamel, ceramic, glass and handmade paper items. They will also pack and ship your purchases home.

Galería De Arte Sans Souci
If you are serious about an art purchase, try this shop.

Centro Comercial Chacaíto
An art gallery in the New York sense. Sans Souci features a variety of Venezuelan paintings. Open Sun. mornings.

Arte & Estilo
Galerías Colbert
☎ 959-0214
This lovely shop features the best in Venezuelan paintings and art. The selection is enormous.

Fabrics

Many well-dressed Caraqueñas still rely on a seamstress for their wardrobe essentials. These shops feature fine fabrics.

Raymar
Centro Comercial Chacaíto
(Main Level – Rear)
We were told of Raymar by a Caraqueña businesswoman who insists that Raymar has no equal in Venezuela, particularly in silk crepes from France and Italy.

Fabrics are sold by the meter and the salespeople are very helpful. Raymar also has fine linens.

Selecta
Paseo Las Mercedes
☎ 927-364
Similar to Raymar. Compare fabrics before purchasing.

Jewelry Shops (Joyerías)

Gold pins, earrings, pendants, and the like are the items to buy here. Some less expensive pieces made of cochano gold (gold with a low luster finish) are particularly good values in Caracas. There are many reliable jewelry shops here. Don't limit yourself to our few selections, which are a sampling. We start with the best.

H. Stern
Hotel Tamanaco
International Airport
This Rio-based chain, with outlets in 13 countries worldwide, specializes in gemstones with unique settings crafted by native artisans. You'll find excellent values in cochano gold and pearl items designed by Venezuelan artists. Orchid and gold nugget motifs, both symbols of Venezuela, make wonderful gifts. Any purchase can be exchanged within a year at any outlet worldwide. The service is first-rate and the shops are conveniently located. H. Stern has always been our first choice for jewelry.

The fine cochano jewelry has a low-luster finish and is a great buy here.

Joyeria El Arte
Av Lincoln, No. 229
(Sabana Grande District)
Well regarded by its loyal patrons, this shop offers cochano necklaces and earrings that are good values.

Italcambio
Av Casanova
(Sabana Grande District)
Italcambio features pieces of Italian design and heritage as well as that of Venezuela, including a 22K Mussolini commemorative coin, and many other fine coins that can be set by your own jeweler as rings, earrings, pendants, etc.

The Gold Market

It's worth your time to visit the Gold Market in the Edificio La Francia Building downtown near the Plaza Bolívar. Here, you will find nine floors of shops featuring gold jewelry, watches, bracelets, necklaces, rings, earrings, and chains. It's best for browsing.

Open from 9 am until 12:30 pm and 2:30 pm until 6 pm Mon. - Fri. The Gold Market is Venezuela's answer to New York City's 47th Street.

For Children

If you take only one thing home with you, let it be a piñata, a reinforced papier mache figure of an animal, or sometimes a comic or superhero like Superman or Popeye. These pieces have special roles at parties. Tradition dictates that the hollow interior of the piñata be filled with small toys, candy and confetti. Then it is tied to a tree, and everyone, usually blindfolded, takes turns whacking it with a broom handle until it breaks.

La Piñata
Av Lincoln
(Sabana Grande District)

The largest piñatas we have seen are sold here. The problem with the really large ones is taking them home. It is difficult, but you can try.

La Gran Piñata
Av Jacinto y Traposos
(El Silencio District)

For the largest Piñata selection in the city, stop here. You will find enormous variety, along with the tiny toys you need for the stuffing. Typical stuffers are whistles, noisemakers, animal figures, yoyos, rings and watches.

Toy Stores

Jugueteria El Rosal
Av Pichincha
(El Rosal District)

After piñatas, you might be ready for a more conventional toy store.

Juguetelandia
Av Francisco de Miranda
(El Rosal District)

This store has a great variety of toys from all over the world.

Indian Hand-Woven Rugs

Tapicestere
C.C.C. Tamanaco

Drop in to view the exquisite Guajiro Indian rugs, which are uniquely woven. Designed by Luis Montiel, these brilliantly colored rugs are handmade in Paraguaipoa, an Indian Village near Maracaibo. Motifs feature birds, animals and flowers.

Blown Crystal

Arte Murano
Urb Potrerito
Via La Mariposa
In a small town, 20 minutes from city center, is this factory where you can watch the figures created. A showroom sells these attractive pieces. Prices start at $1 for small figurines. I purchased a small dog for $10.

If you can't get to the factory (most tours stop there) the airport shops feature Arte Murano at slightly higher prices. Look for the ICET trandemark.

Take the Autopista El Valle toward Maracay and Valencia to the Los Teques/Pan American Highway exit. Follow the Pan American Highway 15-20 minutes to the San Antonio de los Altos exit. Then follow the main avenue (you'll pass several shopping centers and office buildings) several miles to the older part of San Antonio de Los Altos. Bear left at the fork, then make a sharp right at the Potrerito sign. You'll make another right at the intersection. Arte Murano is another half-mile down the road on the right. The Candes Travel Agency offers morning and afternoon factory tours (☎ 571-0987 or 571-1709).

Smoke Shops

There are several smoke shops scattered throughout the city where you'll find high quality cigars, pipe tobaccos and handcrafted pipes. Among the finest are:

Humolandia
1) Paseo Las Mercedes
2) Centro Comercial Chacaíto
☎ 918-119

Inversiones Fumaven
1) Centro Ciudad Comercial Tamanaco
☎ 959-2216
2) Centro Comercial Plaza Las Américas
☎ 985-6980

Prestige
1) Centro Comercial Paseo Las Mercedes
☎ 91-7919
2) Centro Ciudad Comercial Tamanaco
☎ 959-1987
3) Hotel Tamanaco Shopping Arcade
4) Centro Comercial Chacaíto

Music

Two huge record stores are **Don Disco**, Chacaíto Shopping Center, lower level, and **Musical Magnus**, Edifico Arta, opposite the shopping center in Chacaíto. Both offer a wide choice of Latin tapes and records, and reasonably priced guitars.

Another good record store is **Disco Center** in the C.C.C.T. ☎ 924-278.

Books

All the deluxe hotels have bookstores that sell English-language books and magazines. Other bookstores are **Las Novedades**, C.C.C.T. (☎ 92-2055) and **Lectura**, in the Chacaíto Shopping Center. If you're looking for a book in English, the **Librería Inglesa** at Concresa 315 in Prados del Este (☎ 979-1308) is a good resource. If you're looking for a specific title, try **La Gran Pulpería de Libros Venezolanos Pasaje Zing** in Colón a Camejo (☎ 541-1286, fax 541-0046). If they don't have a copy on hand, they may be able to find it for you.

If rare books are your passion and you'd like to add some South American editions to your collection, visit the **Librería Historia** at Monjas a Padre Sierra, Edificio Oeste 2 0 No. 6 in front of the Capital Building (☎ 81-2377).

Caracas Etc.

The following is a glossary of tips, notes and basic data that we have compiled to aid you in your travels.

Airports

The **Símon Bolívar International Airport** and domestic terminal is in Maiquetia on the Caribbean, a half-hour drive north of Caracas. All commercial flights originating in Caracas depart from here. Most privately owned planes use the Aeropuerto Metropolitano and Aeropuerto Caracas, an hour's drive south of Caracas. Inside the city of Caracas is La Carlota, a military base, in current use for twin engines only. (The last dictator, Perez Jimenez, used it for his getaway.)

International Airlines

As of this writing, **United Airlines** has daily flights out of New York (5:05 pm) and Miami (6:45 pm) to Caracas and Maracaíbo. For schedule information and reservations in the United States, ☎ 800-241-6522; in Caracas, ☎ 284-4908.

American Airlines also flies to Caracas. For schedule information and reservations in the United States, ☎ 800-624-6262; in Caracas, ☎ 209-8111. As of this writing, flights depart from New York's Kennedy Airport every morning at 8:40 am, and there are also flights out of Miami.

Viasa, Venezuela's international carrier, flies out of Miami. For information, ☎ 800-468-4272; in Caracas, ☎ 576-2611.

Domestic Airlines

During our last visit to Venezuela we were struck by the growing number of small commercial airlines. **Aerotuy** or **LTA** (Líneas Turísticas Aerotuy) is the largest of those that cater almost exclusively to tourists, offering daytrips as well as all-inclusive overnight packages to Los Roques, the Orinoco Delta, Canaima, Margarita and other destinations. The Caracas office is in the Gran Sabana building on the Boulevard de Sabana Grande (☎ 761-6231 or 761-6247; fax 762-5254). **AeroEjecutivos**, which recently bought out another airline, also offers packages to Los Roques, Margarita, Canaima and El Yaví. They promise to be Aerotuy's chief competitor. AeroEjecutivos has a kiosk in the domestic terminal (☎ 02-929952 or 02-917942; fax 02-953-8181). **Rutaca** also caters to tourists and offers daytrips and packages to Los Roques, Margarita and is located in the domestic air terminal (☎ 31-524412; fax 085-24010).

Aviación Zuliana (☎ US 800-223-8780; Caracas 02-993-9966 or 993-2220) offers service to Maracaíbo, Margarita and Barcelona and also flies to Miami out of Maracaíbo. **Laser** (☎ 02-63-4227 or 263-4274; fax 02-235-8359 or 02-235-5566) flies to Margarita and Barcelona. **LAI** also flies between Caracas and Margarita (☎ 031-52476; fax 073-22668). **Avensa/Servivensa** (US, ☎ 800-428-3672; Caracas, ☎ 02-561-3366; fax 02-563-0225), the largest of the domestic airlines, offers service throughout the country as well as to Miami and New York's JFK airport. Though it once enjoyed a well-deserved reputation for dependability and quality, its performance seems to have slipped in recent years with last-minute cancellations and lengthy delays becoming more the norm than the exception. Their performance may have improved by the time you visit Venezuela. To be safe, ask around before making final arrangements.

American Consulate

The US Consulate is located in Colinas del Valle Arriba on the corner of Calle F with Calle Soapura (☎ 752-0532 or 752-4712).

Babysitters

Your hotel may be able to arrange for a sitter (probably a chambermaid). Establish a rate in advance at the desk. US baby foods and disposable diapers are available in local markets. Drugstores carry a good selection of US over-the-counter medicines.

British Consulate

The British Consulate is located on Avenida La Estancia in the Torre Las Mercedes building, Chuao District (☎ 751-1022).

Cada

Cada supermarkets are found in shopping centers throughout Caracas. Originally launched by an investment group headed by the Rockefeller family, stores in this chain are uniformly clean and well-stocked with North American as well as Venezuelan products.

Canadian Embassy

Located on the 7th floor of the Torre Europa on Av Francisco de Miranda in Chacaíto. ☎ 951-6166.

Car Rentals

Though there are several local agencies, we prefer the North American ones, which generally have branches in the airport and at the major hotels.

Avis:
Centro Ciudad Comercial Tamanaco. ☎ 959-5822.
Av. Principal de Bello Campo. ☎ 261-1135.
Budget:
Av Luis Roche, Altamira. ☎ 800-28343; fax 283-4698.

Dollar:
Av Venezuela, El Rosal. ☎ 953-5837.

Hertz:
Centro Ciudad Comercial Tamanaco. ☎ 959-2478.
Caracas Hilton. ☎ 503-4304.
Hotel Tamanaco Intercontinental. ☎ 208-7294.

Chocolate

Savoy is Venezuela's major chocolate and candy manufacturer, with shops scattered throughout the city. A major outlet is on Sabana Grande at the corner of Los Jabillos.

Churches

Catholicism is the predominant religion in Venezuela as it is throughout Latin America. Your hotel clerk will have a list of nearby churches with mass times. Many Protestant churches conduct services in English. Check *The Daily Journal* for listings.

Coffee

Venezuela grows its own which is somewhat stronger than Colombian coffee. Main brands are Imperial and Fama de América. International hotels have started to offer American-style coffee, although most Venezuelans drink espresso-style coffee. Served in demi-tasse cups it is "negrito" (no milk), "marroncito" (little milk) or "con leche pequeño" (milk coffee). You also can order your choice in larger cups. Order the negro grande (no milk), the marrón grande (little milk) or the con leche grande (milk coffee). Finally, if you prefer American-style coffee, order a "guayoyo."

Credit Cards

To report a lost or stolen credit card, it's best to place a collect call to the the United States office. Be sure to keep a copy of those numbers somewhere in your luggage. When paying by credit card you will usually have to write your passport number on the receipt.

Currency Exchange

It's often best to exchange money in the morning since the exchange windows may close without notice by late morning or early afternoon. Most banks will change dollars at the official rate, which is often slightly lower than that offered by the casas de cambio. Hotels generally offer the worst rates.

Department Stores

Maxy's, one of the most popular department stores, has a Caracas branch in Bello Monte, and **Beco** is in Chacaíto.

Departure Tax

You will pay a $20 tax when leaving Venezuela by air at the International Airport. There is also a nominal tax on all domestic flights.

Drugstores

These are quite common throughout the city. All are stocked with US cosmetics, drugs and toiletries. Pharmacies rotate Sun. and 24-hour openings so that one in each district is always open. Look for the illuminated Turno sign.

Electricity

Venezuela operates on 110 AC (identical to North America), so you will not need an electrical adapter.

Emergency

In case of any type of emergency, ☎ 171.

Flag

Venezuela's colors are red, yellow, and blue.

Government

Venezuela is a Democratic Republic of 20 states and a Federal District. The President and Legislature (Senate and Chamber of Deputies) are elected.

Hotdogs

Vendors are almost as common as in New York, and the toppings far more interesting than the standard saurkraut. You can top your *perrito caliente* with an enticing mix of *guasacaca* (avocado sauce), hardboiled egg, salad, mayonnaise, mustard, ketchup and whatever else may whet your appetite.

Jams & Jellies

Pick up a jar of Niña or La Vienese fruit jelly at any grocery store. First rate.

Kilometers

Instead of miles, kilometers are used here. One kilometer equals .62 (about 3/5ths) of a mile.

Magazines & Newspapers

Most popular is the Latin American edition of *Time* (in English), available at news stands for 75¢ on Wednesdays. *The Daily Journal*, in English, is 40¢. You can also buy all sorts of American and European magazines and books, which are sold in most major bookstores and hotel shops throughout Venezuela.

Maps

Huge revolving maps of Caracas are in the Centro Capriles, Plaza Venezuela. Another is in Centro Comercial Chacaíto, near Papagallo. Maps of Caracas and the country are available in bookstores and sometimes in gas stations along the way. Make sure you have one before you leave on a trip with a rented car; street signs outside Caracas are rare.

Mayor y Detal

This sign over many shops simply means wholesale and retail.

Medical Care

Hopefully someone at your hotel will be able to assist you in the case of a medical emergency. If you are in need of medical attention go to the nearest private clinic rather than a public hospital. You will need to pay by cash or credit card.

Population

Caracas has 4.5 million residents, while Venezuela has over 20 million.

Presidential Palace

This is located downtown on Av. Urdaneta and is called Miraflores Palace.

Radio

Check *The Daily Journal* for the English-language broadcast schedule of the Voice of America and Radio Canada.

Siesta

Business hours are generally 8 am - noon and 2 pm - 6 pm. Shops may close until 2:30 pm. This results in traffic jams at noon and at 2, besides the normal morning and evening rush hours.

Synagogue

The main temple is the Unión Israelita, one block from the Avila Hotel at Avenida Marquez del Toro, San Bernadino. B'nai Brith has an active chapter in Altamira on Transversal 9 and Avenida 7. Another important temple, Asociación Israelita de Venezuela (Seferdim), is in front of Plaza Colón next to Plaza Venezuela.

Taxis

It's best to avoid gypsy cabs. Licensed cabs have a yellow plate that says "Libre." Always agree on the fare before getting into the cab, and don't be afraid to bargain. Trips within Caracas should run around $2 to $3. It's best not to pay in large bills since the driver may tell you he doesn't have change. If you're out at night, ask the maitre d' to phone a cab or do so yourself. Call **Tele Taxi** at ☎ 752-4155 or 752-9122, or **Taxi Móvil Enlace** at ☎ 577-0922 or 577-3344.

Public Telephones

The Venezuelan phone system is relatively efficient and easy to use. You must purchase a phone card from either a kiosk or a pharmacy which displays the CANTV logo. Cards are available in 1,000 and 2,000 B denominations. Insert your card in the slot on the phone and dial the number. There is a screen on the phone which will tell you how much you have left on the card.

To call overseas, dial 00, then the country code and number you want to call. To reach the AT&T overseas operator, dial 800-111-20 or 800-111-21.

Street Crime

Street crime has become a serious problem in Caracas. Leave your expensive jewelry and watches at home or, if you must bring them with you, in the hotel safe. Don't make the mistake of wearing a good fake. The last person you want to fool is a thief. The same goes for lots of cash. Don't keep all your money in one place. It's best to carry bills in small denominations. Keep some in your pockets for paying cabs, bus fares, etc., with the rest in a money belt along with credit cards and your passport. When you're out at night, phone a cab from the restaurant or nightclub. Don't leave valuables in your rental car. Remember, Caracas is a big city. Exercise the same caution, if not more, as you would in any other big city.

Temperatures

Heat is measured in Centrigrade not Fahrenheit.

Centigrade	Fahrenheit
0	32
5	41
10	50
15	59
20	68
25	77
30	86
35	95
37	98.6

Tipping

Bellhops expect 10 Bs per large bag. Cab drivers are not tipped. Waiters should be tipped 5% over the service charge for satisfactory service.

Tobacco

Marlboro and Viceroy are made in Venezuela and sell for about 40¢. Local brands include Astor and Belmont (30¢). Pipe tobacco made in the US can cost $3. Try local brands, Bond Street or Caporal (65¢).

Travel Agents

For day and evening tours of Caracas as well as day trips to Colonia Tovar and the Murano Glass Factory, contact **Candes Tours** at ☎ 571-1709 or 571-0987.

At the airport in Maiquetía you will probably be besieged by tour operator and agency representatives hawking trips. Unfortunately, not all are as reliable or as trustworthy as you would hope. Thankfully, this does not hold true for the folks at **Loggage Care** in the domestic terminal. Knowledgeable, friendly and honest, they won't steer you wrong. Staff members speak English, German and Italian in addition to Spanish. ☎ (031) 55-2564 or (031) 55-1577, fax (031) 55-1055; cellular (016) 22-5764.

Yogurt

A delicious local brand is Yoka, sold in many markets.

El Litoral

"The Beach"

On the other side of the mountains that dwarf Caracas lies the Caribbean. Since the airport is there as well, this will be the view that greets you as your flight approaches Venezuela. The beach area, El Litoral, is well equipped with hotels and restaurants. Caracas is only 30 minutes away.

The towns along the beach are quieter than Caracas, yet still active and energetic. But you'll have to wait for Puerto La Cruz or Margarita if you want to swim, as the shores are mostly rocky and the strong current is unsafe for swimming in most places. There are, however, a few *balnearios*, places where jetties have been built to create safe swimming.

From the airport, the main beach thoroughfare is **Avenida La Playa**, which runs through all the major beach towns. From Caracas, the main route to the beach is a four-lane autopista. But there are several other routes. The Old Road, also connecting Caracas and El Litoral, winds for 16 miles from Avenida Sucre, just east of the autopista, to Maiquetía, the town where the airport is located.

Reaching your beach hotel from Maiquetía airport is as easy as hailing a cab, and that's just what you must do. The taxi ride is only 20 minutes to the hotel furthest from the airport. Heading East from Maiquetía you will travel along Avenida La Playa, the main beach road that winds through El Litoral's several communities. First is **La Guaira**, a port town, then **Macuto**, where the cable car from Caracas terminates, and **Caraballeda**, where the majority of the beach hotels and restaurants are located. It's followed by **Naiguata**, home of the Puerto Azul, a private luxury club; and finally to **Los Caracas**, a community comprised largely of government-sponsored weekend houses for Caraqueño workers.

What to Wear

The Caribbean side of the mountains is much hotter than the Caracas side. Average temperatures are 85° to 90° in the afternoons, and a balmy 75° to 80° in the evenings. Dress accordingly, keeping in mind that most hotels, restaurants, and clubs are air-conditioned. Both men and women will want at least one dressy (lightweight) outfit for an evening in Caracas. Men will not need a tie at any beach hotel or restaurant (in Caracas, ties are generally required).

Getting Around

Cabs and *por puestos*, five-passenger sedans that operate as mini-buses along Avenida La Playa, are the most popular modes of transportation. Within each town, everything is within walking distance, but to get from Macuto, let's say, to La Guaira, you'll need some form of motor transportation.

Cabs will cost you $1 to $5, depending on distance. The *por puestos* continuously pick up and discharge passengers. Cost is 50¢. A sign in the front window notes their final destination. Since most of our restaurants and clubs are within walking distance of Avenida La Playa, you might consider this mode of rapid transit.

Beach Hotels

Caraballeda Hotels

The area's two five-star hotels, the Macuto Sheraton and the Melia, are not far from each other in Carabelleda. In Macuto there are a number of alternatives that offer comfortable accommodations at moderate prices. Most have private pools and good restaurants, although none are right on the beach.

Sheraton Macuto Resort Hotel ☆☆☆☆☆
(Caribe District, Carabelleda)
600 rooms, two buildings
☎ (031) 944-300
Fax 944-318
In US: 800-325-3535
Deluxe

All rooms have terraces. The marina is always bustling. You'll never have to leave the hotel, except to go home.

This self-contained hotel offers all of the services you would expect of a deluxe hotel, although the staff seems to get easily overwhelmed at times. Whether you seek a beauty salon, cinema, gift shop, boutique, bookstore, airline office, bowling alley, discotheque, gourmet restaurant, or marina, it is all here. Both buildings – the newer "A" and the blue-hued "B," somewhat dated – offer total contemporary comfort. It has its own marina and two pools, one huge and irregularly shaped, the other smaller and circular. You have swimming, boating, scuba diving, and fishing during the day; cinema and nightclubs in the evenings; and fine restaurants open at all hours. Air-conditioned.

Hotel Melia Caribe ☆☆☆☆☆
Caraballeda, La Guaira
300 rooms
☎ (031) 945-555
Fax 942-998
Deluxe

Tennis, golf, fishing and watersports are available here.

Easily on a par with the best Caribbean hotels, the ultramodern five-story Melia is an ideal vacation retreat. This spectacular resort complex is only a 20-minute drive from Maiquetía International Airport and 45 minutes from downtown Caracas. All rooms feature color

TV and terraces offering stunning views of the sea. On the premises are both a grill and an excellent seafood restaurant, as well as a discotheque, beauty salon, gym and sauna. Air-conditioned.

Meeting facilities, hosting up to 1,000 persons, were inaugurated at the hotel's opening in 1977 by the OPEC conference.

Reservations can be made here for the Melia Puerto La Cruz, another of this chain's luxurious resorts.

Royal Atlantic Hotel ☆☆☆
Av Principal Del Caribe, Blvd. Naiguata
(Caraballada)
20 rooms, 4 floors
☎ (031) 941-361
Opposite the Macuto Sheraton, this small hostelry has unpretentious rooms with air-conditioning. There is a pool and a good Italian restaurant. Guests are permitted to use the Sheraton's pool and beach for a small fee.

Hotel Fioremar ☆☆
Av Principal, Caraballeda
(front of Macuto Sheraton)
23 rooms, 4 floors
☎ 941-743
Inexpensive
The Fioremar features an Italian restaurant, and clean air-conditioned rooms.

Hotel Villamare ☆☆
Av La Playa, Caraballeda
13 rooms, 1 floor
☎ 91-691
Inexpensive
This hotel offers a pool in the rear and a scenic mountain setting. Not many extras, but the price is right. Air-conditioned.

Hotel Sierra Nevada
Av La Playa
Urbanización Los Corales
21 rooms, 2 floors
☎ (031) 943-035
Inexpensive
Another basic choice in Caraballeda, this one faces the sea. It has a small pool and a bar but no restaurant, Fine if your budget is tight. The price is hard to beat.

Macuto Hotels

Hotel Posada Del Hidalgo
Av La Playa, Macuto
34 rooms
☎ (031) 44-107
Moderate
If you want a room here, you'd better reserve in advance. This popular hotel fills up very quickly. That's not surprising. The Spanish colonial decor is lovely, rooms are comfortable and the price is right.

Hotel Santiago
Av La Playa, Macuto
57 rooms
☎ (031) 46-1754
Moderate
Located across from the water on Avenida La Playa; if you have a room in the front you'll hear the waves crashing against the rocks whenever cars aren't whizzing by. Traffic can be very noisy at times, so if you want peace and quiet, request a room in the back. All in all, this Spanish posada look-alike is a fine choice. Rooms are simple, yet very clean. All are air-conditioned and have color television. The management is friendly. The outdoor restaurant across the street is very good.

Hotel Las Quince Letras ☆☆☆
Av La Playa, Macuto
80 rooms, 8 floors
☎ (031) 461-551 or 44-152
Moderate
Thanks to the success of the renowned Quince Letras Restaurant, this modern hotel under the same management won an immediate following. Small and without frills; guests enjoy bright carpeted rooms facing the sea. There is a fine seafood restaurant. Air-conditioned.

There is a ramp directly from the hotel to the restaurant.

Hotel Macuto ☆☆☆
Av La Playa, Macuto
75 rooms, 6 floors
☎ (031) 461-310
Fax 461-854
Inexpensive
Nearest to the airport (10 minutes), the Macuto is among the oldest of the beach hotels. It was once noted for a first-rate restaurant, though nowadays it faces lots of stiff competition in that regard. Also legendary was its large salt-water pool. Good service more than makes up for the no-frills furnishings. And the value is unbeatable. Air-conditioned.

And for Longer Stays. . .

Albatross Suites
Av Granada, 84, Urbanización Caribe
Caraballeda/La Guaira
☎/fax (031) 945-519
If you're planning an extended stay in Caracas, a suite hotel makes good sense. And what better location than the beach. It's basic, yet comfortably furnished. Albatross Suites offer solid value. All are air-conditioned and have an equipped kitchenette and color television. Daily maid and linen service is provided. Just minutes

by foot from the beach, the marina, the golf course, restaurants and night life.

At the Airport

Puerto Viejo Hotel & Marina
Av Principal de Puerto Viejo
Catia La Mar
107 rooms
☎ (031) 544-044
Fax (031) 521-211
Expensive

The Puerto Viejo is not a bad place to spend a day if you need to catch an early flight the next morning. Though the surrounding town does not measure up to Macuto or Caraballeda, the hotel is fairly nice. Facilities include a large pool area with an outdoor restaurant, a private beach, an indoor restaurant, a tennis court, and a small gym. Rooms are quite comfortable and virtually all have an ocean view. If you're planning to travel to Venezuela by private yacht, you can dock at the marina. Just call ahead to arrange for a slip.

Beach Restaurants

Seafood is the dominant dish here. But you can find good beef and poultry selections on most menus.

During our last visit we were saddened to find that, after 25 years, one of our favorite restaurants, Tomaselli, had closed. Always crowded, it was a great place for pizza and burgers. Still, there is no shortage of restaurants in this area. Prices are comparable to those in Caracas.

Las Quince Letras
Av La Playa, Macuto
11 am - 11 pm (daily)
☎ (031) 461-750
Moderate

Considered among the finest in El Litoral, this restaurant extends out on a peninsula into the Caribbean, within view of the big jets taking off and landing at Maiquetía Airport. In the evening, the sound of waves lapping against the rocks below completes the ambience. As for the food, whether you order shrimp cocktail from the Spanish-English menu, *cazuela de mariscos* (seafood casserole), the paella, or any of the beef dishes, you won't walk away hungry. Good for lunch too.

Cruise liners and pleasure boats pass by, providing you with a changing seascape to go with the succulent seafood.

Timotes
Callejón Libertador, Maiquetía
12 pm - 3 pm; 7 pm - midnight
☎ 22618
Inexpensive
Timotes is among the best "Venezuelan" restaurants on the beach. The fare rivals that of El Portón in Caracas. Try any of the typical Criolla dishes – delicious. The huge air-conditioned restaurant offers excellent service. Timotes is in a shopping center off the main avenue near the airport. Take a cab. Informal.

A very refreshing local drink, called cocada, is made with coconut milk and served in a coconut shell.

El Porton De Timotes
Av Principal
Caraballeda
11 am - 11 pm
☎ 943-530
Inexpensive
The sister restaurant of Timotes, Portón de Timotes is more easily reached from the beach and has the same fantastic food. It's in a private house. A knight in armor stands in the middle, giving the house a strange, antique look. Once again, excellent food.

La Choza Del Santiago
Av La Playa
Across from the Hotel Santiago
Moderate

As long as you're able to get a table away from the street, and preferably along the rail next to the water, dining at this open-air restaurant is delightful. The extensive menu features fine seafood dishes at reasonable prices.

El Farallón
Av La Playa
Playa Lido, El Palmar
Caraballeda
☎ 940-054
Moderate

It's hard to imagine getting any closer to the water than at this lovely open-air restaurant. It juts out into the sea on its own jetty, You'll dine on wonderfully fresh seafood to the sounds of the waves lapping against the rocks as sea breezes drift through the open sides of the restaurant. Even if you don't like seafood, the setting is so delightful that you should try to get here at least once. Pizza is also on the menu.

El Bodegón De Lino
Av Principal, Urbanización Caribe
(Caraballeda District)
11 am - 11 pm
☎ 944-992
Moderate

Traditionally, a *bodegón* is a large eating house with long tables, offering little privacy but lots of hearty cooking and cameraderie. Here, the requisite Spanish hams and strands of garlic hang above the enormous bar and the ample grill is ever at the ready to prepare fish and shellfish to order. There is a long list of Spanish and international dishes on the menu. El Bodegón is a fine choice for informal dining.

Hong Kong Chef
Av Principal
(Caribe District)
11 am - 11 pm
☎ 941-656
Inexpensive
For tasty Chinese food head to the Hong Kong Chef. Dine al fresco at one of the front tables. We particularly enjoyed the shark fin soup, and the sweet and sour dishes. Bilingual menu.

Restaurant Neptuno
Av Principal
(Caribe District)
11 am - 1 am
Inexpensive
Across from the Macuto Sheraton is this combination seafood-Italian eatery. Dine at one of the outdoor tables. Try the *espaguettes con salsa chipi chipi* (spaghetti with clam sauce) or the *pargo* (red snapper). If pizza is your dish, no problem here. Informal and inexpensive.

Hotel Restaurants

The finest dining in El Litoral is in the Sheraton and Melia hotels. Prices are surprisingly reasonable.

El Jardin
Sheraton Macuto Resort (see page 144)
Moderate
The poolside El Jardin is a terrific spot any time of the day or evening. All three meals are served in this informal outdoor restaurant, which doubles as a sports bar most evenings. Fine international cuisine, ranging from salads to more substantial fare, is served here.

Fontanella
Sheraton Macuto Resort (see page 144)
☎ (031) 944-300
Moderate
Despite the air of formality lent by the red and white tablecloths and fancy place settings, dining at the Sheraton's Italian trattoria is decidely relaxed and casual. Generous antipasti and artfully prepared seafood dishes featuring risottos and pastas highlight the menu. The carpaccio, tri-color salad with balsamic vinegar, and the roasted sea bass (*róbalo al horno*) are our recommendations.

Tarantela
Melia Hotel (see page 144)
7 pm - midnight
Moderate
Among the most elegant restaurants on the beach, Tarantela features fine Italian cuisine. There's even Italian music every night.

Tasca Mar
Melia Hotel (see page 144)
12 Noon - 1 am, Tues. through Sun.,
Moderate
The festive atmosphere of a Spanish tasca has been artfully recreated by the Melia. Spanish wines and hearty Spanish fare, including paella (of course), along with live music and a show most nights, are reminiscent of the madre patria.

La Posada del Hidalgo
Av La Playa
Urbanización Alamo, Macuto
☎ 461-138
Moderate
Though not in one of the deluxe hotels, the Posada del Hidalgo is on a par with the restaurants in the Sheraton

and the Melia. In keeping with its medieval exterior, the restaurant specializes in traditional Spanish cuisine. Seafood dishes such as the *parrillada de mariscos* (mixed seafood grill) and the *paella marinera* are artfully prepared and served with panache.

La Gran Paella Del Caribe
Hotel Fioremar
8 am - 12 pm
☎ 941-743
Inexpensive
Small, with high wooden chairs, La Gran Paella serves Spanish food, and does it well.

Quick Snacks

Tropiburger, a McDonald's-like eatery, has an outlet on the main street a few blocks from the Macuto Sheraton. Try the *Guapo*, the Venezuelan answer to the Big Mac.

Days at the Beach

Aside from beaching it and dawdling at poolside, what is there to do in El Litoral before dusk? For a start, check in at the marina near the Macuto Sheraton. You have a choice of fishing, boating, or waterskiing at reasonable rental rates. For information call the hotel, ☎ (031) 944-300, extension 846.

Fishing

You can rent a launch, complete with a crew and fishing gear, that holds six passengers. The per-person half-day rate is not a bad deal since the captain throws in lunch and drinks as well as equipment.

Boat Rentals

A sunfish or catamaran usually rent by the hour at reasonable rates. Boats are in good shape and you may be able to get a special half-day rate.

Waterskiing (Esquí Acuático)

For under $20 an hour, you can rent a boat, a driver and water skis at the marina. Share the cost with friends.

Tennis

Enthusiasts need go no further than the Macuto Sheraton, which accommodates non-guests and guests for the same $5 per-hour rate. Rackets can be rented for $1, but a deposit is required.

Golf

You can tee off at the 18-hole Caraballeda Golf Club, a short ride from the Macuto Sheraton. Greens fees are $10 and you can rent clubs. Most hotels have arrangements with the club for guest privileges on weekdays. Ask your hotel clerk to make plans for you.

Bowling

Club Sheraton offers bowling for about $1, including shoes. The four alleys are open from 11 am - midnight. There is a snack bar and air-conditioning.

Other Beaches

El Litoral has many fine beaches along Avenida La Playa. The most popular by far with North Americans is the **Playa Sheraton** next to the Macuto Sheraton hotel. Venezuelans tend to use the Macuto Beach, nearer to the cable car terminal. A third beach in a visually stunning area is **Los Angeles**, about three miles beyond the Macuto Sheraton Hotel. The buses marked "Los Caracas" pass Los Angeles.

Probably the best beach for tourists is **Camuri Chico Balneario**, about one mile from the cable car terminal. The beach is free and you can rent lockers and chairs. There is a cafeteria and showers too.

Sightseeing in La Guaira

Founded in 1589 as San Pedro de la Guaira (St. Peter of the Wind), La Guaira was a major defense station against attacks from the sea. Behind the town there are a string of five forts that served as watchpoints, from which soldiers could warn the city of attackers.

La Guaira is a major world port.

Casa Guipuzcoana

Built in 1734 as the headquarters for La Real Compañía Guipuzcoana, this building is considered an important landmark in Venezuelan colonial history. It has wooden balconies, intricately carved doors and windows, and is a wonderful relic of times past.

La Real Compañía was installed in this La Guaira building to defend Venezuela's shore and spur commerce. It was a trade monopoly approved by King Philip V of Spain to boost Venezuela's economy; and in its 50-year tenure it did a fairly successful job, although much was skimmed off the top.

Aside from the building's historic significance, it also has an art gallery and offers fantastic views of the mountains.

Museo Boulton

In the former house of John Boulton, founder of Boulton Enterprises in Venezuela, the museum has the dual aim of tracing the history of La Guaira port and paying homage to John Boulton's business.

Open Tues., 9:30 am - 1 pm; 3 pm - 6 pm; weekends, 9 am - 1 pm. (Closed Mondays.) ☎ (031) 25921.

Nights at the Beach

While nightlife in El Litoral will never compare to the upbeat cabarets, boites, and clubs in Caracas, there are discotheques, cocktail lounges and live entertainment clubs here as well.

Clubs & Cabarets

Unlike Caracas and elsewhere in Latin America, clubs here generally welcome singles, but this is hardly heaven for the unattached since couples seem to dominate the beach hotels.

Don Bosco
Melia Hotel
10 pm - 4 am, Tues. through Sun.
Unfortunately for the ladies, the hottest spot at the beach is the Don Bosco nightclub in the Melia. It features a "tastefully choreographed" striptease show every night. We've been told it's lots of fun, but deny any firsthand knowledge.

Vertigo
Caribe Building, 20th Floor
Calle Los Baños
Maiquetía
Wed. - Sun. evenings
Located on the top floor of the highest building on the beach, hence its name, Vertigo has been among the most popular nightspots for years. Needless to say, the views are fantastic.

Calypso Club
Macuto Sheraton Hotel
Discotheque and live music
8 pm - 3 am (daily)
A sensational rum punch gets you in the mood quickly at this swinging music club, which alternates soft rock discs with a good combo. Comfortable leather chairs ring the tables; floors are carpeted; and the motif is Spanish. Perfect for an after-dinner drink.

A Casino

Royal Flush Casino
Av Principal
Urbanización Caribe
Caraballeda
Located next door to El Bodegón de Lino, Royal Flush is a small, friendly casino, one of very few in the area. Craps and blackjack are featured at the tables.

A Piano Bar

For relaxing music along with your cocktail, try the **Bar Almirante** at the Melia Hotel.

A Day in Caracas

If you are based at the beach, you will obviously want at least a day in Caracas.

After breakfast, and perhaps a morning swim, hop a cab to the city. The ride will run about $20. Ask the driver to let you off at Plaza Bolívar, the historical part of the city, where you can stroll around and see the **Bolívar Museum** and the **Casa Natal**, where Simón Bolívar was born. Stop in too at a marvelous toy store, La Gran Piñata, near the museums.

When you've had enough of old Caracas, take a cab to new Caracas, represented by the **Centro Ciudad Comercial Tamanaco**, the most modern of Caracas' shopping centers. Here you'll find major department stores, elegant boutiques and good dining choices.

Take a cab to Chacaíto, then look for the Broadway cinema. Walk toward that movie house (heading west) and just beyond it is the start of the Sabana Grande shopping district. Avenida Lincoln is the center for great shopping. After that you should be ready for an early dinner or at least a cocktail. Check our restaurant guide for recommendations and take a cab. After dining, if you still have not exhausted your energy, why not go to one of our recommended clubs. Have the club manager phone for a cab to take you back to El Litoral.

Margarita Island

I have visited Margarita Island frequently since 1968 and the incredible thing to me is the rapid evolution of this once rustic holiday island – 40 minutes by air from Caracas. Not too long ago, the island was little known outside of Venezuela – which was fine with the Caraqueños who thronged the main town of Porlamar every weekend and holiday. Now Margarita has been discovered by North Americans and Europeans and the island is booming.

Island Overview

Margarita is the largest of three islands that form the Caribbean state of Nueva Esparta (New Sparta), so named by Simón Bolívar because of the valor of the residents during the 19th-century revolution that overthrew Spanish domination. Today, Margarita has a population of over 300,000 while the other two islands – Coche and Cubagua – are sparsely settled. Coche has only about 5,000 residents, mostly in the village of San Pedro. Cubagua, abandoned in 1550 after two tidal waves inundated the island, was discovered by Columbus in 1498 and was home to Venezuela's first foreign settlement, Nueva Cadiz. Today, the island is mostly uninhabited.

Background & History

Columbus discovered the islands of Nueva Esparta in 1498. It was an insignificant discovery at the time, but a year later Cristobal de la Guerra and Pedro Alonso Niño found a hidden bed of pearls off Cubagua, and eventually went back to Spain with 80 pounds of them. This brought settlers to the small island, the first Spanish settlement in South America. The mad frenzy for pearls drove the Spanish to subjugate and enslave the native Guaiqueri Indians as pearl divers. Many young males died from the incessant forced diving. The abuse was so intense that eventually it ignited a revolt, and the Spanish were forced off the island in 1520. Years later, on December 25, 1541, Cubagua's civilized history was ended by a massive tidal wave and earthquake. The island has been uninhabited ever since.

On March 8, 1525 Margarita was given by the Crown to Licenciado Marcelo Villalobos and his family. They were entrusted to begin a society there. He died before actually reaching the island, but his wife, Doña Isabel Manrique, governed until 1535. The Villalobos family ruled the island until 1593, when the last of the family died. The island was then reinstated under the Crown.

When the first troops from Spain, 15,000 soldiers, landed on Margarita in 1815 to quell the revolution, a spurious peace was made with them by Generals Juan Bautista Arismendi and José Francisco Bermudez. Aware that they couldn't defeat them, the rebellious generals were submissive until the troops' departure. Immediately afterwards, the truce was broken and the people of Margarita once again began fighting for independence. Bolívar used Margarita in 1816 as the launching pad for his third expedition into Caracas. On Margarita, in Santa Ana, he declared the 3rd Republic and was proclaimed Commander-in-Chief.

Margarita is the Greek word for pearl, and pearls are the theme running through the entire history of the islands. Providing Spain with shiploads of wealth, pearls were sought frantically. Overmining led to a hiatus in the 17th, 18th, and 19th centuries, but in the 20th century, the industry began anew, primarily for export to Paris. Then, once again, conservationists put an end to pearl diving, outlawing it indefinitely in 1962.

Margarita was a sleepy fisherman's island until January 8, 1975 when it was declared a free port. At that point, the island, particularly its main city, Porlamar, became a shopping mecca. Venezuelans seeking international goods flock there. North Americans, however, will not find any great bargains.

Climate, Terrain & Industry

Margarita's gently rolling terrain is perfect for strolling or motoring. The weather is predictable all year round, with warm, sunny days offering 12 months of swimming and boating. The evenings are cool and breezy, the humidity low.

Today Margarita's principal industries are fishing and tourism. Officially, there are 18 beaches, but I've counted at least a dozen more. You can swim year-round and the waters range from pond-like to North Sea-like. In short, you can choose your wave. More about the beaches later.

A Personal Note

Over the centuries, the once-spartan nature of the people here has apparently softened, for today they are extremely warm and open with strangers. On one visit in Porlamar I tried to buy a soft drink from a passing delivery truck. The driver happily passed me a couple of bottles but refused payment, explaining that he only delivers, he doesn't sell. Later that day, a *por puesto* driver waived my fare when he was unable to make change. Good people here. I'm sure you will share my warm feelings for Margarita.

Orientation

Margarita is 43 miles long and 300 square miles in all. It is actually two islands connected by a narrow isthmus. The second island is called Península de Maca-

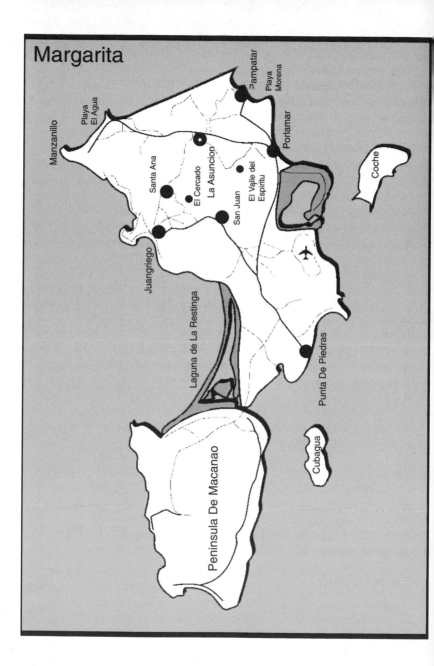

Margarita

Pampatar
Playa Morena
Playa El Agua
Manzanillo
Portamar
Coche
Santa Ana
El Cercado
La Asuncion
San Juan
El Valle del Espiritu
Juangriego
Laguna de La Restinga
Punta De Piedras
Cubagua
Peninsula De Macanao

nao. Largely unpopulated, it is used for local fishing, and has many isolated beaches.

The Península de Macanao is at the western end of Margarita, and Porlamar is southeast. The Aeropuerto Internacional del Caribe is on the southern rim of the island, and is 30-45 minutes by taxi ($12-$15) from Porlamar. The island's thick section is a three-quarter circle from Porlamar to Juangriego, which is center-north. Along the perimeter are Margarita's finest beaches, and the ride between the two towns is spectacular – twisted, cliff-hanging roads that have the sea laid out in front and the green rolling hills behind. **La Asunción**, the capital, is the nose of the fat face formed by Margarita's east side, and **Santa Ana**, a historical city, is the bridge of the nose. **Pampatar**, another wonderful colonial site, is a curve east of Porlamar. And finally, Punta de Piedra, the dock for the ferry to Puerto la Cruz, is in the southwest part of the island, very near to the Península de Macanao. The infrastructure of the island is well-developed and no ride should take you more than an hour.

There are actually two distinct sections of Porlamar. As your cab first enters the city limits, the small crowded, somewhat rusted apartment buildings of the residents are visible. That huge dome you see dominating the skyline belongs to the St. Nicholas Church, site of lovely candlelight processions on Christmas Eve and other religious holidays. The streets are jammed with stores, houses, dogs, and humans. Moving east on either Calle Zamora or Calle Igualdad, you pass several pedestrian thoroughfares that are strictly for shopping.

Then, suddenly, you come to Hotel Bella Vista, and the streets are filled with tourists. The rusted apartments become shiny glass clothing stores. You've reached the tourist section of Porlamar.

The tourist part of the city is dominated by two streets: Avenida Santiago Mariño and Avenida 4 de Mayo. They are crowded with stores selling international goods, fast food joints and restaurants; off one of these streets will inevitably be your hotel. Stores selling Nike, Ralph Lauren, Polo, Finlandia, Lindt, etc., are everywhere.

Avenida 4 de Mayo, east, leads to Pampatar, and the northeast rim where Margarita's best beaches are found.

Arrival/Getting to Your Hotel

Since several airlines, both domestic and international, fly to Margarita, you shouldn't have much trouble making flight arrangements either in Caracas or at home prior to your departure. Your flight will touch down at the modern **Aeropuerto Internacional del Caribe Santiago Mariño**, which is on the southwestern coast of the island in the town of El Yaque.

You can make hotel reservations in the Información Turistica Kiosk at the airport. Local maps are available at the Camara Nueva Esparta, also at the airport. Most banks in Porlamar are on Calle Igualdad. Boulevard Guevara is closed to traffic.

After breezing through customs, stop by the welcome booth of the **Camera de Turismo de Nueva Esparta**, the government tourist office, where you'll be given a welcome pack full of island maps, brochures and coupons for island attractions, including hotels, restaurants and shops. Then head outside and catch a cab to your hotel. A cab to Porlamar should run between $12 and $15. If you're staying at one of the resorts outside town be sure to request an airport transfer as part of your package.

Car Rentals

With so many different beaches and sights around the island to explore, renting a car is definitely worthwhile on Margarita. Given the fine condition of the roads, driving here is relatively easy. Several agencies have outlets both in the airport as well as in town or at the major hotels. You can either pick up your car at the airport or arrange to have one waiting for you at your hotel. It's best to make arrangements prior to your arrival. As we prefer to rent from the large agencies whenever possible, the following are the local numbers of the major chains:

Avis: Airport - ☎ 691-236; Hotel Bella Vista - ☎ 618-920

Budget: ☎ 616-413

Hertz: ☎ 623-333

The Best Hotels

The island, blessed with beaches, is devoted to tourists. While hotels were once concentrated in Porlamar, new hotels and resorts have sprung up all around the island. Prices are still surprisingly affordable for the Caribbean and you'll find all price ranges, starting with the most basic one-star hotels to luxurious five-star resorts. The majority are three-star or two-star and all are nice and clean. Hotels often fill up quickly so advance reservations are strongly recommended.

Margarita Hilton &
Hilton Suites International ☆☆☆☆☆
Calle Uveros, Playa Moreno
Hotel: 291 rooms, 11 floors
Suites: 490
☎ 503-5000 (in Caracas)
☎ 800-HILTONS (in US)
☎ 800-268-9275 (in Canada)
☎ (095) 624-111 or fax 620-810 (In Margarita)
Deluxe
New and magnificent, featuring balconied rooms facing Playa Moreno, the Hilton is a welcome addition to Margarita. Amenities include lighted tennis courts, a health club with sauna and steambaths, four restaurants, a lobby bar, discotheque, casino, fine shops and

a fantastic free-form swimming pool. The Hilton Suites were added in 1995 and operate primarily as a time-share, though it may be possible to stay there on a non-time-share basis. A three-foot wall complete with waterfalls, bridges and slides, joins the hotel with the suites and makes for a delightful walk.

The Hilton features a well-rounded selection of dining options. Breakfast and dinner are served both buffet style and à la carte in comfortably elegant surroundings at **Los Uveros**. The beachfront **Las Morenas** is ideal for a poolside lunch or romantic dinner under the stars and features live music nightly. Haute French cuisine is served at **Le Chateaubriand**, a formal restaurant (dinner only).

Los Veleros is the most spectacular of the Hilton's restaurants. Overlooking the pool and ocean, you'll be dining under the stars. See *Food & Restaurants,* below, for details.

Marina Bay
Calle Abancay, Playa Moreno
(Urbanización Costa Azul)
170 rooms
☎ 621-256; fax 624-110
In Caracas: (02) 979-2513; fax 979-3713
Deluxe

This is one of Margarita's newest five-star hotels. Amenities include queen- or king-size beds, deluxe bathrooms and minibars in all rooms, along with AM/FM radio, satellite TV, and, of course, air-conditioning. The hotel wraps around the large pool, which has both children's and adult sections. Additional facilities include: tennis courts; a fitness center with sauna and solarium; watersports; conference facilities; a casino pub; disco; and a shopping arcade. Dining options include classic French cuisine at La Petite

France; international fare at Canta Claro; or typical island cuisine at Cubagua.

Hotel Margarita Omni ☆☆☆☆
Urbanización Costa Azul
Av Guayacan Oeste
138 rooms (12 floors)
☎ (095) 622-856; fax (095) 620-845
Moderate
Another of the newer beachfront high-rises, the reasonably priced Omni is a great deal for a group of budget-conscious young people vacationing together. It features rooms for as many as eight persons and offers transportation to and from the beaches. It also has an outdoor pool with poolside bar, two restaurants, a sundries shop and a discotheque.

Hotel Bella Vista ☆☆☆☆
Av Santiago Mariño
309 rooms
☎ (095) 617-222; fax 612-557
Moderate
Once Margarita's only luxury hotel, the Bella Vista has now lost that status to the Hilton and other newcomers. Outstanding features include a lovely lobby sitting room, shops, paintings, couches, games, travel agencies, mosaics on the wall, rushing bell boys and waiters with drinks. The Bella Vista is still the hub of Porlamar, with all the travel and rent-a-car agencies, plus government tourist offices, here.

The hotel has several restaurants, a fine pool with a bar and restaurant adjacent, and its own beach. There are occasional poolside films, a nightly barbecue (9 pm - midnight), and poolside chefs prepare the island's special seafood dishes for lunch.

The rooms, although comfortable, do not quite measure up to the rest of the hotel in decor or amenities.

Lake Plaza ☆☆☆☆
Av Bolívar, Urbanización Dumar
☎ (095) 616-945; fax (095) 618-442 or 618-165
Moderate
Conveniently located in the heart of Porlamar, the Lake Plaza provides easy access to the scenic beaches, historic attractions, night-time entertainment and duty-free shopping of Porlamar. Suites, all with an ocean view, are tastefully furnished. On-site amenities include the Caribbean Bar, specializing in tropical cocktails, the Caribbean Grill, a lovely restaurant with both local and international cuisine, separate adult and children's pools and a sauna and jacuzzi – all in a beautifully landscaped setting. The Lake Plaza also provides free shuttle service to island beaches.

Hotel La Perla ☆☆☆☆
Calle Los Pinos
(between Av 4 de Mayo and Rómulo Betancourt)
343 rooms
☎ (095) 636-120
Moderate
The Hotel La Perla is a terrific four-star value next door to Hotel Los Pinos. Highlights include a large outdoor pool with a lovely terrace and bar, along with tennis courts, two restaurants and a lobby bar. Rooms are spacious, tastefully furnished and have queen-size beds and satellite color television.

Stauffer Hotel ☆☆☆
Av Santiago Mariño at M. Patiño
98 rooms
☎ (095) 612-911; fax (095) 618-708
In Caracas: ☎ (02) 793-3101 or fax (02) 782-0944
The Stauffer Corporation bought this three-star hotel and spruced it up. It has a rooftop terrace, restaurant, casino, tour desk and gift shop. Rooms are quite comfortable.

Hotel Los Pinos ☆☆☆
Av Los Pinos and San Francisco
90 rooms, 5 floors
☎ (095) 612-211 or 611-301; fax (095) 612-101
Moderate
On a street running parallel to Avenida 4 de Mayo, Los Pinos is on the same block as the four-star Hotel La Perla. At the bar on the patio you hear the clink of drinks and the hum of soft conversation. Breakfast is included in your room rate.

Hotel La Perla, next door, has the same owners.

Flamingo City Hotel ☆☆☆
Av 4 de Mayo
50 rooms
☎ (095) 644-557, 645-564
Moderate
New and clean, this is in the impressive row of stores and other hotels that line this strip. In the midst of all the action of Porlamar, Hotel Flamingo has a bar and restaurant, and provides good tourist information.

Real Flamingo ☆☆☆
Av 4 de Mayo
34 rooms
☎ (095) 611-311, 619-326
Moderate
Further away from the action than the Flamingo and not as modern, the Real Flamingo is pleasant, clean, and near the popular bowling alley.

Hotel Colibrí ☆☆☆
Av Santiago Mariño
70 rooms
☎/fax (095) 615-386 or 612-195
E-mail: ghibli@enlared.net
Moderate
When we first visited Margarita, the Colibrí was a quaint family-owned hotel. Needless to say, a lot has

changed since then. Extensive renovations have turned it into an elegant tropical hotel and it has the best casino on Margarita. 'Swank' best describes the casino with its elegant decor and gaming tables featuring baccarat, blackjack, French-American roulette, and poker. There's even a Royal Ascot Horse Machine for lovers of the track, and, of course, slot machines. Live music is featured most evenings. The Colibrí also has two restaurants. One is Spanish and the other Italian, each with its own ambience. Rooms are tastefully furnished and comfortable.

Hotel Maria Luisa ☆☆☆
Boulevard Raul Leoni
98 rooms
☎ (095) 637-940; fax 635-979
Moderate
The Maria Luisa features an outdoor bar on the terrace beside the small pool, as well as an indoor bar with room for dancing and a fine seafood restaurant. Rooms are comfortable and tastefully furnished. You won't go wrong for the price.

Hotel Imperial ☆☆☆
Av Raul Leoní
89 rooms
☎ (095) 616-420, 615-056
Inexpensive
The Hotel Imperial is next door to the María Luisa and on the same street as three good restaurants: Cocody, Coco Beach and Ruben. It retains much of the style of a traditional small Caribbean hotel, with simple rattan furnishings and plants throughout. Rooms are air-conditioned and come with a mini-fridge. The restaurant specializes in international and local cuisine.

Hotel Le Parc ☆☆
Calle Quilarte with Paez
☎ 617-097; fax 612-653
Inexpensive
Right outside downtown Porlamar, near Plaza Bolívar, Hotel Le Parc has a pool, playground, piano bar, restaurant and air-conditioning. A popular place.

A Super-Budget Choice

Posada La Marina
Calle La Marina 21-42
(between Fajardo and Diaz)
☎ (095) 485-666
Currently operating as a residence hotel, the Posada La Fontana is slated to open its doors to backpackers in the near future. Call ahead to make sure. Both hotel-style and private rooms (with fan and private bath) are off a breezy, plant-filled courtyard. Guests are permitted use of the kitchen and will share in the family atmosphere. This terrific budget choice is in the colonial part of Porlamar, four blocks from the Plaza Bolívar.

Suite & Apart-Hotels

Margarita Dynasty ☆☆☆☆☆
Calle Los Uveros (across from the Hilton)
160 suites
☎ (095) 621-622; fax (095) 625-101
The new five-star Dynasty offers studios and two-bedroom luxury suites equipped with kitchenettes. It has a large outdoor pool and guests enjoy the use of the Hilton's facilities for a small fee (which is often overlooked). Other features include three fine restaurants and a casino.

Port L'Mar Suites ☆☆☆☆
Calle 5
Urbanización Dumar Country Club
Porlamar
307 suites
☎ (095) 639-537; fax 614-221
Moderate

Guests at Port L'Mar Suites enjoy outstanding service at a price that's hard to beat. Facilities include a swimming pool, lighted tennis court, small shopping center, and hourly shuttle service to tax-free shopping and Moreno Beach. It also operates as a time-share.

Fine international and regional cuisine is on the menu at the L'Green House, Carney Grill and L'Churuata restaurants, while less formal fare is available at the L'Plaza Coffee Shop and the L'Terraza Snack Bar. Poolside cocktails, including exotic tropical drinks, are accompanied by live music at the L'Bonche Bar.

Port L'Mar is also a favorite for conventions and conferences.

Howard Johnson Tinajero Suites and Beach Club
Calle Campos between Marcano and Cedeño
66 Suites
☎ (095) 638-380 or 639-049
In Caracas (02) 241-7321

One of the newest all-suite hotels on Margarita, this has little in common with a motor lodge. It offers one- or two-bedroom apartment-style suites. All are air-conditioned and feature a jacuzzi, satellite TV, and a kitchenette equipped with a refrigerator, microwave oven, range top and coffee maker. The hotel has a pool and its beachfront Restaurant Mandinga is just one block away.

Arrecife ☆☆☆
Av Bolívar, Playa Moreno
☎ 623-033; fax 979-5455
Telex 21038
Moderate
The reasonably priced Arrecife is a great choice if you prefer an apartment to a hotel room. All suites, one- and two-bedrooms (sleep four and six respectively), have a living room, two baths and fully equipped kitchen, as well as cable TV and central air-conditioning. Facilities include a nursery, shopping, two pools, a game room, laundry facilities, a snack bar and restaurant.

Margarita International Resort
Av Bolívar
Urbanización Dumar Country Club
Porlamar
☎ 634-622; fax 636-011
Telex 614-221
Moderate
The Margarita International Resort is a favorite with vacationing families. Kids love the waterslide and playground. Parents love the great prices. All suites have two bedrooms, two baths, fully equipped kitchen, living room, color TV and air-conditioning. Tennis courts, restaurant/bar, rent-a-car, rent-a-motorcycle, and a delicatessen and souvenir shop round out the list of facilities.

Margarita Suites ☆☆☆☆
Av Santiago Mariño at Av 4 de Mayo
210 rooms, 14 floors
☎ (095) 639-960 or 639-796
Moderate/inexpensive
In the heart of Porlamar, the Margarita Suites offer comfortable accommodations. Facilities include an outdoor pool, a restaurant serving international and

Italian cuisine, and a game room featuring electronic gambling machines. Since you're in walking distance of many fine restaurants, you can economize by eating in some nights and splurge on a few nights out. You also have the option of including breakfast in your room rate for $12 more.

Hotel Daisy Suites
Calle Fermín at the corner of Cedeño
☎/fax 619-565
Inexpensive
A terrific budget choice in the heart of Porlamar, this is a small, charming hotel with a typically Venezuelan feel to it. You can tell by the friendliness and warmth of the staff. Rooms are small and simply furnished. All come with a small refrigerator, air-conditioner, and color TV.

Studio Apartments

If you'd like to rent a fully equipped studio apartment for one to four persons in a luxury building (swimming pool, jacuzzi), contact Grant Holmes at ☎/fax (095) 48566.

Resorts & Hotels Around the Island

In former times, accommodations on Margarita were primarily small and mid-sized hotels in Porlamar and a few others in Juangriego. This has changed dramatically in recent years, with large all-inclusive resorts cropping up along the eastern and northern coasts.

Isla Bonita Golf & Beach Hotel
Playas de Puerto Viejo Y Puerto Cruz
Pedro Gonzalez
312 rooms, 4 floors
☎ (095) 657-111; fax (095) 657-211
Deluxe

The newest and most magnificent of the resorts on Margarita, the Isla Bonita deserves every one of its five stars, and then some. Plus, it's surprisingly affordable in comparison with similar resort hotels on the leeward islands. Designed to recapture the elegance and sophistication of the old world, the Isla Bonita pampers its guests in an atmosphere of modern splendor. Sunlight reflects off the polished marble floors of the lobby atrium hinting at the many pleasures that await throughout the rest of the beautifully landscaped grounds. Not only does the Isla Bonita boast the only 18-hole golf course on the island, it also features a European health spa with a fitness center, dieticians, masseuse, jacuzzi and beauty salon, two lighted tennis courts, two outdoor pools, watersports, and world-class dining at four different restaurants. Modern conference facilities are also available. The hotel provides a shuttle to Porlamar several times daily, except Sundays and holidays. Rooms and suites are spacious and impeccably furnished, and overlook the pool area and the beach. Located on the western side of the island, just minutes from Juangriego. It's hard to imagine a lovelier location at sunset.

Dunes Beach Resort
Puerto Cruz Beach
Pedro Gonzalez
204 rooms, 2 floors
☎ (095) 631-333; fax 632-910
US 800-858-2258 or fax (305) 444-4848
Deluxe
A refreshing change from the high-rise hotels in Porlamar, the Dunes Beach Resort features colonial-style rooms in buildings scattered throughout the grounds. Facilities include three pools, six tennis courts, watersports, a playground, several restaurants and bars. Evening theme parties and a disco round out the

entertainment. The fishing village of Pedro Gonzalez is 10 minutes away by foot and the hotel offers shuttle service to Juangriego. There's also an in-house car rental service.

Margarita Laguna Mar
Via Pampatur
Pampatar
☎ 620-711; fax 621-363
US 800-858-2258
Deluxe

Once strictly limited to time-shares, the five-star Laguna Mar is now an all-inclusive resort. Guests enjoy sunbathing at its private beach or many pools, riding the waves in the safety of a state-of-the-art wave pool, sailing, and wind surfing or waterskiing on the lagoon. There are five meals daily. There's a tennis center with eight regulation courts, a competition court and two training courts, as well as a complete health spa (spa treatments are not included in the standard rate) and recreational center. When they're not at the beach or on the courts, guests can be found at the cinema, the large screen TV and video room or enjoying a meal at any of the Laguna Mar's five restaurants. Choices range from informal to Mexican to world-class seafood and international gourmet fare.

The Laguna Mar's 409 suites have been designed to provide guests with all the comforts of home and more. The Laguna Mar is one of the largest resorts on the island. Reservations must be made in advance.

Hotel Flamingo Beach ☆☆☆☆☆
Calle El Cristo
Sector La Caranta
Pampatar
☎ 624-822; fax 622-672
US 800-221-5333 (in Miami, 305-599-2124; fax 599-1946)
Moderate

The Hotel Flamingo Beach is an all-inclusive beach-front resort on Pampatar Bay. Guests enjoy unlimited watersports on the beach, tennis, a gym with sauna, and live music poolside by day, plus the Flamingo's own disco, nightclub and casino by night. Restaurants include an outdoor grill and a pizzeria featuring authentic brickoven pizza.

Playa El Agua ☆☆☆☆
Av 31 de Julio
Playa El Agua
228 rooms, suites and bungalows (some with jacuzzi)
Moderate
This hotel is right on Playa El Agua, the most popular beach on Margarita. Bright colors, accentuated by the verdant grounds, create an air of festivity throughout the rooms, restaurants and public spaces. Another all-inclusive, the hotel has four restaurants, including a beachside barbecue and an Italian restaurant. Tarps and lounge chairs are provided on the beach. The hotel has a large pool with poolside refreshments as well as three smaller pools and two tennis courts. Operated by the same management as the Isla Bonita.

Tamarindo Guacoco ☆☆☆☆
Carretera, Vía Guarame
Playa Guacuco
132 rooms, 31 Cabaña Suites
☎ (095) 622-355; fax (014) 95-5896
Moderate
Delightfully casual, the all-inclusive Tamarindo is located on the northern edge of Playa Guacuco. Rooms are decorated in cool pastels and wicker and most have a small balcony looking out onto the Caribbean. Relaxation comes easy here, either on a cushiony lounge chair under an umbrella by the pool or on the beach below. Those more inclined to be active can spend their days snorkeling, waterskiing, mountain biking or

working out on the beach or in the gym. A poolside café, seafood restaurant, and piano bar on a terrace overlooking the beach round out the amenities. The Tamarindo is operated by the same management as the Isla Bonita.

Pueblo Caribe
Carretera Costanera
Playa El Tirano
96 rooms, 5 floors
☎ (095) 48166 or 48852; fax (095) 48737
Inexpensive
Surfers would be well-advised to consider staying at the all-inclusive Pueblo Caribe, on the east coast between Playa Guacuco and Playa El Agua. Beachgoers generally overlook Playa el Tirano in favor of the other two. Hence, guests at Pueblo Caribe enjoy a little more solitude than at other beachfront hotels. Since the waves and undertow tend to be stronger here than at other beaches, you may want to limit your aquatics to the hotel pool, which is rather large and shaded by palm trees. There's a thatched-roof bar at poolside, along with music and live entertainment most evenings. The Pueblo Caribe is popular with Germans, Italians and Danes.

Portofino Mare Hotel ☆☆☆☆
Manzanillo
295 rooms
☎ (095) 490-544; fax (095) 490-980
US 800-221-5333 or 777-1250
Europe, ☎ (01372) 466-944; fax (01372) 470-057
Popular with Europeans and Argentineans traveling on economically priced all-inclusive packages, the Portofino is on Playa El Agua, one of Margarita's most popular beaches. If you're looking for seclusion, you probably won't find it here. Facilities include three

probably won't find it here. Facilities include three restaurants, two outdoor pools, kayaking, snorkeling and windsurfing, a game room and satellite television. Aerobics and tropical dance class, along with activities for adults and children, are often scheduled. Evening entertainment features folkloric shows and there is also a discotheque.

Hotels in Juangriego

Quaint and picturesque, staying in Juangriego, the largest town on the north coast, is a low-key alternative to all-inclusive resorts and the hotels of Porlamar. Juangriego's best known attraction is sunset over its quiet fishing harbor.

Villa El Griego ☆☆☆☆
Calle Picaquinta with Calle El Sol
Juangriego
☎ 254-382
246 rooms
Villa El Griego is perfect for those who are on vacation to relax. Located on a tranquil bay in Juangriego, it blends right in with the perfectly landscaped surrounding gardens. Most of all, Villa El Griego is famous for its spectacular, multi-colored sunsets.

There are eight swimming pools on the grounds and the hotel has its own car and motorcycle rental service. Fine cuisine is served at La Grande Lumière Restaurant, while the snack bar and pizza restaurant offer less formal dining. Le Chat Rouge discotheque is a popular after-dark meeting place. All 168 suites are comfortably equipped with kitchenette, covered terrace, color TV with satellite antenna and central air-conditioning.

Hotel Juangriego
62 rooms
Moderate
Predominantly condos and apartments for rent to long-time residents or tourists, but 62 rooms in the large modern building are available for short-term hotel use. The rooms are as modern as the structure, and there is a restaurant and swimming pool on the premises.

Hotel Clary ☆☆☆
Calle Martires
☎ 54-037
Inexpensive
A family-run hotel in the quiet western town of Juangriego, the Clary is relaxing and wonderfully clean. There are seven individual apartments for rent. The hotel has the out-of-the-way serenity of Juangriego's great sunsets.

Restaurants

As you would expect, seafood, prepared a variety of ways, dominates most menus. Sauces are unusual and piquant. Typical of Margarita cuisine is a clam consommé called *consommé de chipi chipi*. Other "must" dishes are *arroz con mariscos*, a rice and shellfish platter that usually comes with fried plantains; *hervido de pescado*, a fish stew; and our all time favorite, *cazuela de langosta*, lobster chunks baked with creole sauce. The island's favorite drink is a rum punch, pink and potent.

Most of the restaurants we've listed here are in Porlamar and are best reserved for dinner. Since you will probably be spending your days at the beach, and having lunch there as well, we've listed the beachfront restaurants in that section.

International

Vandelvira
The Isla Bonita Golf & Beach Hotel
Continental
Open dinner only
☎ 657-111
Expensive

Ultra-elegant by Margarita standards, the Vandelvira is definitely worth the drive from Porlamar. Arrive in the daylight so you can take a walk around the grounds before dinner. Since the Isla Bonita is on the west coast, you should definitely plan to be there at sunset. Time it right and you should be having cocktails on the terrace as the sun dips below the horizon.

A pair of heavy wooden doors at the end of the long lobby corridor open to reveal tables impeccably set with fine crystal stemware. The subtle lighting and classic decor of the dining room would be best complemented by a string quartet and the occasional pop of champagne corks. The menu is equally inspired, its exquisite presentation rivaled only by the understated flourish with which it is served.

Los Veleros
Margarita Hilton
Calle Uveros
Continental
☎ 624-111
Dinner only

Los Veleros is the newest and most spectacular of the Hilton's restaurants. Set in a glass enclosure overlooking the pool and ocean, you'll literally dine under the stars. The menu takes an innovative approach to local seafood. Highlights include carpaccio of swordfish and grouper in a Japanese ginger sauce, grouper filet served on a bed of pumpkin, and *churrasco de mero*.

Brasas

Opposite the Banco Provincal
Open noon - 3 pm; 7 pm - midnight
☎ 619-956
Moderate

A modern white, large-windowed restaurant located near Los Pinos Hotel, Brasas has a continental menu that leans toward American tastes. Meats dominate, primarily steaks, chops and barbecued dishes, accompanied by a fine selection of wines and champagnes. You will enjoy dining here.

Cocody

Av Raúl Leoni (Bella Vista)
French
☎ 618-431
Open 6 pm to midnight
Moderate

As you sit on the beachside terrace contemplating the menu – blanquette de pargo, steak au poivre, and boeuf bourguignon – you may begin to think you're in the French Caribbean. Though husband and wife team, Jacqueline and Jacques, may make light of the careful planning and attention to detail that went into their restaurant, they can't deny it. Many agree that theirs is the loveliest terrace on the island. As you sit under the palms and listen to the waves rolling into shore, you'll be glad you reserved ahead. If you didn't, not too worry, the dining room is beautiful.

Coco Beach Club

Boulevard Raúl Leoni
Californian and Thai
☎ 633-101

Like its neighbors Cocody and La Casa de Ruben, Coco Beach offers a unique dining experience. A terrific option for those who prefer light dining, local seafood is prepared both California and Thai style.

The Grill Room
Centro Comercial Aquarius
Av 4 de Mayo
☎ 611-509
Open noon - 3 pm; 6 pm - midnight
Just as the name suggests, The Grill Room is a bar and grill featuring a fine international menu. Meat dishes are your best bet. A favorite lunch spot of local executives.

Cheers
Av Santiago Mariño
International
☎ 610-957
Open 12 noon to 11:30 pm
Though the decor is reminiscent of that well-known neighborhood pub in Boston, you won't find mozzarella sticks, buffalo wings or burgers on the menu. You will find a long list of soups, salads, appetizers and main courses, along with daily specials. With so many dishes to choose from, there's certain to be something on the menu for everyone in your party.

Venezuelan Seafood

The Lobster House
(La Casa de la Langosta)
Av Francisco Esteban Gómez,
between Av. Bolívar and 4 de Mayo
☎ 636-076
The Lobster House boasts one of the most extensive seafood menus we've ever seen. Boiled, grilled, thermidor, Margariteña – the chef will prepare your lobster any way you want it. Fish and shellfish entrées run the gamut from grilled to Stroganoff to grouper filet "Doña Lina" (in pear sauce). Pastas and risottos are prepared with or without seafood, and there are also steak and chicken dishes for landlubbers. Decor is clearly nautical, with waiters dressed as sailors and fishnets, sails

and pirate scenes throughout. The bar is a popular meeting place and features live music several nights a week. The original Lobster House is in Chacachare, not far from La Restinga. This one opened in April 1997.

El Gallo Pinto

Av 4 de Mayo at Av Aeropuerto
☎ 617-702
Open noon - midnight
Moderate
Flowers all around, with live piano music in the background, finished brick walls, hardwood floors and a large polished wood bar create a lovely setting for a leisurely evening meal. The house specialty is *asopado a la marinera*, a hearty soup of rice and seafood seasoned to perfection. The *pargo a la plancha* (grilled red snapper) is equally good, as are most fish dishes. Appetizers include guacamole with shrimp, *ceviche de mero*, and gazpacho.

La Casa de Ruben

Av Raúl Leoni
☎ 642-046
Open 11:30 am to midnight
Ruben is on the same block as Cocody and several other recommended restaurants. The colorful glass-enclosed dining room offers lovely views of the outdoor gardens. Specializing in the *alta cocina Margariteña* (haute Margaritan cuisine), the menu takes an innovative approach to regional cooking with entrées such as *medallones de bacalao* (cod medallions) and *mero marinero* (grouper in a seafood sauce). The large upstairs bar is a popular gathering place.

El Chipi

Calle Cedeño at Santiago Mariño
Open 11 am - 11:30 pm
☎ 636-101

El Chipi features a pargo dish that is a must, *filet de pargo pampatar* – red snapper stuffed with ham and cheese with a delightful marisco sauce. Excellent. Also popular are the *mejillones marinera* (mussels) and the calamares (squid). Specially recommended for lunch or a quick bite anytime is the remarkable consomé de chipi chipi.

The consomé de chipi chipi is a must.

María Guevara
Hotel Bella Vista
Open all day
☎ 22-695
Moderate
Large, open-air (under a picturesque thatched roof) and by the sea, the poolside María Guevara is in the back of the hotel and has fine fish dishes. The clams are especially good. Juggling elegance and informality, the restaurant can supply both.

Martín Pescador
Av 4 de Mayo
Open noon - 4 pm; 6 pm - 3 am
☎ 24-364
Moderate
With a huge neon sign announcing its presence, Martín Pescador makes a show of its meats, stacked up on racks, and its fish. A deli-type setting, this place has panache. Steaks and shrimp dishes are great.

Bahia
Av Raul Leoni via El Morro
Open noon - 11 pm
☎ 614-156
Expensive
A large wood and glass restaurant with a flower garden in the back, Bahia is an institution. Its lobster is outstanding. Many locals reserve it for special occasions.

Los Tres Delfines
Calle Cedeño
Open all day, from 11 am onwards
☎ 617-557
Moderate
With a piano bar and large neon entrance, Los Tres Delfines is another seafood restaurant with fine food.

Italian

Jardín De Las Orquideas
Calle Campos
Dinner only, 7 pm - 11 pm
☎ 619-271
Expensive

This is a popular choice with Margarita's international visitors. Service is provided in English, French or Italian. At $15, the four-course prix-fixe menu (appetizer, pasta, entrée and dessert) featuring both French and Italian dishes, is a terrific value. Pasta and bread are homemade. Owner/chef Italo Parodi, a well-known entrepreneur from Monaco, is on hand to make sure all his guests are well-cared for. He'll even pick you up at your hotel if need be.

La Italiana
Av 4 de Mayo
Open noon - 11 pm
☎ 612-756
Inexpensive
A small restaurant on the main strip, right after the bowling alley, with an old-fashioned setting, and pictures of Italy on the wall. Excellent food. The pastas, particularly the bolognaise, are fantastic, and the four-spiced pasta is other-worldly.

O Sole Mio Da Rosetta
Calle Cedeño con Molave
Open 6:30 pm - 11 pm
☎ 611-220
Moderate
A large restaurant with couches and red tablecloths. There is a piano bar and photos of Italy on the walls. The Italian fish dishes are fantastic, with shrimp the star.

El Canalete
Av 4 de Mayo
Open all day
☎ 613-275
Moderate
A trailer-like structure, with wood walls and quilt tablecloths, El Canalete features typical Italian fare, with pastas and fish heading the bill.

Restaurant Da Genarino
Calle Patiño with Malavé
☎ 619-701
Pizza is the mainstay at this very rustic outdoor restaurant. After dinner, head across the street to the Heladería Italiana for espresso, cappuccino, Italian pastries and gelato. You'll be lucky to get a table; it's a popular spot. The gelato is excellent and well worth the wait.

El Pinero
Av Raul Leoní
Open all day
☎ 619-079
Moderate
Popular and tasty, El Pinero has a trilingual menu, specializing in shrimp, pizza, and exotic drinks.

Il Castello Romano
Calle Cedeño
Moderate
Another good Italian restaurant, it's located in an air-conditioned red brick house next door to El Chipi.

Chinese

Dragon Chino
Av 4 de Mayo
Open all day
☎ 618-253
Moderate
Dragon Chino has a huge menu and a flashy Hong Kong entrance. It serves typical Chinese dishes, with fish being the best. Chop suey and egg rolls are fine too.

Spanish

Sevillanas
Av Bolívar; ☎ 638-258
Open 12 noon - 8:30
Expensive
Sevillanas proves that joie de vivre is a Spanish concept.. The spirit of Andalucia has been reproduced in the white-washed stucco and polished wood decor of the mesón-style dining room. Traditional Spanish cuisine is featured – *gazpacho Andaluz, paella Valenciana, arroz marinera*, and *cazuela de mariscos*, but Venezuelan *asopado de mariscos* is served as well. Come for dinner, but plan on spending the evening. Live flamenco starts at 9 pm and lasts into the wee hours of the morning.

Fast Food

Cremis
Calle Cedeño
Cremis serves pizza, ice cream and hamburgers in an open-air setting.

Copp Cafe
Av 4 de Mayo at Calle Fermin
☎ 635-228
This outdoor restaurant is crowded at breakfast, lunch and dinner. The brickoven pizzas, 20 varieties, are reputed to be Margarita's best. They even deliver!

Paris Croissant
Av Santiago Mariño
On the Hotel Bella Vista end of Santiago Mariño, this features croissants in endless varieties, along with other baked goods, sandwiches and ice cream. Plenty of outdoor seating.

Juangriego

Restaurant Clary (Hotel Clary)
Open 8 am - 12 midnight
☎ 53-0297
Moderate
With just a few tables, Restaurant Clary has great snapper and paella, with a serene setting for a quiet but informal dinner as you watch the sunset.

El Viejo Muelle
Calle El Fuerte
☎ 53-0073
Moderate
This simple beachfront restaurant offers wonderfully fresh, homestyle seafood. It's next to the lighthouse.

El Fortín Marisqueria
Calle El Fuerte
Juangriego
☎ 55092
Moderate
Not fancy, but the food is good. The outdoor El Fortín features shellfish and Spanish cuisine. El Buho next door is a similar and equally good choice.

In La Asuncion

If you are in Asuncion at lunchtime and feeling exceptionally hungry, try **Fogonazo**. The steaks and parrillada are tops.

Beaches

Aside from exploring the endless sands – two dozen or
so magnificent beaches encircle the island – you will
wish to poke around the out-of-the-way fishing villages, old Spanish forts and Catholic shrines. Time
permitting, plan a daytrip to one of the nearby islands.

Since roads for the most part are exceptionally well
maintained and distances are short, it makes sense to
rent a car. If you prefer not to drive, you can hire a taxi
or have your hotel make the arrangements for you.
Establish the rate and time period in advance.

If you're like us, the beaches are likely to be your top
priority, so we'll start with them. Don't forget to pack
plenty of sunscreen (and use it generously), a beach
umbrella for shade, sunglasses and a hat. A picnic
lunch is optional since there are excellent outdoor restaurants at most of the beaches.

Yes, the beaches here are virtually endless as they ring
this enchanting island. With so many to choose from,
you would do yourself a terrible disservice by not
venturing away from the Bella Vista or El Morro
beaches, neither of which are representative of Margarita's lovely strand. Many hotels offer transportation to
the more popular beaches around the island. But if
you'd like to go to some of the less frequented ones,
you'd be better off renting a car. We've described the
beaches traveling counterclockwise along the east
coast and then turning to travel down the west coast to
Juangriego. However, you needn't travel this route to
get to the west coast beaches. With the help of a map,
you should have no trouble finding a shorter route.

One general rule: swimming is generally safest during the early part of the day. The undertow is quite powerful and by 3 pm the waves begin to roll in at the open beaches, sometimes rather suddenly.

It is advisable to swim during the early part of the day.

Heading east out of Porlamar on Avenida 4 de Mayo, you'll soon arrive in **Pampatar**. The beach here is calm and tranquil, dominated by a cluster of fishing boats. The setting is quietly majestic, with the beach shaded by Pampatar's castle and fort.

Margarita's best beaches are outside Porlamar.

The beaches on Margarita's east coast are favored by island visitors and locals alike. The first is **Playa Guacuco**, which you will reach by continuing north out of Pampatar. It was so named by Margarita's earliest inhabitants, the Guaiqueri Indians, for the abundance of clams there.

Digging for clams is still a popular pastime. Look around and you may see island residents digging their heels into the sand and twisting to bring the tiny clams out of their burrows. The beach is near-perfect, with the surf rough enough for playing but not overpowering, and the sand as soft as a mattress. There is not much shade on the beach, but you can rent a tarp for a few dollars. A healthy dose of sun protection won't hurt either. There is a restaurant/bar on the beach, as well as showers and restrooms.

Playa Guacuco ends at the fishing port of Puerto Fermín. It is popularly known as El Tirano, named after its infamous resident, the cruel Lope de Aguirre, El Tirano. Legend has it that he killed his only daughter rather than have her be known as the daughter of a Tyrant. The beach here, **Playa Tirano** and its neighbor **Playa Parguito**, nestled in a secluded inlet to the north, are both popular with surfers.

On the other side of Playa Parguita lies **Playa El Agua**, Margarita's most popular beach. It is 2½ miles of powdery sand, waves, and palm trees. Don't get overconfi-

Watch the strong undertow here!

dent in the water, however, and keep a close watch on young children as the undertow is exceptionally strong. Weekends are especially busy, with frequent beach volleyball tournaments, musical concerts and other events. Several restaurants rent beach chairs and umbrellas. Showers and restrooms are provided as well. There is a bazaar featuring clothes and souvenirs on the road behind the restaurants.

Restaurants line the beach. All feature an open dining terrace with a central bar and specialize in fish dishes.

Restaurants include:

El Nuevo Trapiche
Moderate
The snapper here is fantastic; so are the chicken dishes.

El Pacífico
Moderate
Lobster and shrimp are available here, as well as exotic drinks.

Dunas 2000
Moderate

A private club, dress here tends to be more formal. Men may need a jacket to get in.

Dunas 2000 specializes in *paella de mariscos* for approximately $10. They don't always have what's on the menu, and the waiter will try and bully you into getting the dishes he is currently pushing.

A quiet alternative just north of Playa el Agua is the solitary **Playa El Humo**. However, deep water and rough seas make the water better suited for strong swimmers.

The twist around Margarita's northern spur, **Cabo Negro**, and the ride south to Juangriego, is inexpressibly spectacular. The road curves and narrows like Big Sur, and you rise to see the face of northeast Margarita. The mountains loom behind as you drive alongside a series of seemingly abandoned beaches on the coast below.

The first beach you'll come to is **Playa Manzanillo**. Located on one of the island's most picturesque fishing harbors, early in the morning and then again in the afternoon it buzzes with activity as the fishermen set off and return with the day's catch in tow. Help bring in the catch and you may find yourself generously rewarded. The beach is lined with huts, boats, nets, and other fishermen's gear.

Gazing south along the coast, several of the other west coast beaches and villages come into view, including **Los Morros de Constanza, Puerto Viejo, Puerto Cruz, Bahia Pedro Gonzalez, Playa Caribe,** and **Bahia La Galería**.

Just beyond Manzanillo is **Playa Guayacán**. At the base of a sharp incline, this small beach is not easily reached by car. It's best to walk down the narrow road until you find yourself on a beautifully secluded bay. Far more accessible are the beaches at **Puerto Viejo** and **Puerto Cruz**. Just follow the road out of Playa Manzanillo. Among the most breathtaking of Margarita's beaches, Puerto Cruz is swept by strong winds that drive the waves into shore and build sand dunes. Needless to say, it's one of Margarita's most popular surfing beaches. The surf at Puerto Viejo is calmer, making it a popular destination for families with young children. Parking, restaurants and comfort facilities can be found at Puerto Cruz.

Continuing along the coast towards Juangriego, you'll pass the beach at **Pedro Gonzalez**, another fishing village, and **Playa Caribe**, which, once unknown to all but a few residents, is well on its way to becoming one of the most popular beaches on the island. New restaurants and facilities have opened here in recent years, including the Mosquito Coast Beach Club. Finally, you'll come to the tranquil waters of Juangriego Bay and **Playa La Galera**. Shaded by palm trees, it is the

Seeing the sunset from here is an absolute must.

loveliest spot on the island for watching the sunset over Juangrieo Bay.

There are numerous other beaches around the island, including **El Yaque** on the southern coast, whose shallow waters are ideal for windsurfers and small children, and the beaches to its west near Punta de Piedra. The beaches at the Laguna de la Restinga and the Península de Macanao as well as those on the islands of Cubagua and Coche are discussed below.

Around the Island

Porlamar

The city of Porlamar is best visited on foot during the cooler hours of the early morning and late afternoon. Concentrate on the main streets – **Calles Igualdad** and **Guevara**. Calle Igualdad runs from the Bella Vista Hotel to Plaza Bolívar, the city's largest plaza, a six-block stretch dominated by multi-storey apartment buildings and duty-free shops. Just as in cities towns and villages throughout Venezuela, **Plaza Bolívar** is the social center of the city. Friends meet on its benches; hard-fought chess games are played there; and you'll even hear the occassional strumming of a guitar. Porlamar's principal church, **San Nicolás de Bari**, whose huge dome is visible throughout the city, is sits on the plaza. It is the site of religious festivals, particularly the Feast of St. Nicholas, the patron saint of Porlamar, on December 5 and 6.

A pleasant stroll along Calle Guevara (in front of the church) for five blocks will put you at Porlamar's outdoor market on the sea, **El Mercado de Conejeros**. Along the way are jewelry, perfume and other duty-free shops. The market, which runs for five or six short blocks, offers avocados, oranges and pineapples, not to mention fish and soft goods. Watch the women maneuver the baskets perched atop their heads.

At the intersection of Calle Igualdad and Calle Fraternidad is the **Museo de Arte Contemporáneo Francisco Narváez**. It features works by the Margaritan-born sculptor as well as those of other painters and sculptors from Margarita and eastern Venezuela. The museum is open Tues. through Sun., 9 am to noon and 2 pm to 6 pm.

Worth exploring too is the **Urbanización Bella Vista** on the Punta El Morro beach. Fishermen live on the strip closest to the sea and their boats are anchored nearby. Goats, donkeys, pigs and assorted fowl seem to have free rein as they wander in and out of the homes. Many families sleep in hammocks, with double-sized versions for couples. Stroll a block or two off the beach and you will find yourself in the city's most attractive residential area, with colonial-style homes and fashionable cars. Quite a contrast.

Pampatar

A huge castle converted to a Spanish colonial museum makes a trip to this seaport, six miles from Porlamar, a must. Along the road, take a five-minute detour and visit **Playa Angel**, where a rock formation resembles a praying angel.

A small colonial town, Pampatar is strikingly different from Porlamar. The town is largely its fort, **San Carlos Borromeo**. Destroyed in 1662 when Pampatar was burned by the Dutch, the fort had protected the town diligently until then. Rebuilt almost immediately, it has a central square surrounded by four towers. A moat, now dry, encompasses the proud fort. Completely restored in 1968, it is now a museum that contains paintings of independence heroes and war scenes, historical weapons and a replica of Columbus' Santa Maria. Most popular is the Battle of Matasiete painting commemorating an important revolutionary battle fought in Margarita. The fort is open every day from 8 am - 12 noon and 2 pm - 6 pm. West of the fort is a row of opulent colonial homes.

Directly across the street is the Iglesia del Cristo del Buen Viaje, which contains the figure of Christ of the Safe Voyage. Originally destined for Peru, the statue was unloaded here because the ship carrying it from Spain couldn't raise its anchor with the statue aboard.

La Casa Amarilla is the pink neoclassic building next to the Municipal Building. It was the seat of the transitory Republican Government during the War of Independence.

Nestled in a valley between Ausunción and Porlamar, El Valle del Espíritu Santo is the home of the Virgin of the Valley, patron of fishermen and of the Venezuelan fleet, and the spiritual capital of eastern Venezuela. Throughout the year and especially on September 8th, many pilgrims make their way here to pay homage and pray to the Virgin.

As the story goes, after being severely bitten on the leg by a shark, a fisherman prayed to the Virgin, offering her his first pearl if she would save his leg. His leg miraculously healed, the fisherman kept his promise and saved his first pearl, which was in the shape of a leg, for the Virgin. This legend still holds power for the local residents. If anatomically suffering, they will pray to the Virgin and, if healed, will have a piece of jewelry molded in the shape of the relevant body part as a gift for the Virgin. The original pearl is displayed in the parish building across the street.

The Virgin is said to have been discovered in a cave by a Guaiqueri Indian. Ornately clothed, she is in a glass case above the church altar. Year after year, the Virgin continues to receive a multitude of gifts, which are displayed in the small museum in front of the church.

Founded in 1529 by Isabel Manrique, the island's first governess, El Valle was the original capital of Margarita.

The parish house is open every day from 8 am to 6 pm.

La Asunción

Six miles from Porlamar is the city of La Asunción, where the imposing Santa Rosa Fortress dominates the skyline. La Asunción, an authentic colonial town, is a find for history buffs.

The city is a fine example of colonial architecture and style, and is the capital of Nueva Esparta. Inland from Porlamar, the highlights of La Asunción are mostly centered around the Plaza Bolívar. The **Nueva Señora de la Asunción** dates from the late 16th century and is one of Venezuela's earliest churches. The facade is plain, almost sterile (this may have been a security precaution because of Margarita's constant attacks from pirates), except for its door. The inside is as streamlined as the outside; the left lateral tower dates back to 1599 and is the oldest in Venezuela.

La Asunción is the capital of Nueva Esparta and is where that state's government buildings are found.

The **Museo Nueva Cadiz** is a potpourri. Displays vary from pre-colonial artifacts to local handcrafts. The museum used to be the Casa Capítular, the seat of the colonial government. It is open from 8 am - 12 pm and 2 pm - 5 pm.

Also in town are the **Casa de la Cultura**, which houses samples of all the varying kinds of pottery in Venezuela, and the **Casa de Juan Bautista Arismendi**, devoted to the Margarita-born Independence War hero. The government buildings are also worth seeing.

La Asunción's most special attraction, in my mind, is the **Castillo de Santa Rosa** (Santa Rosa Fort). Located high up on a hill, across from the hospital, the fort opens up most of the island for viewing.

Begun in the late 17th century, the fort's obvious strategic value is its prominence as an observatory and the fact that it was inland. It was built with a tunnel that led to the Governor's house, the convent of San Francisco and the church. The Castillo de Santa Rosa's most famous prisoner was the wife of Juan Bautista Arismendi, Luisa. The cell in which she languished with her stillborn baby has been kept almost the same as it was when she was in it. The inscription above the door reads, "Luisa Caceres de Arismendi for her virtue and valor and martyrdom for her husband and country as prisoner in this jail at 16 years of age."

Several rooms contain colonial weaponry, knights in armor, paintings of Bolívar, iron balls that were attached to prisoners' legs, and a bottle dungeon. The fort itself retains its colonial feel of militarism.

The view of the island is magnificent, showing off the mountainous interior and landscape descending to the sea. The fort was obviously efficient in defending against attacks from the east, north, and south, but the western part of the island is invisible.

The fort is open every day from 8 am to 6 pm. A small donation is requested.

Santa Ana del Norte

Often referred to simply as Santa Ana or El Norte, this quaint colonial village 12 miles west of La Asuncíon is home to the 18th-century church where Simón Bolívar signed the decree proclaiming the Third Republic on May 7, 1816. The patron virgin of the village and the church is Santa Ana, patron saint of maternity. Hanging outside the handicraft shops that line the main street are the handwoven hammocks known as chinchorros. On a hill overlooking the village and westwards to Juangriego and the Península de Macanao are the ruins of the Fortín España.

El Cercado

Located not far from Santa Ana, the village of El Cercado is best known for lovely ceramic pots and vases. Generally soft brown or chocolate colored, they are relatively inexpensive. Visit the local factory for the best selection.

Juangriego

Juangriego was the site of the final and bloodiest of the battles fought on Margarita in the War of Independence: El Fortín de la Galera. On August 8, 1817 the Spanish troops brutally overpowed the last of the Venezuelan forces on Margarita. Though defeat was inevitable, the Venezuelans chose to fight to the end rather than surrender. Such was their valor that the Spaniards christened them the New Spartans, comparing their fierce tenacity with that of the ancient Greek warriors. The Laguna de los Mártires nearby was also named in honor of this battle.

Nowadays, Juangriego is a peaceful alternative to Porlamar. It has two main streets, one paralleling the beach and the other perpendicular to it. Both are full of shops, and the street leading away from the beach has a pretty white church in the center.

Juangriego is the place for sunsets. The most spectacular spot to see the sunset is from El Fortín de la Galería. Located on the hill overlooking the bay, it offers a panormaic view of the surrounding area. La Gran Bahia Pizzería is on Avenida Jesus Rafael Leandro, the main road leading into town.

El Caserío Tacuantar y El Museo de Arte Popular Venezolano is a living museem dedicated to preserving traditional Veneuzuelan culture, El Caserio Tacuantar is a faithful reproduction of a typical turn-of-the-century village. Its small homes and public buildings were constructed enirely of indigenous materials – ceramic tiles, wood, mud and stones – by local artisans who make their living much in the same way their predecessors did. A small museum dedicated to handicrafts from all over Venezuela is located in the main building. There is a small shop as well. Just minutes east of Juangriego via the coastal road, the museum is open every day from 9 am to 5:30 pm.

Macanao & La Restinga Lagoon

If you were to study a map you would notice that Margarita is not just one island but two, connected by a narrow isthmus of mangroves, marshland and beach known as the Parque Nacional Laguna de La Restinga. Up until now we've concentrated on the more developed eastern island. Now it's time to move west to the rugged, desert-like Peninsula de Macanao and La Restinga Lagoon.

La Restinga is best visited in the morning when the ocean is calm and your chance of seeing many of the birds that make their home or feed in the mangroves is better. Afterwards you can either spend a few hours or the rest of the day at La Restinga beach or continue on to the Península de Macanao.

Getting There

If you're traveling from Porlamar, head west on Avenida Juan Bautista Arismendi (also known as the Porlamar-Punta de Piedras espressway). From Juangriego follow the coastal highway toward the airport. The drive from Porlamar should take you around 35 minutes.

About 14 miles outside Porlamar is the turn-off to La Restinga, which is on the right-hand side of the road. Shortly after making the turn, you'll pass a local landmark known as **Las Tetas de María Guevara**, two hills resembling a woman's breasts. They were jokingly dedicated to a 19th-century heroine of the War of Independence who, according to a local historian, was flat-chested. Also along this road is the turn-off to the town of **Chacachacare**, home of the original Casa de Langosta Restaurant.

The road will take you to the entrance of the **Parque Nacional de La Restinga**. There is a large parking lot opposite the entrance.

Touring La Restinga

The only practical way to visit the park is in a peñero or wooden launch. The launches are docked at El Indio, a pier located just a short walk from the parking lot. Most will carry no more than five passengers and charge under $20 per boatload. The brackish water of the lagoon is no more than eight feet deep and is populated by red snappers, grunt fish, sardines, swordfish, black mullets and beds of oysters, which are commonly found clinging to the hard roots of the mangroves. Among the indigenous and migratory birds that feed in the lagoon are scarlet ibis, red-legged tinamous, frigatebirds, blue herons, green herons, great egrets, ground doves, cormorants and flamingos.

After crossing open water, your peñero will travel through a a labyrinth of mangrove channels with names like Canal de Mi Dulce Amor (My Sweet Love Channel), El Tunel de los Enamorados (the Lovers' Tunnel), the Canal de Maria Guevara and the Canal del Beso (the Channel of the Kiss). Your final destination will be Playa La Restinga, atop the barrier reef that connects the main island with the peninsula. Made of crushed fossil shells rather than sand, the beach is the longest on Margarita, stretching over 15 miles from La Guardia to Punta Tigre. Not only is La Restinga usually less crowded than other island beaches, the water tends to be warmer and the waves are a little tamer. Prior to setting off, you should make arrangements with your driver about the amount of time you want to spend there. There are several open-air restaurants on the beach so you may want to plan on having lunch before continuing on to the Península de Macanao.

Península de Macanao

The abundant greenery of La Restinga is replaced by the rugged arid hills of Macanao. Picturesque fishing villages replace the high-rise hotels, all-inclusive resorts and busy throughfares of Porlamar and eastern Margarita. The most popular and probably the best way to tour the Macanao is by jeep. This is especially true if you're planning to visit the more remote beaches, as they are accessible only by dirt road. The following is a rundown of the principal beaches and towns on the peninsula, heading clockwise.

From La Restinga follow the coastal road to **Boca del Río**, the largest and most important of the villages. If you need gas or supplies, you should get them here. Worth visiting here is the **Marine Museum of Boca del Río**, a modern museum devoted to the history of fishing, the marine life and ecosystems of La Restinga and the waters off Venezuela. The museum is open Tues. through Sun. from 9 am to 5 pm. The **Instituto de Investigaciones Científicas**, a marine biology research center, is just outside Boca del Río.

As you follow the coastal road you'll pass several beaches and villages, including Guayancito, Barrancas and Manglillo. Continue along the western perimeter of the island to **Boca de Pozo**. The second largest and one of the most traditional and picturesque of the fishing villages on the penninsula, it features lovely vistas of the Bay and the mountains of the interior, including Macanao, which, at 2,200 feet, is the highest peak on Margarita. If you're ready to "beach it" for awhile, take the turn-off to **Punta Arenas**, a sandy beach on the westernmost tip of Margarita. Or push on to **Playa la Pared** or **El Tunal**, considered by many to be the loveliest of the peninsula's beaches. Be sure to bring a sun shade and water with you as there is little or no shade at either of the two and facilities are limited.

Just as its name suggests, La Pared (the Wall) is set into a cliff. There is a small outdoor restaurant overlooking the beach that features fresh fish and a panoramic view of the beach and beyond. Just west of La Pared, El Tunal sits next to a small fishing village. If you are at either of the two in the late afternoon, you should plan on staying for sunset.

At El Tunal the paved road heads inland and back to **Boca del Río**. If you have the time, you may want to visit **San Francisco**, a traditional inland village.

As an alternative, if you're in a four-wheel-drive vehicle, you can explore some of the dirt roads that head back out to **Punta del Tigre** and along the northeastern borders of the peninsula. The waters of **Punta el Maguey** are popular with windsurfers.

Exploring the Macanao by Jeep Safari

Although not our preference, an organized jeep safari is one way of visiting the Macanao. The tour includes open bar, lunch, a bilingual driver/guide, and insurance. Contact **C.C. Tours** on Calle Tubores in Porlamar (☎ 640-297).

Or on Horseback

Cabatucan Ranch offers guided tours of the Macanao on horseback. For more information, ☎ (016) 819-348.

Daytrips to Cubagua & Coche

Margarita's sister islands to the south, Coche and Cubagua, offer what may be a welcome respite from the hustle and bustle of Porlamar. Markedly absent are the hotels and restaurants that line many of the beaches on Margarita, along with the casinos, shopping and nightclubs of Porlamar. Instead, you'll find tranquil beaches and little or no development.

Coche, the larger of the two, has 19 miles of shoreline. Around 7,000 residents live in the quiet fishing villages of **San Pedro, El Bichar, El Guamache, Güinima** and **Zuliaca**. Coche is attracting windsurfers in increasing numbers. Snorkeling and other watersports are also popular, as is cycling. There are two hotels in San Pedro, the largest of the villages: the **Hotel Isla de Coche** (☎ 095-991-431) and the **Coche Speed Paradise** (☎ 014-952-182 or 952-726), which caters especially to windsurfers. Both offer air-conditioned rooms with private bath, and have a pool and restaurant. The **Conferry** ferry line offers daily departures from Punta de Piedras at 5 pm Mon. through Fri. and from Coche to Punta de Piedras at 6 pm. Weekend departures are at 8 am and 6 pm with returns at 6 am and 5:30 pm.

Cubagua has been uninhabited ever since Christmas Day 1541, when an earthquake and tidal wave devastated Nueva Cadiz, the first South American settlement and the first and last settlement on Cubagua. It had been founded by Spanish explorers who had come to Cubagua after discovering that the tiny island was the source of the pearls worn by the Guaiquiríes Indians on Margarita. Nowadays Cubagua and the ruins of Nueva Cadiz are a popular destination for divers and snorkelers.

Several party boats offer day trips to the islands, complete with lunch, drinks, snorkeling and beach games. These include a full-day sail to Coche aboard the *Amazonia* (☎ 642-173) or aboard *Catatumbo*, "the world's largest day charter catamaran" (☎ 631-072). There is also a day in Cubagua hosted by Viola Tourism, whose main office is in the Centro Comercial Makro on Calle Colegio (☎ 630-715).

Other Day Time Activities

Golf: The 18-hole golf course at the Isla Bonita is open to non-guests. For information and starting times call the pro shop at ☎ 657-111, ext. 5370.

Scuba: The **Pablo Montoya Diving Center** offers PADI and NAUI certified diving and instruction as well as equipment rental. Packages include trips to La Blanquilla and Los Testigos islands as well as Los Frailes and other nearby islands. ☎ 610-124.

Windsurfing: The Vela Highwind Center on El Yaque beach offers equipment rentals and instruction. You can book packages in advance in the US by calling ☎ 1-800/223-5443 or 415/525-2070/fax 415/525-2086.

Margarita After Dark

Margarita is no longer the sleepy island we visited 20 years ago. With so many nightclubs, bars and casinos to choose from, you would be well-advised to take a nap before heading out for the evening. There's a good possibility you may not make it back to your hotel much before sunrise. Luckily, most clubs and casinos are on or not far from Avenidas 4 de Mayo and Santiago Mariño, within walking distance of each other and of area hotels.

Casinos

No sooner had Venezuela legalized gambling in the early '90s, than casinos opened on Margarita. No threat to Atlantic City, Las Vegas or the Indian reservations, most are fairly small and have a few gaming tables plus with a fair number of slots and other gambling machines. The basic games are here, including blackjack, Caribbean poker, baccarat, and craps in a few places. Most offer free drinks to gamblers at the tables. Stakes are low enough ($2 blackjack) that you can spend a night at the tables and, even on a bad night, still walk away with money in your pockets. Many of the slots offer fairly generous payouts.

The casinos are generally open by 7 or 8 pm (slots may open earlier) and don't close until 4 or 5 am. Virtually all are open 365 days a year. Dress codes are very relaxed and even T-shirts are permitted. But, since you'll be treated according to how you're dressed, it's best to save the T-shirt and sandals for the beach.

Our favorite casino is the **Flamboyant**, in the Hilton Hotel. Quieter than most and perhaps on the small side, it features blackjack, roulette and poker, as well as slot machines. The **Casino Costa Azul**, located downstairs in the Marina Bay Hotel, is also small, yet quite nice, and features blackjack, roulette and slot machines. **Le Casino** in the Port L'Mar Suites is one of the few spots in town that offers craps in addition to blackjack, roulette, poker and baccarat. Located in one large room, slot machines line the walls.

The largest traditional-style casino in Porlamar is the **Casino Colibri** in the Hotel Colibri on Avenida Santiago Mariño. Table games include blackjack, a few different varieties of poker, baccarat, and French and American roulette. High stakes gamblers can adjourn to the private gaming room. The Colibri also has over a hundred slot machines and electronic horseracing. Unlike most casinos on Margarita, the **Oasis Casino** at the Stauffer Hotel has more tables than slots. The **Luxor Casino** in the Margarita Princess Hotel on Avenida 4 de Mayo is open 24 hours.

The largest gambling establishment in Margarita is **Bingo Charaima** on Avenida 4 de Mayo. Spread out over two floors, it features mechanical games on the first floor and bingo on the second.

Discos

Dancing is not a spectator sport on Margarita, nor should it be. Loud Latin music and crowded dance floors are the norm.

Sevillanas
Av Bolívar
☎ 638-258
Open Mon. - Sat.
You don't have to travel to Spain for pure Flamenco. Margarita has its very own Tablao at Sevillanas, one of the island's hottest nightspots. Reminiscent of an Andalusian posada on the outside, the interior is just as Spanish. The entertainment alternates between live flamenco and merengue. Luckily, there's plenty of room between the tables since no area has been designated a dance floor and patrons find it impossible to stay seated. You probably will too. It's a great place to meet people. If it's too loud for conversation, send a rose to someone you like and you'll get your point across.

Mosquito Coast
Paseo Guaraguao (behind the Bella Vista Hotel)
☎ 613-524
Open 7 days, from 9 pm
North American owners Jake Edgar, a Californian, and Terry Bannon, a Canadian, knew precisely what they were up to in 1989 when they combined a casual tropical atmosphere with a state-of-the-art sound system playing non-stop dance music from across South America. This has been the island's most popular night spot with international visitors and Venezuelans alike since opening night. There is an indoor disco, plus an outdoor patio bar overlooking the beach.

Mosquito Coast Beach Club
Playa Caribe
☎ (016) 951-207
From 8 pm
High season only
Jake and Terry did it again, this time on the north coast. Their new Mosquito Coast serves double duty as a beach club by day and a non-stop beach party by night. You can come for sunset and dance till dawn. No smokey bar or crowded dance floor here. Palm trees may be all that separates you from the stars overhead.

Discoteca Eye
Calle Marcano at Igualdad
One block in from Santiago Mariño, Eye rarely goes unnoticed. If you miss the huge sign – rather unlikely – look for the white building with the black masks. Stop for a drink at the bar and then pass through the doors to the dance floor. Eye is living proof that strobe lights will never be outdated. The music changes nightly and there's a live show several nights a week.

Subsuelo
Galería Fente
Av 4 de Mayo
☎ 642-954
Open 10 pm - 3 or 4 am
Cover charge $5
If cover charge and location are any indication of quality, Subsuelo should receive a high ranking. It's located in the basement of one of the largest and loveliest of the island's shopping centers. Its outstanding features are a large bar and dance floor and lots of video screens.

Barra Cuba
Calle Cedeño, between Fermín and Campos
Open 10:30 pm

Live Latin music guarantees a crowd every night at this popular dance club. There's a large bar area and a perpetually crowded dance floor.

Nickel
Av 4 de Mayo
Across from Buccaneers between Bingo Charaima and Gold Finger, Nickels features videos all around, two bars, pool tables and loud music.

Village Club
The Santa Cruz Building
Santiago Mariño
☎ 613-668
Open 7 days, from 9 pm
Cover charge
Located downstairs, this modern club is popular with a younger crowd. In keeping with most clubs today, it features a video dance floor, as well as three bars and comfortable seating.

The Bar Scene

Though Latin music dominates the dance floors, the bars definitely take their cue from the good old US of A.

Dugout
American Sports Bar & Grill
Av 4 de Mayo
☎ 639-511
If you didn't know better, you'd think you were in Cooperstown. This "All American" sports bar brings back the days when the Dodgers were still in Brooklyn and Babe Ruth could do no wrong. Baseball memorabilia, including signed baseballs and photos of the 1955 Dodgers and the local New York teams, will take you out to the ball game, while the Tex-Mex menu promises more than just peanuts and crackerjacks. The bartenders are even dressed in baseball uniforms. Among

the most popular bars in Porlamar, Dugout attracts a fairly young crowd of sports fans who gather to watch their favorite teams, baseball and otherwise. You can even go home with a souvenir T-shirt or jersey from the gift shop.

Buccaneers Sports Bar & Grill
Av 4 de Mayo
☎ 956-386
Open 5 pm

In true swashbuckling spirit, the energy runs high at Buccanneers and so does the noise level. You can keep up with the teams back home on the large screen TV, which is perpetually tuned in to one sports network or another. Challenge all comers to a game of darts, fussbol, air hockey or pool. Or dance the night away to the live band. And if all this activity makes you hungry, the menu features a satisfying selection of American fast food and Aisan specialties. You climb a flight of rickety steps to get to this spacious bar. Depending how your evening went, going back down may not be as easy.

Cheers
Av Santiago Mariño altos de Don Lolo
☎ 610-957

Except for the fact that it is jam-packed with young Venezuelans every night, the bar here is a near-perfect replica of the bar in the popular television series it's named for. A little piece of Boston in the Caribbean? Stop in and see for yourself.

Woody's Pub
Centro Comercial 4 de Mayo, Local 18
☎ 632-063

"Woody's Pub Algo Diferente" ("Woody's Pub, Something Different") is the slogan of this popular meeting place. Always noisy and always crowded, live music and dancing is featured on Tues., Thurs. and Sat. nights.

The atmosphere may be a little more subdued at our final recommendations:

Piano Blanco
Calle Patino, next door to the Stauffer Hotel.
☎ 640-936
10:30 pm - 4 am
You'll enjoy Latin and Venezuelan music in an informal setting at this combination nightclub/restaurant. The restaurant specializes in pastas, pizzas and seafood.

Bella Vista Hotel
☎ 617-222
8 pm - midnight
There's live music and dancing poolside seven nights a week. With the palm trees and stars above and the Caribbean just steps away, it's hard to imagine a lovelier setting.

Bowling

Pin enthusiasts can assuage their passion at the six-lane **Margarita Bowling Club** on Avenida 4 de Mayo near the old airport. It is open nightly from 5 pm to 2 am (Sun. until midnight), and a line will cost you $1.50. Shoe rentals are $1. Snack bar in rear.

An Amusement Park

Diverland, also known as Isla Ventura, in Pampatar has a huge ferris wheel and roller coaster, along with loads of other rides. All rides are included in the $4 admission fee. The park opens at 7 pm Wed. through Sun.

Best for Men only...

Gold Fingers
Av de Mayo
Reservations: 615-557
$5 cover charge

If further proof is needed that Margarita has passed from the sleepy island of the 1970s to the 1990s, Gold Fingers is it.

Whether you call it exotic dancing or striptease, Gold Fingers is the hottest place in town. Women in varying stages of undress are stationed throughout the club. Hoping to attract an upscale clientele, it advertises itself as the "Rolls Royce of the Gentlemen's Establishments" and boasts "the best in table dancing" and a state of the art sound and light system. Adult videos and books are displayed in the first-floor entrance. The club is upstairs. Reservations are advised.

Shopping

Local pearls and handicrafts are best buys on Margarita.

Given Margarita's status as a duty-free zone, a tempting array of European fashions, French perfumes, Asian electronics, Swiss watches, and elegant jewelry fill the shops lining Avenidas Santiago Mariño and 4 de Mayo, Gomez and Guevara Boulevards, and Calle Igualdad in Porlamar. Benneton, Tommy Hilfiger, Nautica, Gucci, Cartier and Sebago are not unknown here. With such a selection, it's no surprise that shopping ranks high with many visitors to Margarita. However, while prices on imported goods may be low by South American standards, North Americans would be advised to check prices carefully, especially on electronic items. Prices are often just as good, if not better, at home.

You'll also find shops selling typical Venezuelan handicrafts, along with those from other Latin American countries. If you're traveling to other destinations in Venezuela, we'd advise you to wait until later to buy something. Prices may be better and you don't want to be lugging your purchase around. Otherwise, shop to your heart's content. And don't be afraid to bargain. Not only is it acceptable in all but the most exclusive shops, it is expected.

So what should you buy on Margarita?

Pearls

In colonial times, the abundant pearls from the waters of Margarita and nearby Cubagua attracted both pirates and Spanish colonists. Shops still sell jewelry set with these irregularly shaped pinkish gems. You'll also find cultivated pearls from Japan. These come in whites, grays and blacks and are good buys too.

Shops are open from 9 am - 1 pm and 2:30 - 7 pm weekdays; from 9 am - 8 pm Saturdays.

For loose pearls, try first the **Casa Avila**, Calle Gomez 47, which owner Juan Avila Guerra operates from his home. Prices start at $10 and go up depending on color and size. Bargaining is advised.

Local Handicrafts

On the route from La Asunción to Tacarigua there are several stalls selling native crafts. Chief among these are **hammocks** or **chinchorros** handwoven by artisans in the villages of Santa Ana del Norte and La Vecindad.

El Cercado, a village on the west end of the island, is known for its pottery. You can visit the workshop in town. El Cercado is one mile from Santa Ana.

Shops in Porlamar

Artesanía
Calle Igualdad
For reasonably priced Venezuelan handicrafts, you'll do well at this second-floor shop a few doors in from Santiago Mariño. Not as overpriced as other handicraft shops, but it still won't hurt to bargain.

Artisan's
Calle Malave between Cedeño and Patiño
Not unlike Artesanía, Artisan's features handicraft items from throughout Venezuela and other Latin American countries.

Los Makiritares
Calle Igualdad, a half-block west of the Bella Vista Hotel
Los Makiritares is also devoted to crafts from all over
Venezuela. Most noteworthy are the colorful rugs and
tapestries woven by the Guajira Indians.

Imagen Gallery
Margarita Hilton Shopping Arcade
Imagen features handcrafted items of the highest quality, including handcarved wooden objects and colorful
ceramics. I bought a beautiful handpainted pelican
figurine here. The main shop is here in Porlamar.

Arte Venezuela
Calle Igualdad
☎ 638-437
This lovely gallery is devoted to sculpture and paintings by Venezuelan artists.

No Fear Gear
Boulevard Guevara
Centro Comercial Big Power
No Fear Gear is home to an outrageous selection of
funky T-shirts and beachwear.

Don Lolo
Av Santiago Mariño
☎ 611-860
Don Lolo has a fine selection of European-style men-
swear.

Joyería Ivan
Av 4 de Mayo in the Cosmos Building
Ivan is Margarita's most prestigious jeweler. From
Swiss watches to precious gemstones, all purchases are
guaranteed.

Mi Sueño
Calle Igualdad
Whether you're looking for big dangling earrings or a frivolous pendant, you'll find a great selection of costume jewelry here.

El Reino del Juguete
Calle Igualdad with Amador Hernández
A fun shop to visit. You'll especially enjoy the colorful selection of piñatas.

NBA Sports
Calle Igualdad, between Fraternidad and Fajardo
☎ 615-278
Nike and other popular brands are featured at this sporting goods shop. Check the prices. Though you may find some bargains, you may do just as well shopping at home.

Don Coco
Av Santiago Mariño, next door to Cheers
Don Coco's selection of fine perfumes, French and otherwise, is hard to beat. There are five locations in all. The largest is on Santiago Mariño. Others are in the major hotels, including the Hilton and the Laguna Mar.

Mermelada
Calle Igualdad
If you've left your sunglasses at home or lost them, you'll find a replacement at this sunglass boutique.

El Mercado de Conejeros
This flea market is on the outskirts of Porlamar on Avenida Juan Bautista Arismendi. Open seven days a week from 7 am to 2 pm, it is housed in two buildings. The blue building features clothes and accessories and the yellow building, food.

Shops in La Asunción - La Aldea

Shops selling watches, pearls, leather goods, coral jewelry and Cuban and Dominican cigars are clustered in this quaint shopping hamlet. It's a popular stop with tour buses.

Margarita Etc.

Airlines

Aerotuy
Airport, ☎ 691-129
Porlamar, ☎ 632-211

Avensa
Airport, ☎ 691-301
Porlamar, No. 47 Calle Mariño, ☎ 617-111

Aeroejecutivos
Porlamar, ☎ 632-642

Laser
Airport, ☎ 691-329

Rutaca
Av Santiago Mariño
☎ 691-346 or 691-245

Zuliana de Aviación
☎ 632-852 or 632-926

Bank/Currency Exchange

Change money at **Cambios Febres Parra** in the Hotel Bella Vista lobby (☎ 616-043); **Cussco** at the corner of Calle Velasquez and Santiago Mariño or at the **Banco Consolidado** on Santiago Mariño in front of the Bella Vista.

Car Rentals

Avis
Airport, ☎ 691-236
Hotel Bella Vista, ☎ 618-920

Budget
Airport, ☎ 616-413
Hotel Bella Vista, ☎ 618-920

Hertz
Airport, ☎ 623-333
Hotel Margarita Hilton, ☎ 615-822

National
Airport, ☎ 691-442

Drinking Water

Drink only bottled water.

Dr. Scholl

A local branch is at Calle Zamora 18 and is open 8:30 am - 12:30 pm; 2:30 pm - 6 pm, Mon. to Fri. Sat. am only.

Emergency Phone Numbers

Police, ☎ 169

Firemen, ☎ 166

Ferry

Arrangements and information regarding passage from Punta de Piedras to Puerto La Cruz or Cumaná can be made at **Conferrys** on Calle Marcano. ☎ 619-235. To reserve by phone, ☎ 800-FERRY (33779).

When we last visited, departures to Puerto La Cruz were at 9 am, 1 pm, 3 pm, 9 pm and 1 am daily. There were 8 am and 11:30 am departures to Cumaná. Conferry also offers service to Coche.

Gourmet

The **Bodega de Blas** on Avenida Santiago Mariño is a terrific shop for gourmet items.

Newspapers

The Daily Journal and *Time* magazine are sold at the Hilton and Hotel Bella Vista's gift shops .

Pharmacies

These are plentiful and well-stocked with US drugs and sundries. There is always a drugstore open 24 hours.

Post Office

Located at the corner of Calle Gomez and Calle San Nicholas; you can also send radiograms here.

Supermarket

Try the **Supermercado Ultramar** on Calle Guevara for any foodstuffs you might require. There are many others all over town, such as **Cada, C/M** and **Prika**.

Tours

Holiday Tours offers a wide range of possibilities, not only on Margarita but across Venezuela, as well as day trips to Tobago, Grenada and Los Roques. Branch offices are in all the major hotels, but we recommend you make arrangements with Fulvio in the Hotel Bella Vista (☎ 617-227, ext. 169).

Tourist Information

The tourist information office is in the Bella Vista Hotel.

Transportation

Taxis have no meters, so fix a price in advance. To most parts of town you will pay between 50¢ and $1. Por puestos (jitneys) are common.

Puerto La Cruz

This is Venezuela's gateway to the Caribbean, a now well-furnished small city that has the contagious laziness of salt air and the high energy of a vacation spot. Puerto La Cruz is on the bay, not far from Margarita, separated by water, of course. It hugs the larger town of Barcelona – capital of Anzoátegui state – and is an hour and a half by car from Cumaná, another Caribbean beach resort.

Puerto La Cruz itself does not offer fantastic beaches. Visitors instead are attracted by the breathtaking islands of Mochima National Park, which offer some of the county's best snorkeling, diving and birdwatching. In Puerto La Cruz you'll find fine hotels, water taxis and organized excursions to the islands, and a strip of restaurants, shops and entertainment.

The town (or small city) is growing, with condos and more hotels going up. It is becoming a stomping ground for weekend tourists from Caracas, and is popular with an international crowd. It does seem as if Canadians and Italians have found the treasure of Puerto La Cruz; they dominate the international population.

Watersports abound. The coral formations off Puerto La Cruz are ideal for snorkeling and scuba. There is also boating, sailing, fishing, waterskiing and parasailing. With its fantastic climate – not searing in the day but definitely hot – and warm spring-like nights, its lyrical promenade on Paseo Colón, the main street, and rejuvenating atmosphere, Puerto La Cruz is a gem.

History

Oil has a way of bringing attention. For close to 400 years Puerto La Cruz, lost in anonymity, languished as a fisherman's pit-stop. It was known simply as "la playa" (the beach), and was just that for fishermen from the interior and Margarita, who used it to rest and dry out their catches.

The first transformation for Puerto La Cruz, although minor, was in the early 1800's when the fishing grounds around Cumaná were discovered. Instead of stopping for a few hours, a night perhaps, Margariteños began to spend longer periods of time on the beach of Puerto La Cruz. Eventually, some of them started building homes.

The second surge of popularity came with Venezuelan tourists, mainly from Caracas, who came here for the beaches and the alkaline waters of the **Spring of the Sacred Cross.**

Finally, in 1937, the first quarts of oil were found in the savannahs south of Puerto La Cruz, and this led to the oil terminal at the foot of Guaraguao Hill, east of the town.

Puerto La Cruz/Barcelona now has a population of 350,000 and growing – the fifth largest port in the world in volume of oil shipped. This has made it a thriving commercial center. With its fantastic beaches Puerto La Cruz has also grown as a tourist spot, and the city is responding with new hotels and a tourist-oriented infrastructure. Officials are eagerly and optimistically looking to the future.

Orientation

Puerto La Cruz is a 200-mile drive from Caracas on highway CT9. If you fly, you'll land at the General José Antonio Anzoátegui Airport in the city of Barcelona, which is adjacent to Puerto La Cruz. The taxi from the airport to the Melia Hotel, one of the main hotels, takes about 20 minutes and should cost around $8 US. The Doral Hotel and the Maremares Golden Rainbow Resort in the Complejo Turístico El Morro are closer. Hertz and Avis both have counters in the airport.

Activity revolves around **Paseo Colón**, which runs along the beach with a pedestrian promenade alongside it. The promenade is a nucleus of activity. You'll find an artisan's market here most evenings, along with street musicians. The eastern border of Paseo Colón is marked by the beachfront Melia Hotel. The Hotel Rasil is at the westernmost point at Calle Anzoátegui. Puerto La Cruz is small enough that you should not have a problem finding your way around.

About 20 minutes away by cab is the **Complejo Turístico el Morro**, a new development of condominium apartments and houses of five-star quality. The Doral Hotel and Golden Rainbow Resort are here.

Hotels

Melia Puerto La Cruz
Paseo Colón
220 rooms
☎ (081) 653-611; fax (081) 653-117
In Caracas, (02) 762-9314
Deluxe

The beachfront Melia was one of the first deluxe hotels in Puerto La Cruz. You'll find no shortage of amenities. Dining options include a bar and grill, a seafood restaurant, a semi-formal Italian restaurant and a coffee shop. There's also 24-hour room service if you'd prefer to dine alone on your private balcony overlooking the Caribbean. There's a disco for night time fun, and two pools, tennis courts and a full line-up of watersports including scuba, sailboats, and launches to keep you occupied during the day. Guides and instructors are available. Hotel shops include a newsstand/sundries shop, a sports shop, and a hairdresser, as well as car rental desks and tour operators. The conference center can accommodate up to 1,000 people.

Maremares Golden Rainbow Resort & Spa ☆☆☆☆☆
Av Américo Vespucio
Complejo Turístico El Morro
500 rooms
☎ In the US, (800) 472-4626 or (800) 772-1227
In Florida, (305) 569-7700; fax (305) 471-5623
Toll-free in Venezuela, 800-7367
In Puerto La Cruz (081) 813-022; fax (081) 814-494
Deluxe

A world unto itself, The Golden Rainbow is the largest and most luxurious resort in Puerto La Cruz. Active guests fill their days with golf, tennis and racquetball, while others lounge at the spectacular lagoon-style swimming pool with its cascading waterfalls, tropical islands and wave machine. All will enjoy the daily excursions to Mochima National Park, which include lunch, drinks and snorkeling equipment. The Maremares also has its own marina with 50 slips, and offers deep-sea fishing charters as well as yacht and sailboat cruises. Scuba equipment and instruction are also available. The health spa features fitness facilities, massage and spa treatments and even has its own restaurant. If you don't want to leave the kids home but would like some time for yourself, there's a program for kids under 12 and babysitting can be arranged.

The resort boasts five restaurants ranging from bathingsuit-informal to casually elegant. Additional amenities include car and motorbike rentals, resort shops, dry cleaning, laundry and medical assistance.

Punta Palma Hotel & Marina
Av La Península
Complejo Turístico El Morro
181 rooms (five floors)
Toll-free ☎ 800-78682; (081) 817-052; fax (081) 818-277
Expensive
The Punta Palma is one of the few hotels in Puerto La Cruz that can truly be described as beachfront. Nestled into the side of El Morro, the setting is lovely. All rooms have terraces overlooking the palm-lined beach and Puerto La Cruz or the mountains across the bay. Watersports equipment is available for rent and the Punta Palma also has tennis courts. Dining options feature a choice of three restaurants, including the elegant Guacamaya, which serves international and Venezuelan cuisine with an emphasis on seafood. Entertainment includes live music at poolside by day and a disco for after dark. There's regular shuttle bus service to Puerto La Cruz.

Doral Beach Hotel ☆☆☆☆
Av Américo Vespucio
Complejo Turístico El Morro
1,312 rooms
☎ (081) 817-510, fax 817-574
Expensive
This is another fine hotel in El Morro. More sprawling than high, there is a vast central pool, tennis, golf, and the other things that come with a deluxe hotel. But what the Doral really specializes in is water activities. Aquaventure on the premises offers parasailing, aqua rocket rides, waterskiing, windsurfing, kayaks, tube rides, water sledding, pedal boats, fishing, sailing, snorkeling, scuba diving, and boat excursions. Enough to keep you active for weeks. The Doral's two restaurants serve continental and Polynesian food.

Venezuela

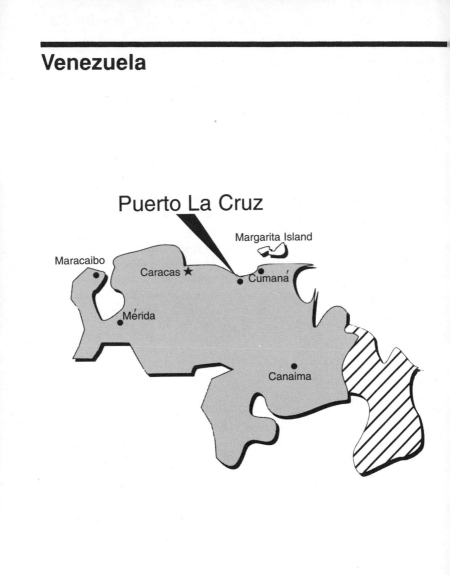

Hostería El Morro
Complejo Turístico El Morro
146 rooms
☎ (081) 811-311; 811-312
fax 814-226
Moderate
Near the Doral, this is a basic hotel on the beach. It has a pool and serves buffets at poolside; there is also a snack bar. The rooms are small, but comfortable and air-conditioned. Popular with Venezuelan families.

Hotel Rasil ☆☆☆☆
Paseo Colón #6 (Corner of Monagras)
345 rooms, 24 floors
Toll-free ☎ 800-RASIL, 672-422; fax 673-121
Moderate
The high-rise Rasil offers US television in all guest rooms, air-conditioning, a rooftop pool, formal and informal restaurants, nightclub and a small fitness center.

Hotel Cristina Suites
Av Municipal at Maneiro
250 rooms (17 floors)
☎ (081) 674-712; fax (081) 675-058
In Caracas (02) 993-8204 or fax 920-377
Expensive
The Cristina Suites caters primarily to business travellers and conventions. All rooms are suites and most have kitchenettes. It has a fitness center and two pools along with a poolside snack bar and an international restaurant.

Hotel Terramum
Av Principal del Lecherías
112 rooms (8 floors)
☎ 812-392, fax 810-696
Moderate
Just outside Puerto La Cruz in Lecherías, the Terramum offers comfortable accommodations at a great price. It has a pool and a ground-floor restaurant.

Hotel Gaeta
Paseo Colón
52 rooms (4 floors)
☎ 650-536, fax 674-717
Moderate
The Hotel Gaeta is in the thick of things on Paseo Colón. Its top-floor restaurant offers great views of the city and sea.

Hotel Senador
Calle Miranda, Plaza Bolívar
34 rooms
☎ 673-522
fax 652-338
Moderate
Only one block off Paseo Colón, this small but pleasant hotel has the comfort of a good soft bed, a nice hot shower and cool air-conditioning, but nothing else outstanding.

Hotel Riviera ☆☆☆
Paseo Colón 33
74 rooms
☎ 672-111; fax 651-394
You'll find furnishings here to be adequate and clean. Rooms can get noisy since the hotel is across from the busiest section of the promenade.

Hotel Montecarlo
Paseo Colón 119
☎ 685-677
Inexpensive
This Italian-run hotel is small and basic.

Two Final Choices...

If you prefer a more typically Venezuelan setting to the summer resort atmosphere of Puerto La Cruz, you may want to consider staying in Barcelona. Just keep in mind that the town itself does not really cater to non-

Venezuelan tourists. Truthfully, we prefer to stay in Puerto La Cruz.

Hotel Oviana ☆☆
Av Caracas
30 rooms (3 floors)
☎ (081) 764-147, fax (081) 764-953
In operation since 1990, the two-star Oviana is the newest of the hotels in Barcelona. It has its own bar/restaurant and rooms are basic yet comfortable.

Hotel Barcelona
Av 5 de Julio
Barcelona
70 rooms
☎ 881-065
Moderate
The Barcelona is an adequate second choice. It is a pleasant hotel, large and modern in its look, but doesn't have much to offer.

Restaurants

Most of Puerto La Cruz's best restaurants are on Paseo Colón, although there are some off the main drag. Prices are not steep, though the fancy restaurants in the Melia and Golden Rainbow are more expensive than the rest.

Try some of the local dishes. A fine choice is *cuajao*, made with mullet or loach roe, stewed fish and braised sawfish in round slices. Otherwise, the fare is comparable to that of other Venezuelan cities. Italian restaurants are by far the most numeruous. This is not surprising given the number of Italians who vacation here.

You should definitely try the cuajao at least once.

Tasca Mar
Melia Hotel
Open 7 pm - 11 pm (closed Sun.)
Expensive
One of the best restaurants in the city, Tasca Mar specializes in Spanish and seafood dishes. The interior matches the food, with a strange mixture of colonial and nautical designs. There is live music. The dishes to try are the *Catalana esqueixada* (cod fish stew), *paella*, *mero en cazuela* (casserole of bass), and gazpacho.

La Pequeña Roma
Calle Bolívar
Centro Comercial Mar
☎ 668-624
Moderate
Billed as "a small piece of Italy in Puerto La Cruz," La Pequeña Roma has a homey setting, with couches and lounge chairs, and serves great pizza and ravioli. Giorgio Cherubini is a fine host.

Da Luigi
Paseo Colón
☎ 655-737
Da Luigi is another of Puerto La Cruz's fine Italian restaurants. You'll find traditional fare, including fine antipasti to start and plenty of seafood dishes, with and without pasta.

Porto Vecchio
Paseo Colón (next door to the Brasero Grill)
☎ 652-047
Noon to midnight
The colorful Porto Vecchio features live music in the evenings and a more upscale menu than the other Italian restaurants in Puerto La Cruz. If you're hungry, start off with a plate of bruschetta for the table. Entrées include *rigatoni puttanesca*, *linguine del pescatore* and *cordero al horno* (baked lamb with sautéed potatoes).

Your friendly host, manager Juan Montelongo, will make sure you're well cared for.

Las Brisas
Golden Rainbow Resort
☎ (081) 813-022
A great choice for casual dining. Breakfast, lunch and dinner are served here. High wooden ceilings and ceiling fans. The restaurant is open to the outdoors, creating a very refreshing ambience.

Al Fresco
Golden Rainbow Resort
☎ (081) 813-022
7 pm-11 pm, Wed.- Sun.
Al Fresco is the Golden Rainbow's more formal alternative. Fine Italian cuisine is served in a luxurious dining room overlooking the marina.

La Tarantella
Melia Hotel
☎ (081) 653-611
Closed Sun.
Moderate
Adjacent to the lobby, La Tarantella offers formal dining, with marble floors, green tablecloths, organ music and the dim lighting of a hushed-tone eatery. Except for an Italian-influenced *cazuela* or fish stew, main courses are typically Italian.

Brasero Grill
Paseo Colón
☎ 688-655
Moderate
Also concentrating on fish and meat, Brasero prepares it skillfully.

Chic e Choc
Paseo Colón
☎ 652-551
Moderate
Despite its French menu, the food is surprisingly affordable, even by Venezuelan standards. Crêpes stuffed with vegetables, seafood or meat run from $4-$6. The filet mignon steak au poivre at $7 was an appetizing choice. Given our location, we opted for the brochettes de la mer, $8, and weren't disappointed. The wine list features Chilean wines, which did seem a bit pricey.

La Bella China
Paseo Colón
☎ 691-685
Inexpensive
This is the city's best Chinese restaurant, serving good Chinese food at reasonable prices. It's near the Melia Hotel.

Tio Pepe
Paseo Colón #11
☎ 653-654
Moderate
Very much a Spanish motif with posters of Spain on the walls and waiters dressed in typical Spanish clothes. Try the *bacalao a la gallega* and *calamares en su tinta* (squid in its ink).

Bonasera Pizzeria
Paseo Colón
☎ 651-946
Moderate
One of Puerto La Cruz's best Italian restaurants, Bonasera usually fills up before the others. Reserving ahead is a good idea. The veal pizzaola is a personal favorite. The pizzas are quite good as well. If you can't get a table here, there are a string of Italian restaurants

at the opposite end of Paseo Colón that are worth trying – **Da Luigi** (☎ 653-757), Torno a Sorrento, and **Casa Napoli** are representative.

La Bahia
Paseo Colón (in front of Hotel Riviera)
☎ 650-177
Moderate
A large outdoor patio dining room right on the beach makes La Bahia balmy and fun. The food is excellent, with filet, *pargo, mero* (bass) and lobster the highlights.

Los Napalitos
Paseo Colón (next door to the Hotel Rasil)
We were attracted by the busts of Diego Rivera and the old photographs of Mexico. As you've probably already figured out, the menu is Mexican.

Fuente Mar
Paseo Colón
☎ 687-623
Moderate
This was once an informal (inexpensive) outdoor eatery, but on our last visit to Puerto La Cruz we were surprised to discover that Fuente Mar had changed its look (and prices) entirely. It is now enclosed and fairly formal. A waterfall spans the length of the front windows. The menu is fairly extensive with an emphasis on seafood. Specialties include *arroz marinera* (rice with shellfish) for two and paella, also for two.

Tong Sing
Paseo Colón
☎ 22-850
Typically Chinese in style, Tong Sing runs a close second to La Bella China. The lo meins and seafood dishes are worth trying.

El Rancho Del Tio
Paseo Colón (not far from the Melia)
☎ 674-301
Expensive

This was obviously designed to appeal to tourists from outside Venezuela who want to sample typical Venezuelan cuisine. You can't miss the large, white stucco ranch-style building down the strip from the Melia Hotel. The extensive menu emphasizes typical Venezuelan dishes from around the country, including *sanchocho*, *churrasco* and *pabellón*.

Restaurant Cafeteria
Hotel Doral
Open 7 am - 10 am; 12 noon - 2:30 pm; and 6:30 - 9:30 pm
☎ (081) 817-510
Moderate

More formal than most of the restaurants described here, this place specializes in Spanish, international and local cuisine.

Piccolo Café
Centro Comercial La Galería
Calle Colón

The first time we visited, the Piccolo Café had literally just opened for business two hours earlier. We were glad to see it was still around during our most recent visit. Located in a relatively new building, this bi-level café is a lovely spot for coffee in the afternoon or drinks and soft jazz in the evening. The light menu includes pastas, soups, salads and sandwiches. The bar upstairs doubles as a small gallery where local artists can exhibit.

La Goleta
Melia Hotel
☎ (081) 653-611
Opens at 6:30 am

A snack bar serving salads, soups, sandwiches, and burgers, the Goleta is a great place to relax and have a light meal. There is also more substantial fare such as *pabellón criollo* (beef, black beans, rice and plantains) and stewed fish.

Fast Food

Tropiburger & Other Local Favorites

Similar to Burger King, **Tropi** has many branches, the closest one in front of the Melia. It serves burgers, hotdogs, shakes, pizza and other fast foods. **Priazzi**, a relatively new chain of Italian eateries springing up throughout the country, has opened next door. There is a large **Arturo's** on Paseo Colón. The menu is similar to, although more extensive than, Tropiburger's.

Pizza Hut & Burger King

These two have outlets on Paseo Colón. Burger King is across from the Hotel Rasil, while the bi-level Pizza Hut is on the other side of the beach across from the Melia.

El Paseo de Los Canales

Located on the Hotel Rasil end of Paseo Colón, this small complex is home to **Tony's Big House Deli**, which features deli-style sandwiches both hot and cold. Another North American staple, frozen yogurt, has been steadily working its way south and is now available in Puerto La Cruz. Following the example of its US counterparts, **Yog N. Fruz** offers this "low cal" treat with plenty of toppings.

Italian Gelato

Given the large number of Italians who seem to be settling or at least vacationing here, it is not surprising to find more than one gelateria in Puerto La Cruz. If you'd like a *barquilla* (cone) to go, stop by the **Heladería**

Italiana 4D, next door to the Piccolo Café on Paseo Colón. The very popular **Gelatería Torino**, on Calle Maneiro one block up from Colón, has both indoor and outdoor tables and offers espresso, cappuccino and pastries in addition to numerous gelati.

Sunup to Sundown

Mochima National Park

Without a doubt, the best reason to visit Puerto La Cruz is Mochima National Park. Created in 1973, it stretches along the coast from Puerto La Cruz to Cumaná in a breathtaking combination of coastal mountains rising out of the sea as rocky walls of cacti and scrubby trees ending in peaks of lush cloudforest, sparkling beaches in quiet inlets, coral islands, and mangroves. Of the park's approximately 370 square miles, 155 are on the mainland; 20 are islands in Mochima Bay, and the remaining 195 square miles extend downwards to the seabed. The park's singular vistas are best experienced by making the drive along the coastal route between Cumaná and Puerto La Cruz.

The drive is described at the end of this chapter.

The park harbors a fascinating combination of ecosystems. Alternating with steep rocky cliffs, mangroves weave intricate channels along the shoreline, both above and below the surface. While storks, herons, scarlet ibis, cormorants and boobies are often to be found perched among the branches, crabs can be seen scurrying up the tangled roots. Shrimp, worms, shellfish and mollusks feed on the algae and plankton that grows along the base of the mangroves, only to become fodder for the parrotfish, surgeon fish and angelfish that come in from the coral reefs to feed. Shore birds such as the brown pelican, the frigatebird, seagulls and the falcon-like coracora are invariably at the beach and along the rocky sections of the shoreline.

As you climb into the cloudforest, the foliage thickens and the wildlife becomes more elusive. Armadillos, jaguars, pacas, foxes and capuchin monkeys make their home here, as do rabbits, deer, snakes and sloths. In sharp contrast to the arid landscape below, the moisture-rich soil nurtures tall trees, palms and flowering vines.

Second only to Los Roques, Mochima offers some of the country's best diving and snorkeling. Its waters are home to an extensive coastal coral reef system made up of both hard and soft corals. Thanks to the mangroves along the shoreline, which provide an ideal spawning and feeding ground, the area is able to sustain an abundant fish population. Colorful parrot fish, angel fish, manta rays and other tropical fish are easily spotted in the shallower waters around the reefs, while red snapper, shark and blackfin and yellowfin tuna prefer the deeper waters.

Many of the finest snorkeling and dive sites surround the islands. The most popular islands are **Isla de Plata**, **Las Borrachas**, **Chimana Grande**, **El Faro**, **Isla de Monos**, **El Saco**, **Las Islas de Caracas**, **Conoma**, and **Conomita**. In addition to great snorkeling, some have beautiful sandy white beaches, though there is usually very little shade. The island landscapes are similar to that of the coast, with spectacular rocky cliffs jutting out from the sea. Black lizards and iguanas are often the only inhabitants of these arid islands. Since the coral reefs double as a barrier, the waters are usually quite calm.

For a day of island hopping and snorkeling, consider a day trip to the islands of Mochima Park offered by **Explosub**. Based in the Melia Hotel (☎ 653-611 or 650-574, fax 673-256), Explosub also offers a full-day cruise aboard a luxury yacht complete with open bar, snacks, barbecue on the beach, snorkeling, and music; sunset cruises; deep-sea fishing excursions; and scuba packages, including certified instruction.

The **Aquaventura** agency in the Doral Hotel offers a gamut of activities. There are snorkeling trips to the nearby islands for either half a day or the whole day at very reasonable prices. It is a 20-minute ride to the islands, and snorkeling gear and refreshments are included.

Aquaventura also offers a resort course in scuba diving followed by one or two dives. The diving trips are at volcano mouths, marine canyons, blue lagoons and coral reefs. Aquaventura also has aquarocket rides, waterskiing, windsurfing, tube rides, water sleds and boat trips, as well as parasailing.

Aqua Joy in the Golden Rainbow Resort also offers a wide range of activities, including snorkeling tours of the islands, scuba courses and dives for the certified, jet ski rentals, deep sea fishing and chartered tours.

If you'd like to head out to Mochima on your own, you can take a water taxi. The cost per boat should be somewhere between $10 and $15, depending on which island you go to. The "taxi stand" is on Paseo Colón behind the El Rancho del Tío parking lot. Taxis run all day long so you needn't worry about a schedule. Just arrange for the driver to pick you up again at the end of the day. Be sure to bring plenty of water, an umbrella for shade and whatever you may need for the day, as most of the islands, with the exception of Isla de Plata, have no comfort facilities.

Sailboat and deep sea fishing charters can be arranged at the Americo Vespucio Marina in the El Morro Tourist Complex. Contact **Max Rasitours** at ☎ (081) 811-295 or fax 812-863, or **Nelson & Nelson** at ☎/fax (081) 778-232.

Walking Tour

A walking tour is a good way to orient yourself to the city and see a bit of its history. The main street is **Paseo Colón**, the hub of tourist activity. Walking its length, about a mile, starting from the Melia Hotel, you'll take in the beach and outdoor artisan market, where you can buy jewelry, leather goods, belts and other items.

On Calle Sucre turn left (south), and in one block you will reach **Plaza Bolívar**, a lovely square. Two blocks from there, off Calle Anzoátegui, is the lovely **Iglesia de Santa Cruz.**

Although it is slightly out of the way, the **Mercado Principal** is worth the walk if you're interested in experiencing some truly local flavor. Follow Calle Anzoateguí to Avenida Cinco de Julio where you should turn right and then left onto Calle Venezuela, which will bring you to the market. The open-air market operates from about 6 am until 1 pm and features stall upon stall of vendors selling handicrafts, T-shirts and souvenirs, household items, and fresh fruits and vegetables. The market is also a great place to sample typical Venezuelan foods.

Municipal Gallery of Modern Art

A small permanent collection of paintings and sculptures by local artists is exhibited. It is just past the Alfonso Carrasquel Stadium in a small one-story building. Open Tues. - Fri., 9 am - 12 pm; 3 pm - 6 pm and Saturdays and Sundays, 3 pm - 6 pm. Free.

El Morro Tourist Complex

The Complejo Turístico El Morro is a massive project that began several years ago and is nearing the final stages of construction. It is home to the Americo Vespcucio Marina, the Plaza Mayor Shopping Center, and the exclusive Pelicano Resort, a development of beautiful waterfront homes.

The Maremares Golden Rainbow Resort, Doral Hotel and Punta Palma Hotel & Casino are located here as well.

Amusement Park

On the Paseo Colón is **Guayanaven**, which has bumper cars, ferris wheels, and other rides.

Sights in Barcelona

If history is what interests you, your energy would be better spent on a walking tour of Barcelona. Capital city of the state of Anzoátagui, Barcelona is about 20 minutes from Puerto La Cruz and offers more historic sites.

Casa Fuerte

With a strange and exciting history, Casa Fuerte was a Franciscan Convent in the 18th and 19th centuries. The austere Franciscans considered themselves caretakers of the poor, sick and alienated. They also used the edifice as the departure point for their missionary activities in the south. During the War of Independence in 1811, it was converted to a fort which, unfortunately, suffered at the hands of Spanish troops.

Refusing to accept the constitution of Venezuela during the independence battle caused the Franciscans to lose the Casa Fuerte. Their tenure there ended tragically in a battle that took place on April 17, 1817. General José Adama pummeled his enemies in a forceful attack. Unfortunately, he became so intoxicated by his victory that he killed everyone in sight, regardless of age and gender. Among the best known of his victims was Major Chamberlain, an Irishman from Jamaica who swore allegiance to Bolívar's cause. Chamberlain's death became legend in Europe where tales and poems were written about him. The ruins have been a national landmark ever since.

Museo de la Tradición

A potpourri of historic items, the Museum of Tradition is more like an antique shop. The house itself was the fourth to be built in Barcelona in 1671, and is the oldest one standing. It has been restored in its colonial style.

The museum has about 400 items of Indian, colonial and post-colonial interest. There are statues of saints, old stones, street signs warning against leaning on the lightpost after 6 pm because of electrocution, and other odd relics.

The museum is open every day from 8 am to 12 noon and 3 pm to 6 pm.

Opposite the Casa Fuerte is Plaza Bolívar, and not far from the Plaza is a cluster of interesting sights. These include the **Plaza Miranda**, **Plaza Boyaca**, the main plaza of the city and government, and the **Cathedral of Barcelona**. All are easily visited in a short stroll. If you allocate an hour or two you can tour these places at a leisurely pace and savor their history. We recommend it.

Ferry to Margarita

Rather than fly to Margarita, many travelers take the ferry from Puerto La Cruz. The trip is very affordable and takes under four hours. There are four Conferry departures every day (8 am, 1 pm, 8 pm, and 1 am). A round-trip first-class ticket is under $15, including the port tax. Tourist class is about $5 cheaper. There is also an express, which departs at 7 am and 2 pm and takes just two hours. A ticket is $25. If you're traveling by car, the ferry makes it possible for you to include Margarita in your driving itinerary. The fare for a passenger car is around $18 round-trip.

The ferries are conveniently located just beyond the center of town.

Although not absolutely necessary, unless you have a car, Conferry recommends you reserve in advance. You can do so at the ferry terminal itself; in the Melia Hotel; or call **Conferry** at ☎ 677-847 or 678-253. You can also reserve ahead in Caracas. Their office is in the Banhorient building on Avenida Casanova (☎ 782-8544).

Shopping

On Paseo Colón you'll find a string of shops and boutiques, as well as street vendors selling art, leather items, masks, jewelry, hats, belts, and tapes. These are fun to stroll through because they are the most active and alive.

Puerto La Cruz is not a place for serious shopping.

The Gold Market
Paseo Colón, next door to the Hotel Riviera
The Gold Market features a lovely selection of 18 kt. gold jewelry, much of which is set with precious and semi-precious stones. Prices are reasonable.

INBYDCA, C.A.
Paseo Colón, #55
Beycardennys Building
☎ (081) 650-126
Indian handicrafts are the specialty here. Masks, rugs and hammocks make excellent gifts. **El Aquario**, next door, features similar items.

Playmon Artesania Y Deportes
Paseo Colón 35
☎ 24-569
For local handicrafts and souvenirs this is a good place. It's also the shop for masks, snorkels and beach toys.

Mareblu
Paseo Colón 67
Handicrafts, including woven items and hammocks, are featured here along with beachwear.

After Dark

Once relatively subdued, nightlife in Puerto La Cruz has really come into its own in recent years. There are several discos in town and, of course, casinos.

Harry's Bar/Pub
Calle Bolívar 53
☎ 688-319
Marilyn Monroe, Marlena Dietrich, Humphrey Bogart and Elvis are all represented at Harry's Bar, Puerto La Cruz's top nightspot. Speakeasy-like in its decor, the glass-topped tables sport US license plates and there's no shortage of video screens. Things don't get started until after midnight and it doesn't quiet down until around 6 am. Harry's Bar is in a yellow building one block off Paseo Colón.

Bar Whiskey
Maremares Golden Rainbow Resort
☎ (801) 813-022
With live Latin music and a crowded dance floor every night, Bar Whiskey is another popular locale with the after-midnight crowd.

Malibu
El Morro Tourist Complex
Near the Doral Hotel. This is another lively club which attracts a young crowd.

12 y 23
Av 5 de Julio
☎ 668-803
The ambience here is reminiscent of Cuba in the 1950's. Indeed, much of the music is from that era. Live music and dancing. Open Tues. - Sat.

Ibiza
Paseo Colón
☎ 675-258
The bi-level Ibiza is a popular choice with the 25-and-up group. It's open every night.

Club Guatacarazo
Paseo Colón
☎ 652-594
A flamboyant spot called the best club in Venezuela on TV, Club Guatacarazo is a trip.

How about getting married and not worrying about alimony? This club is structured for lovers, for flingers, for one-night-standers. You are greeted at the bar with a cup, in the shape of a breast, filled with champagne. With a marriage confession, and Club Guatacarazo, you are hitched. You even get a marriage certificate and waiters singing "Here comes the bride." Inside it's swinging and wild. Costumed waiters add to the festivities. Don't miss it.

Caribiano
Melia Hotel
Open 9 pm - 3 pm; weekends, 9 pm - 4 am
(Closed Sun.)
A hopping place, Caribiano has a large dance floor with tables surrounding it and couches lining the wall.

Bar Moriche
Melia Hotel
For a more relaxed evening, the bar in the Melia is plush and intimate – a good place to meet people. Location: right in the lobby of the hotel.

Casinos

When gambling was legalized in Venezuela, casinos seemed to spring up overnight. Service and surroundings run the gamut, from video arcade to classy. Puerto La Cruz is certainly no exception.

Bingo Casino Star 33
Av Alberto Rabell, The Star 33 Building
Open noon to 4 am every day
Star 33 is by far the most attractive and best casino in
Puerto La Cruz. There are blackjack, craps and roulette
tables and the service is top notch.

Casino Cristal Palace
Calle Guaraguo
Open 24 hours.
Located across the street from the Banco Provincial, the
Cristal Palace is a big step down from the Star 33. In our
opinion, however, it's the second nicest casino in
Puerto La Cruz.

Sahara Club
Paseo Colón, next door to the Hotel Gaeta
(across from the Melia)
☎ 800-566
The Sahara Club was Puerto La Cruz's first casino.
Although not fancy, it offers the standards – blackjack,
roulette, Caribbean poker, and baccarat.

Gran Salón 77
Paseo Colón 77
Open 24 hours
Video arcade-style, the Gran Salón features electronic
machines only.

Puerto La Cruz Etc.

Cambio

You can change money in the Hotel Riviera and at the
Casa de Cambio on Paseo Colón.

Casa Scholl

Calle Anzoáteguil
☎ 23-162
For aching feet.

Avensa/Servivensa

Centro Pepsi, ☎ 663-101

Aeropostal

☎ 770-315

Puerto La Cruz to Cumaná

The 50-mile coastal road from Puerto La Cruz to Cumaná is poetic, a link of nature that makes you feel awed. Viewers are staggered with offshore islands, the hidden beaches, and coves which hint at the shore's beauty. You feel as if you can see forever and that the view will probably stay with you, maybe even after death.

This trip is a must. If you will be staying in Cumaná, drive. If not, it's a wonderful day trip by taxi or rental car.

Head east out of Puerto La Cruz along the coastal highway, CT 9. Just outside town you'll pass a Mexican-owned cement quarry, one of the largest on the continent. It owns the nearby **Vencemos Zoo**. The zoo was set up to show native Venezuelan animals, and is in a coconut grove next to the water. To reach it, you must turn right off the highway at the Pertigalete sign.

Stop for a cachapa, fresh and delicious.

En route you will see women making *cachapas*, a delicious mélange of freshly ground corn, sugar and salt in a flat cake. It is cooked on a wooden fire, and is communally done, with even the children participating. Stop and sample at least one, plain or with cheese. Wash it down with a refreshing *coco frío*, ice cold coconut water which you drink straight out of the fruit.

Shortly after leaving Puerto La Cruz you'll pass the port of **Guanta**. Boats to Isla de Plata leave from the pier here and you can usually find someone to take you to the other islands from here as well. Just past Guanta is a turn-off for **Parque de la Sirena** (there will be road signs), above the village of **Chorrerón**. Well worth a detour, the park's focal point is the **Pozo de la Sirena** (mermaid's well), a beautiful waterfall that cascades into a series of freshwater pools. In the rainy season these pools are great for swimming. Walking and picnicking are other favored activities here.

About 11 miles out of Puerto La Cruz you'll come to **Los Altos de Santa Fe Lookout**, a 2,925-foot natural observatory. From here you can see the beaches, bays and islands that make up the shore of eastern Venezuela. The view is limitless and stunning. It will give you a feeling of eternity that will be stirred only by the salty winds. The road continues on past the lookout into highlands, where you should come to the century-old **Hacienda de Bucares**, a coffee and cocoa plantation. If you phone ahead (☎ 093-664-103), you may be able to arrange a guided tour. If you are planning to arrive at dusk be sure to bring a sweater as it can get quite chilly here after the sun goes down.

Just after entering the state of Sucre, you'll come to **Arapito**, the first of many beaches you'll pass en route. It has a few places to eat, and many small launches or peñeros are available to take you to the offshore islands nearby.

The second beach you come to is **Playa Colorado** (Red Beach), which is narrower than Arapito but more popular. From Colorado you can also rent (on weekends) a boat to take you to the parallel islands of **Arapo** and **Arapito**. There are nice beaches on the islands, and some fishing families live there.

The next beach is **Playa Los Hicacos**, a beach for the professors and students of Club Universitario UDO Los Hicacos. You then come upon **Playa Santa Cruz**, a fishing village 18 miles from Puerto La Cruz. Since it faces west, the sunsets are fabulous.

The fertile **Valley of Santa Fe**, the surrounding area, sits upon the gulf and is home to many fishermen. It is the part of South America where missionaries coming from the island of Santo Domingo first landed.

*Mochima Bay
is the highlight
of this trip.*

The most outstanding part of the stretch between Puerto La Cruz and Cumaná is **Mochima Bay**, 30 miles from Puerto La Cruz. Mochima Bay is part of an entire region of cliffs, bays and waterways that wind and twist between the mainland and the Caribbean. The region is 6% islands, 52% water and 42% mainland, which gives you an idea of its maze-like beauty. The mainland is composed of narrow valleys and rugged hillsides, with an ecology of aquatic vegetation, mangrove trees, and coral reefs. It is obviously a wonderland of nature.

Mochima has been designated a National Park and is popular with water-skiers and boaters. In the town of Mochima you can hire a *peñero* or small boat to take you around the interior bays and cliffs, a definite must. There's no other reason to visit the town of Mochima. Since there are no facilities on the islands or coastal beaches, be sure to bring plenty of water and other supplies.

After Bella Vista you come to the penultimate town of **Barbacoas**. Barbacoas is famous for its dolls, which are sold all along the road. They are colorful and imaginative; even if you are not buying one you should stop and look at them. The next stop is Cumaná.

Cumaná

A magnificent, star-shaped, restored colonial fortress towers over this Caribbean city of 250,000. Its dungeons and cannon are only one reason for visiting Cumaná. South American's first city, it was founded in 1521 and, despite having been devastated by three separate earthquakes in 1684, 1755 and 1929, still retains a bit of its Spanish colonial charm, with red-tile roofs, narrow, cobblestoned streets and 18th-century churches.

If you like your history in small doses, Cumaná does offer something more – miles of nearby immaculate beaches in use year-round. It is a jumping-off point to Margarita; many Caraqueños combine vacations here and in the islands.

A Quick Orientation

If you fly to Cumaná, you will land at **Aeropuerto Gran Mariscal de Ayacucho** in El Pirón, 15 minutes by cab from your hotel. Or you can rent a car at the airport. Driving to town, you will pass through the **San Luis** section along **Avenida Universidad**, which leads into the city center. The inner city begins at the **Plaza Nueva Toledo**, which has at its center a statue of a Cumanagoto Indian holding aloft a fish.

To the left of the Plaza is a major street, **Calle Perimetral**, a two-way thoroughfare (unusual here) that has a number of recommended restaurants. Intersecting Calle Perimetral are the two shopping streets of **Avenida Bermúdez** and **Calle Mariño**. **Plaza Miranda**, which marks the beginning of "colonial Cumaná," is across the bridge on the bank of the **Manzanares River** and is the starting point for our recommended walking tour. Keep in mind that the Manzanares bisects the city. The colonial areas are closest to the river and the modern area furthest from it. The best resort hotels are located on the Caribbean, not far from the airport.

History

It was in 1506 that the first true, but unintended, steps toward colonization began. Although the missionaries that arrived had no specific intention to colonize, the foundation was set for a European presence. The first Franciscan missionaries were welcomed by the pearl diving Cumanagoto Indians, the region's original inhabitants. Once word got out about the pearls, Spanish settlers were quick to arrive. In 1521 Bartolomé de las Casas arrived with a community of artisans and farmers.

Cumaná was the first settlement founded by the Spanish on mainland South America.

Cumaná's colonization was hastened by an Indian rebellion a year earlier. With the glut of pearls found on the island of Cubagua, the Spanish periodically swept the coast of Cumaná, catching slaves like fish. This spurred a revolt, which in turn made the Spanish more militaristic, and led them to build a fort in Cumaná.

In between repeated attacks a unique event occurred. Las Casas, an aristocrat from Spain, became enraged at Spain's inhumanity to the Cumanagotos. As a result of his lobbying the King, he was given a tract of land to begin his own community. His vision quickly evaporated as he discovered that the Indians had gone inland to escape death and to retrench. The final blow to his utopia was inertia; the progress of Spain in crushing its weaker foe was too intoxicating and profitable to be stopped.

Over the next 100 years or so the history of Cumaná was a cycle of warfare and retribution, with the Spanish and Indians trading blows. The outcome is well-known, but it happened less as a result of military conquests than religious ones.

Cumaná was not a quick or easy comrade in the Independence War. It accepted membership in the Captain's Generalcy in 1777, but only on its own terms. It reneged on its oath and reverted to the loyalist side; it was a friendly port for General Pablo Morillo, sent from Spain to quash Bolívar.

Eventually, Cumaná crept into the nation of Venezuela, and modern times have brought the port, fishing, tourism, beaches and its status as the capital of the State of Sucre.

Climate

Meteorologists have an easy time in Cumaná. Warm sunny days with cooling evening breezes persist year-round. Average temperature, 80°.

The Best Hotels

As you might expect, the better hotels are to be found on the nearby Caribbean shores. Unless you have a business reason for staying at a downtown hotel, stick to the beachfront. Hotels below are air-conditioned and come with private bath and phone.

Hotel Los Bordones ☆☆☆☆
Final Av Universidad
(San Luis Section)
115 rooms, 8 floors
☎ (093) 513-111; fax (093) 515-377
Expensive
Los Bordones is the kind of hotel that keeps you busy wondering what to do next. With bright colors, as befits its Latin American style and tropical location, the hotel has elegant rooms. It also has a list of features: several restaurants, tennis courts, jacuzzi, two pools,

watersports equipment, and many shops. There is a casino next door. The hotel has a fun, alive feel to it.

Hotel Cumanagoto ☆☆☆
Calle Mariño, 18
(San Luis Beach)
161 rooms, 4 floors
☎ 653-355, Telex 93173
Moderate
A Sofitel Hotel, the Cumanagoto is in a beautifully landscaped setting. With a feel that is like a small community, the hotel is on a par with Los Bordones for comfort. It has a swimming pool, restaurants, tennis courts, a travel agency and some shops.

Gran Hotel Cumaná ☆☆☆
Av Universidad
50 rooms, 3 floors
☎ (093) 510-218; fax (093) 512677
Moderate
Located just a short walk from the beach, the Gran Hotel Cumaná is a popular choice. Most rooms feature a balcony looking out to the sea or over the pool. There's a poolside restaurant and bar as well as two indoor restaurants. Furnishings are basic yet comfortable.

Hotel Minerva ☆☆☆
Av Cristobal Colón
138 rooms
☎ (093) 662-712; fax (093) 662-701
Moderate
The Minerva is a nice comfortable hotel that has all the needed functions plus more. In front of the hotel is a long promenade along the water. There are two restaurants, a pool, and many rooms have terraces.

Hotel Savoia
Av Perimetral
47 rooms, 4 floors
☎ (093) 321-455; fax (093) 314-379
Inexpensive
A nice relaxing hotel with no extras, the two-star Savoia is a fine place for people on a budget.

The Best Restaurants

Seafood dominates the local cuisine and with justification, for the *chipi chipi* (small clams, usually served in a soup), and *pebre de morrocoy* (turtle steak in garlic sauce) are superb dishes. North American restaurant owners would do well to check out this cuisine. Be sure to sample *mejillones* (mussels), and *empanadas de cazón* (sharkmeat pie).

There are no posh eateries in Cumaná. Informal decor and attire are the rule.

Polinesa
Hotel Los Bordones
☎ (093) 513-111
Open noon - 3 pm; 7 pm - 11 pm
Expensive
Polinesa is justifiably proud of its fish and chicken dishes. The restaurant is large, with beamed ceilings and a colonial look. There is an extensive menu.

Los Castillitos
Av Cristobal Colón
Open 11:30 am - 11:30 pm
Expensive
Across from the Minerva Hotel, Los Castillitos is a glass-enclosed structure that hangs over the water. It specializes in fish dishes; the food is quite good.

Araya
Hotel Cumanagoto
Open 11 am - 11 pm
Expensive

Araya, on the second floor of the hotel, affords a lovely view of the beach and the Caribbean and is a fine choice for casual dining. At the time of our last visit in early 1997, Cumanagoto was closed indefinitely for renovations.

El Colmao
Calle Sucre
Located across from the park in the historic district, El Colmao is reminiscent of an Andalusian hacienda. It's a lovely spot for drinks and dinner.

El Teide
Av Perimetral, Oriente Building
☎ 662-907
Heavy traditional Spanish-style decor dominates the interior of this fine Spanish restaurant. Seafood and garlic lovers will be in their element as the menu emphasizes both. Representative choices include *champiñones al ajillo* (mushrooms in garlic sauce); *cazuela de mariscos* (a typical Spanish shellfish dish served in an earthenware crock); *camerones al ajillo* (shrimp in Garlic sauce); and *pargo a la plancha* (grilled red snapper).

Restaurante Cristobal Colón
Av Perimetral
☎ 312-712
Located in front of the Hotel Minera, Cristobal Colón doubles as a *tasca* (pub) and a piano bar. It's a fine choice for drinks and appetizers or a full meal.

Chef Dinosoff
Los Bordones
Open 12 noon - 11 pm
Moderate
Another good choice for lighter fare. Service and cuisine are first-rate.

Sunup to Sundown

We strongly urge a walking tour to get the "feel" of Cumaná by day. Start in the old colonial section where the buildings all seem to have red tile roofs. At the **Plaza Miranda**, on the so-called right bank of the Manzanares River, immerse yourself in the city's sounds and sights – buses, taxis, fruit stalls, news vendors, shoeshine boys. Follow the river street for two blocks, turn left and you will find yourself on **Calle Rivero**, a narrow colonial street, all of seven feet wide plus a two-foot-wide sidewalk. Stroll along the deserted streets (residents spend their outdoor time on interior patios; the streets are used only to enter and leave their homes). Just ahead on your right will be the **Santa Inés Church**, the city's main church, built in 1572. Note the impressive stained glass windows. The statue you will see is that of Saint Inés, patron Saint of Cumaná.

Half a block beyond the church on your left atop a hill is the yellow-walled **San Antonio Castle**, the city's most important site. Climb the steps to the castle, which resembles a movie set, and then continue to the structure's peak. All of Cumaná is visible. To your left is the Cumanagoto strip (look for the hotel), while on your right is the Araya Peninsula. Originally constructed in the 17th century and since restored, the castle is shaped like a six-sided star with the walls made of local coral. A guide (Spanish speaking only) escorts visitors through the dungeons and onto the outer walls. Note the red-tile roofs of the structures surrounding the castle and don't overlook the sculpted lion heads atop the wall. If you're thirsty, (we usually are at this point), stop at the snack shop here.

After a respite, retrace your steps back to Santa Inés Church; at Calle Sucre turn right and two blocks beyond is the **Plaza Bolívar** and the adjoining **Plaza**

Adjacent to the church is the fortress of Santa María de la Cabeza which, 300 years ago, housed a garrison of 250 soldiers. Only the outer walls stand today. Ask the church priest to let you see the inside gardens.

Venezuela

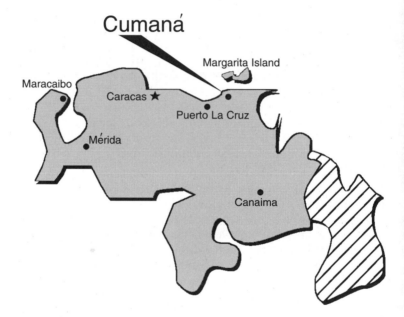

Cumaná

Margarita Island

Maracaibo

Caracas ★

Puerto La Cruz

Mérida

Canaima

Pichincha. Here are the Sucre State Government buildings, including the Governor's home.

A block left of Plaza Pichincha, where Sun. afternoon concerts are held, is the city's **main cathedral**. Note the etched wooden ceiling and elaborate chandeliers.

Among the memorabilia are a golden crown and feather pen presented to the general by the City of Cochabama, Bolivia.

Continue strolling, bearing left, and you will find yourself back at the Plaza Miranda. Just beyond it is the **Plaza Ayacucho** with its statue of General Sucre, revolutionary war hero who was born in Cumaná. That colonial-style building is the **Municipal Palace**. On the second floor is a small museum commemorating General Sucre.

Sucre Museum

This museum is dedicated to the Cumaná-born war hero General Antonio José de Sucre. The General was considered the second most brilliant military mind after Bolívar. On December 9, 1824 he won the battle at Ayacucho, which resulted in the independence of Peru, and later beat the royalist forces in Alto Peru, resulting in the creation of Bolivia. He then became the Gran Mariscal de Ayacucho. His short career spiralled, as he then became Bolivia's first president. But, because he shared Bolívar's vast dream of a united Latin America, he was murdered in the mountains of Colombia.

The museum is in the **Consejo Municipal** (Municipal Palace) and is open Tues. - Fri., 9 am - 12 pm; 3 pm - 6 pm; Sat., 4 pm - 6 pm and Sun., 10 am - 12 pm; 4 pm - 6 pm.

Market

The market of Cumaná is electric and restless. There are foods, from spices to meats and fish; arts and crafts; and other items such as hammocks, coffee and cuatros, a hybrid guitar developed by the local Guaiqueri Indians.

The fort offers fantastic views of the region and should not be missed.

Castillo de San Antonio de La Eminencia

From its perch overlooking the city, this fort offers a widespread view of the surrounding area and out into the Caribbean.

Its history is Cumaná's. Built originally to spot oncoming enemies, the fort served this purpose for years, preempting Captain Henry Morgan's attempt to smash the city. An earthquake flattened the fort and the city in 1684, but the fort was soon rebuilt. In 1853, the fort was again destroyed by an earthquake, and this time it took almost 50 years to rebuild. Again, an earthquake, coupled with a tidal wave, ruined the fort. It was minimally rebuilt in 1959 and more sturdily repaired in 1975.

Araya Península

The main attractions of the peninsula are its natural beauty and the Castillo de Santiago de Araya. The peninsula is reached by Hovercraft or car-ferry from Cumaná or by a jeep road from Cariaco and Chacopata.

Construction of the **Castillo de Santiago de Araya** was forced by the Dutch who were blatantly stealing the abundant salt located off Cumaná. At one point the Spanish sent out a ship to stop them, which resulted in a battle, and, finally, a truce. The truce was ostensibly kept, although the Dutch continued to steal the salt clandestinely. It soon became necessary to build the fort. Construction began in 1621.

Completed in 1665, the Araya fort is considered the best in Venezuela, and superior to any other in the Americas. It could accommodate 300 men, had 45 cannons and was built in an unusual trapezoidal form. It was a huge structure, overpowering in its appearance.

In 1726, a hurricane destroyed most of the fort. To keep it from falling into the wrong hands, the Spanish blew it up in 1762, although by that time salt could no longer be mined.

The bulwarks still stand, powerful monuments to good architecture and the importance of salt.

Mochima National Park

As described in the *Puerto La Cruz* chapter, Mochima National Park and the Bay are quite special and should not be missed.

Museo del Mar

Av Universidad

This interesting aquarium is open Tues. - Sun., 8:30 am - 11:30 am; 3 pm - 7 pm.

After Dark

Though the nightlife in Cumaná is relatively tame, you should be able to find something to do. There are three **film houses** in town: the Paramount in the Plaza Miranda; the Teatro Humboldt on Calle Bermúdez; and Pinchincha, near the Plaza Pichincha. All are air-conditioned and feature fairly recent films.

Free concerts are often held weekends in the main auditorium at the Universidad del Oriente (University of the East).

Casino-goers can try their luck at the **Casino Royale** located in the building next door to the Hotel Los Bordones. It's open from 7 pm to 4 am every day and features black jack, roulette and poker.

Nightowls, primarily singles and young couples, congregate at a few chosen clubs. **Jamaica**, a pop bar on Avenida Universidad, is one of the most popular. More appealing to an older crowd, **El Campanaso** is a piano bar on Avenida Universidad.

Cumaná Etc.

Airlines

Avensa

Main office here is at Calle Armario 18. ☎ (093) 24-505.

Auto Rentals

Volkswagen has offices at the airport and on Avenida Bermúdez. Rates vary with the model you select.

Banks

A good one is the **Banco Unión**, Calle Mariño and Calle Carabobo.

Barber Shop & Beauty Parlor

Try the one on Pasaje Tobia, between Calles Bermúdez and Mariño (downtown).

Books & Magazines

The **Gift Shop in the Hotel Cumanagoto** carries English-language publications, including *The Daily Journal* (published in Caracas). On our last visit in 1997, however, the hotel was closed for renovations. A fine bookshop is the **Librería Cervantes** on Calle Comercio.

Buses

The red and yellow bus marked San Luis will drop you at your beach hotel. Fare is 10¢. Last stop is the Cumanagoto Hotel. Pick it up on Avenida Universidad.

Cabs

General rate is 70¢ to $1.15. Set the fare in advance. Hourly cost is $4.50.

Cada Supermarket

Wide range of edibles. Located on Avenida Perimetral. Open Sundays 8 am to noon, Saturdays all day, and weekdays all day except from 12:30 pm - 2:30 pm.

Casa Scholl

The footsore should head to Casas Scholl, Calle Sucre, near Plaza Bolívar; full treatment is $2.25. Closed noon - 2:30 pm. Open Saturdays.

One-Way Streets

Except for Avenidas Perimetral and Universidad almost all streets have one-way traffic.

Pharmacy

A good farmacia, **Virgen del Valle** is on Avenida Perimetral and Mariño. Another one is **Central** on Avenida Bermúdez near the Bridge.

Post Office

It is near the Plaza Eloy Blanco on Calle Paraíso.

Shopping

Your best browsing is along **Avenida Bermúdez**. You might also stroll through the shops in **Pasaje Tobia**, between Calles Bermúdez and Mariño near the bridge.

Universidad Del Oriente

Among the oldest universities in the Western Hemisphere, its main entrance is on Avenida Universidad. This is by far the most prestigious school in this part of Venezuela.

Mérida

*L*ocals here boast that some of the world's finest trout fishing is to be found in the lagoons in and around Mérida. But that's only part of the reason why you should journey the 400 miles from Caracas to this city in the Andes. It is set 5,400 feet above sea level in a highland valley between the Sierra Nevada de Mérida and the Sierra de La Culata.

For openers, there is the air itself. It reminds us of Vermont in May after the sun has burst forth following an early morning rain. Fresh, crisp, clean. Then there is the charm that can be found only in a colonial-era city – nestled on a mountain plateau surrounded by snow-capped mountains. The people – including the 25,000 students at the local university – treat strangers with an openness that is as welcome as it is rare in the closed-off world of today.

There is also the pleasure of strolling the narrow colonial streets in town and the sprawling seductive countryside beyond. And if all of this is insufficient, there is the world's highest cable car, which sweeps up to a peak almost 16,000 feet high. Little wonder we are rather fond of Mérida, as are many Venezuelans, who use it as a holiday retreat all year round. Temperatures here average 66° over the 12 months. Perfection.

History

Founded on October 9, 1558 by Captain Juan Rodríguez Suárez, the city's birthdate was blackened by crime. Suarez, who was on official business from Colombia (then Nueva Granada), was sent to the Andes to explore and, as was popular in those days, to conquer some Indians. On a tangent he discovered and founded Mérida; but the founding of a city could only be done by royal decree; hence, Suarez, technically, had committed a crime. His rival, Juan Maldonado y Ordóñez, was eager to see him arrested and have him stand trial. If not for the intervention of Bishop Juan Carlos de los Barrios, Suarez would have been drawn and quartered. Suarez was eventually exiled to America.

Since Mérida's incorporation into Venezuela in 1777, its head has been held high. It was the first city to accept Bolívar as El Libertador, and the first city to erect a statue to him in 1842 (you will find the statue in the Parque de las Cinco Repúblicas).

Mérida is dominated by youth. It is the home of Venezuela's second oldest university, the Universidad de los Andes, which was founded in 1785. Merida's unique combination of mountain air and youthful energy make the city even more attractive to visitors.

Orientation

Sometimes called the *techo* (roof) of Venezuela, the State of Mérida is perched atop the highest part of the Venezuelan Andes. Mérida City, the state capital, is built on a plateau in the Sierra Nevada range which, from above, looks like a large roof to a small building surrounded by much larger buildings with smaller roofs. From Mérida's roof you can supposedly take binoculars and peruse the entire Venezuelan Andes. With that image in mind, you should get a sense of Mérida's beauty.

The geography around Mérida is similar to that of the Alps. The lower parts of the mountains are covered with trees, and the peaks are usually snow-capped. The tallest peaks are around Mérida. The highest of these is **Pico Bolívar**, which, at 16,427 ft, surpasses the Alps by at least 3,000 feet. The city is surrounded by four rivers – the Albarregas and the Chama are the main ones; the Milla and Mucujin, the peripheral rivers. It is perpetual Fall in Mérida, and that is why, with the heavenly peaks in the background, the city is so alive.

The streets are clean, uncluttered, and most buildings are five to seven storeys high.

The city, though, with a population of over 250,000, has grown out of its pastoral colonial look. Although, particularly at Plaza Bolívar, the city retains its architectural pedigree, much of it has become quite modern. Nothing overwhelms, except maybe the University's circular hospital by the airport. There is enough of the colonial Spanish look intermixed with the psychedelic Indian style to give a hint of Mérida's past.

Getting There

While many Caraqueños drive to Mérida – it takes about 10 hours – chances are you will fly into the Alberto Carnevali Airport, which is right in town. Avensa offers three flights daily out of Caracas (6 am, 9:30 pm, and 4 pm at press time). Some of the smaller start-up airlines may offer service from Margarita.

Landing at Alberto Carnevali is a breathtaking introduction to Mérida. As he makes his descent right into the center of the city, your pilot will wind his way through a series of snow-capped mountains, practically pausing to point out Pico Bolívar. Just like the rest of the city, the runway is on an incline.

A cab to your hotel should cost less than $3. A *por puesto* (jitney car) is even cheaper. If you are traveling on a budget and your luggage is light, you can even walk to a hotel from the airport.

International flights arrive at the **Juan Pablo Perez Alfonso International Airport**, one hour west of Mérida in El Vigía. It is named for the Venezuelan oil minister who organized and founded OPEC. The country's newest airport, it was completed in 1991 and has the longest runway in Venezuela.

Finding Your Way Around

You can pick up maps and assorted tourist information, including hotel recommendations, at any of the **Corporación Merideño de Turismo** information kiosks scattered about town. Locations include the airport, the bus terminal on Avenida Las Américas, in front of the Las Tapias Shopping Center on Avenida Andrés Bello, at the corner of Avenida Los Próceres and Universidad, on the ground floor of the Mercado Principal on Avenida Las Américas, and the main office at Plazoleta Cruz Verde at the interesection of Avenidas 1 and 2 (☎ 524-359).

To orient yourself quickly, remember that the avenues – the main thoroughfares – run north and south. All are one-way. Streets (calles) run east-west, between the rivers.

Mérida is small and contained. The city is only about three miles long, north to south, and half a mile wide – but it is in its width that Mérida is most visibly expanding.

Finding your way around the center city area is not be difficult. Avenues run north to south and streets (calles) run east to west. Since Mérida is built on a northward incline, just remember that as you walk uphill you're heading north. The streets (calles) are numbered inversely. As you're walking north or uphill on an avenue, the street numbers are declining. Calle 1 is the northernmost street. The avenues are numbered from west to east. The Teleférico is located on the easternmost avenue, Avenida 8.

Technically, the center of the city is the Plaza Bolívar, which starts at Calle 23 and stretches from Avenida 3 (Independencia) to Avenida 4 (Bolívar). Surrounding the Plaza are many small shops, government buildings – wonderful colonial structures – and the imposing cathedral.

Mérida's southernmost point is about half a mile south of the airport, which stretches from Calle 40 at its northernmost point to Calle 52. The area is dominated by parks, eight of them to be exact. Walking north from the airport on Avenida Urdaneta, the main thorough-fare, you'll pass through a quiet residential area, which becomes more active at the Hotel Caribay. Just beyond is the CCCD shopping center. Center City begins at the Parque Glorias Patrias, across from the Park Hotel.

Bounded by the Chama and Albarregas Rivers, the Pan American Highway runs parallel and west to Mérida and, in the city, is called Avenida Los Próceres. The nucleus of the city has narrow colonial streets with high curbs and small squat buildings. Viaducts One and Two, Calles 38 and 26 respectively, link up Avenida Los Próceres and are the routes out of the narrow confines of old Mérida and into the wider and newer streets of the suburbs. Once outside the central part of the city, the buildings become larger and more modern, and the area is dotted with shopping malls, restaurants and clubs. Avenida Los Próceres leads to the suburbs and into the northern Andes. The avenue also takes you to the suburb of Chorros de Milla, where the zoological park and other important sites are located.

Climate

Like New England in Spring, that's the way Mérida is all year. Many afternoons are warm enough for swimming, with temperatures in the 70s, while evenings and morn-ings are cool and crisp, with readings in the upper 50s. Humidity is low. In short, spectacular weather.

The Best Hotels

Since Mérida is strongly tourist-oriented, it's under-standable that the city – for its size – has so many good hotels. These range from two- to four-star hostelries and include a good number of perfectly acceptable standard hotels. There are no five-star hotels in Mérida.

As is generally true throughout Venezuela, rooms with private bath are standard in all hotels. The El Tisure Hotel is the only one to offer air-conditioning. Given Mérida's pleasant climate, you will probably find that you're comfortable without it.

Hotel prices in Mérida are lower than in Caracas and on Margarita.

El Tisure ☆☆☆☆
Avenida 4 (Bolívar) between Calles 17 & 18
33 rooms, 3 floors
☎ (074) 526-072; fax (074) 526-061
Although it is the newest hotel in Mérida, El Tisure features old-fashioned hospitality and personalized service. Its small size allows the staff to dote on each and every guest. Rooms are spacious and feature sitting areas, remote control color television, baths with choice of jacuzzi or shower, and minibar. A sauna and massage in the fitness room is a great way to unwind after a day of hiking or fishing. El Tisure is the only hotel in Mérida with air-conditioning.

El Tisure is named for a remote hamlet in the wilderness northeast of Mérida where, more than 20 years ago, local artist Juan Felix Sanchez built a stone chapel. The hotel has its own adventure tour agency offering excursions to the hamlet, which is only accessible on foot, as well as to other nearby destinations.

Hotel La Pedregosa ☆☆☆☆
Off Pan American Highway in Urb. Pedregosa Norte
75 rooms, 25 cabins
☎ (074) 663-181 or 664-295; fax (074) 661-176
In Caracas: Centro Ciudad Comercial Tamanaco
☎ 959-7333 or fax 959-1605
Moderate
Located beyond the Pan American Highway in a largely undeveloped area, La Pedregosa encompasses a lake, a pool, riding trails, tennis courts and a chil-

The hotel has A-frame cabins, each of which can handle six guests.

dren's play area on 25 acres that resemble a small village. Rowboats, available for rental, dot the man-made lake, which is stocked with fish to please anglers. Launch rides are offered too. Rooms in the main lodge all have enclosed terraces that are pleasant indeed. At night there is a good discotheque too.

Park Hotel ☆☆☆☆

Across from Parque Glorias Patrias at Calle 37, Av 4
125 rooms, 8 suites, 5 Presidential Suites
☎ (074) 630-803; fax (074) 634-582
A modern white building that ascends like a staircase, the Park Hotel has a bustling lobby. With its six meeting rooms, accommodating up to 500 people, the hotel is probably the central place for non-residential business. Its stained wood paneling gives it an international look, and during restful moments, its couches are teeming with reclining visitors. Attached to the hotel is a mini-shopping mall. There is a restaurant, a disco and a travel agency in the hotel. The hotel was recently elevated from a three- to a four-star rating, an indication of its present momentum.

Hotel Don Juan ☆☆☆

Off PanAmerican Highway in Urbanización Las Marías
72 suites
☎ (074) 441-693; 446-366
Moderate
If you plan to spend more than a few days in Mérida, you should consider the Hotel Don Juan. Business travelers do. Its 72 suites come equipped with color TV and a kitchen, as well as three bedrooms, three baths, and a living room. Among the Don Juan's amenities are Il Piatto restaurant featuring fine Italian as well as international cuisine served in a setting reminiscent of a country home in south-central Italy. There is also the Cantina de Don Juan, a perfect place to unwind after a day of sightseeing.

Venezuela

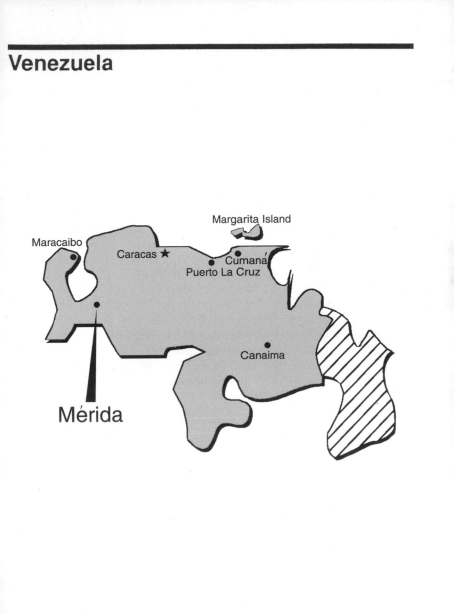

Hotel Caribay ☆☆☆
Av 2 Prolongación
77 rooms, 3 suites
☎ (074) 637-596; fax (074) 634-828
Moderate
The first tall building you'll encounter after leaving the airport, the Caribay has seven floors. It is a mainstay of Mérida, not overly fancy but quite nice. It is a pleasant, comfortable hotel which has a restaurant, bar, conference room and English-speaking travel agency. Its small lobby is functional. The main attraction is the Match Disco, complete with neon lights and black interior.

Hotel Prado Rio ☆☆☆
Av Universidad, Hoyada de Milla
42 cabins, 2 suites, 13 rooms
☎ 520-775; 520-704
Moderate
Operated by the government, the Prado Rio has a holiday air about it – almost like a ski lodge – and features an unusual three-tier dining room. The lower level houses a comfortable bar and TV area, while the middle tier is an informal lounge area with a fireplace and potbelly stove. The grounds, perfect for strollers, house a garden, volleyball area, and pool complete with an adult slide. A recreation room draws ping pong addicts. The red-hued cabins, located a short distance from the main house, are a good value for families. This hotel was created for comfort and relaxation. The lobby and lounge attest to this with comfortable overstuffed chairs and couches. Vivid flower arrangements brighten the lobby. Private entrance as well as parking.

Hotel Belensate ☆☆☆
Off Pan American Highway
Urb. La Hacienda
63 rooms
☎ (074) 662-963; fax (074) 662-823
Moderate

The marvelous wooded grounds are spacious enough to house a stable, a children's playground and a brook stocked with trout, as well as ducks and monkeys. If you're traveling in a group, you might consider renting the three-bedroom cabin with private bath – comfortable and private. Suites are posh, with carpeting, sitting rooms, and tiled baths. The Spanish-styled main lodge features a fireplace nook that draws yarn spinning sportsmen in the evening.

The Belensate is located across the Albarregas River to the south of colonial Mérida, a five-minute drive from the airport. No pool. In a country setting. At night you will find it hard to believe you are in a city.

Hotel Chama ☆☆☆
Av 4 Calle 29
63 rooms
☎ 521-082
Moderate
On Avenida 4, off the main Avenida 3, the Chama is thoroughly entrenched in the center of town, an easy walk to Calle 26 and Plaza Bolívar. Rooms are small yet spotless. There is a bar, snack bar, boutique and pizzeria, which is a loud student hangout and lots of fun.

Hotel La Terraza Karibik
Chorros de Milla
150 rooms
☎ (074) 448-227 or 441-133; fax (074) 448-237
Moderate
In the suburb of Chorros de Milla is the hotel, which is a large white and blue building, with a huge parking lot. The hotel is on the edge of the plateau, with the mountains beginning to climb just beyond it. The Terraza has a desolate feel, with such a large lobby that, even with lots of people, it seems roomy. The hotel has three restaurants, a piano bar, a disco with a caged-in chessboard for a dance floor, and a new casino.

Hotel Gran Balcón
Av Paseo de la Feria
35 rooms, 3 cabins
☎ 524-056; 522-269
Inexpensive

*The front patio
of the hotel is
wonderful for
just sitting and
staring at the
mountains.*

On the eastern edge of town, with the mountain range
as its backyard, the Gran Balcón is a clean, friendly
hotel. It is on a residential block, and at night is quiet.
A restaurant serves really good Venezuelan food. The
breakfast corner in the lobby is equally fine. The rooms
are functional, clean, and cool. There are filtered water
coolers in the hallway.

Hotel Princesa
Av El Valle
19 rooms, 10 cabins
☎ (074) 441-166 or 443-050
Inexpensive

Similar to the Valle Grande Hotel (see below) but less
spectacular and pastoral. With a restaurant, snack bar
and playground, you will be happy here.

Hotel Oviedo
Av 3
63 rooms
☎ 632-009
Inexpensive
On Avenida 3, the main thoroughfare, closer to the
airport than Plaza Bolívar, the Oviedo has a sparkling
new look, as if it were just built. An uninteresting white
structure, the hotel has a restaurant attached.

Hotel Mintoy
Calle 25, Ayacucho 8-130
67 rooms
☎ (074) 520-340; fax (074) 526-005
Inexpensive

Near the Teleférico, the Mintoy is a typical Venezuelan hotel. Clean, basic rooms, restaurant and in-house travel agency.

Hotel Teleférico
Av Parque Las Heroínas
30 rooms
☎ 527-370
Inexpensive
By the teléferico on the eastern edge of town, the hotel is functional and inexpensive. It contains a restaurant, bar and snack bar.

Hotel Mucubaji
Av Universidad (Vuelta de Lola)
63 rooms
☎ 443-461
Inexpensive
A tall modern building on the outskirts of Mérida, the Mucubaji is clean and friendly. There is a restaurant.

Hotel Nevada Palace
Calle 24, No. 5-45
42 rooms, 3 floors (no elevators)
☎ 529-339
Inexpensive
If you're driving you might look at the Palace since it offers underground on-site parking. Beyond that, the hotel is clean and comfortable. Rooms are small and modestly furnished. Bar and restaurant on the main floor. It is within easy walking distance of the Plaza Bolívar and the Teleférico.

Hotel Manchego
Av Urdaneta
☎ 636-656
Inexpensive
Near the airport, the Manchego is a quiet, family-run hotel that has a very hometown feel to it. Smells waft

into the lobby from the kitchen, and the lobby doubles as a living room.

Hotels in the Countryside

If you've rented a car you should consider staying at a hotel outside the city. With the beautiful Andean countryside right at your door and Pico Bolívar always in view, it's hard to imagine a more delightful way to experience Mérida. Our first three selections are all located on the road to La Culata, the Vía a La Culata, and we've arranged them in order, from closest to furthest from the city. Our final selection, Los Frailes, is in Santo Domingo, a two-hour drive from Mérida.

Hospedería San Javier
Vía el Valle
43 rooms
☎/fax (074) 440-585
Moderate
In San Javier del Valle, just a short distance off the main road, the Hospedería is a popular choice for retreats and conferences. It features rooms for up to seven persons. The interior has white-washed walls with wooden beamed ceilings and intricately carved wooden moldings. There is a lovely fireplace in the dining room.

Hotel Valle Grande ☆☆☆
Via La Culata (7 miles northeast of the city)
30 rooms, 30 cabins
☎ (074) 443-011
Inexpensive
The Hotel Valle Grande sits in the valley, all alone, peaceful and serene. If being alone in the midst of your own dreams is important, the Valle Grande will be perfect for you. Rustic decor features plenty of fireplaces and cozy sitting areas, perfect for enjoying the house specialty - *ponche andina*, a warming blend of anise and other secret ingredients. Guest rooms have

wood-beamed ceilings, large frame beds and sturdy wooden furnishings. Individual cabins have a living room with fireplace and a kitchen with refrigerator and stove. The hotel has a restaurant, bar, disco, and travel agency.

Estancia San Francisco
Vía La Culata
20 suites, 6 cabins
☎ (074) 448-338, fax (014) 744-000
Expensive

The colonial-style Estancia San Francisco caters to a very exclusive clientele. A guard at the entrance ensures that access to the beautifully landscaped grounds of the expansive walled-in estate is limited strictly to guests. Although recently built, the Estancia is designed in traditional Andean style with white stucco and heavy wooden beams and trim. Furnishings are representative of the region and are accented by antiques and original artwork. Cabins and bi-level suites are located throughout the grounds to ensure guests additional privacy. Suites feature a living room, bedroom with separate dressing room, and bath. Three-bedroom cabins have two bathrooms, a living room with fireplace, a fully equipped kitchen and dining room.

In addition to complete privacy and tranquility, guests enjoy horseback riding, hiking, trout fishing in the Estancia's private lake, and picnics. Moving indoors there is a reading room and a game room. Fine regional and continental cuisine is served in the restaurant.

Hotel-Resort La Culata
Via La Culata
☎ (074) 748-601
For reservations in Caracas, ☎ (02) 351-000 or 238-895; fax (02) 237-5455
Expensive

Fireside cocktails followed by a relaxing dinner in typical Andean style. This is how you'll end your day at La Culata. Rustic, yet with all modern amenities, the fine hotel/resort is nestled at the foot of the Andes just 35 minutes from the airport. Its 90 rooms and suites are comfortably furnished and all are equipped with private bath, central heating, satellite color television, and minibar.

Hotel Los Frailes
Santo Domingo
☎ (02) 562-3022, ext. 1040, or 522-244 (Avensa)
fax (02) 564-7936
Expensive

"Serene" best characterizes the Hotel Los Frailes, a fully restored/refurbished colonial monastery. You can spend your days accompanied only by your thoughts as you wander the Andean countryside or take part in the hotel's trout fishing and horseback riding excursions. Evening lectures, board games and social hours in the hotel's grand salon, with its lovely open fireplace, are a great way to meet other guests. Fine international and Andean cuisine is served in the hotel dining room, while light meals and snacks are offered in the English-style pub. The hotel's 48 rooms are tastefully furnished and come with private bath and heating units. Los Frailes is owned by Avensa and you can reserve through them directly.

The Best Restaurants

Mérida is not the kind of city to concentrate on world-class or formal restaurants; but that, by no means, is a comment on the food. With a vast array of choices, Mérida is jam-packed with restaurants. The city is so small that you can stroll past 10 to 15 restaurants, and then pop into one. Although we urge you to stick to the local restaurants, the golden arches have infiltrated the

Venezuelan Andes. The region's first McDonald's has just opened on Avenida Las Américas.

Before we note our recommendations, a few pointers. First, Mérideños tend to dine relatively early in the evening. While a Caraqueño dines at 9 pm, residents here usually sit down closer to 7:30 pm. Since the area around Mérida is famous for its trout, and it is a highlight of the regional cuisine. Any hotel you stay in will have a restaurant. As for prices, a four-course meal including tax and service (exclusive of cocktails) should run you less than $12 per person. But a sudden change in international monetary values can affect prices.

Sugar-coated figs called dulce de higo are a local delight, along with domestic cheeses.

Casa Vieja
Av Los Próceres via Av Las Américas
Lunch and dinner
☎ 661-394
Moderate

A restored Spanish mansion, the Casa Vieja is as much a visual experience as a gastronomic one. Specializing in Venezuelan and international meats, the restaurant is complex and large. The Salón para Fiestas (banquet room) abuts a garden and man-made waterfall. It is a large space for dancing, hung with black chandeliers. There is a bar, squashed between the salon and restaurant, that is a cowhide-covered, masculine watering hole, appropriately decorated with Old West ornaments. In keeping with its menu, the restaurant has a leather interior. There is a reception area/gift shop at the entrance, and an open mezzanine to take in the air.

The ambience complements the fine food here.

Prado Rio
Hotel Prado Rio
Open 7 am - 10 am, noon - 3pm; 7 pm - 10 pm
Moderate

Aside from the superb seafood, this tri-level restaurant offers an informal ski lodge ambience amid gleaming

Dine near a window for a nice view of the city and bull ring.

planked flooring, ceiling beams, and original hand-woven Indian rug wall hangings. The restaurant on the upper tier overlooks a lounge and the bar on the lower two levels. Try the trout or red snapper (*pargo*), absolutely fresh and first rate, or the chicken with ham dish. The bilingual menu offers a daily fixed-price four-course dinner – a bargain. Service is expert and efficient. If you like to linger over your cocktail, order your dinner from the lounge. The maitre d' will do the rest. Great value.

El Meson Del Estremeño
Av Paseo de la Feria
☎ 528-208
Expensive
A fine choice for dinner with friends, classic Spanish cuisine dominates the menu, along with international dishes.

Il Duce
Av Las Américas
Centro Comercial Mamayeya
Lunch and dinner
☎ 446-575
Moderate
Probably the most American in look, with candlelit tables, varnished floors, plush seats, fancy silver and plates, and soft music. Specializing in Italian food, it is located in the shopping mall, with the entrance on the first floor. There is a piano bar and sitting room.

La Vuelta Del Zorro
Av Las Américas
Centro Comercial
☎ 449-770
Moderate
Specializing in Mexican food, the restaurant is a haunt for students, and hence it jumps with live music or stereo. The drinks are excellent, and so is the food, with

many Mexican variations. The portions are very large and, with some sangria and nachos already in your stomach, you won't need as many burritos.

Restaurant Gran Balcon
Hotel Gran Balcón
Av Paseo de la Feria
Open noon - 3 pm; 6:30 pm - 10 pm (daily)
☎ 529-055
Moderate

With a panoramic view of the mountains, this restaurant could get by with mediocre food. But that isn't the case, as witness two outstanding dishes – *ternera milanesa* (veal cutlet) and *chuletas de cochino* (pork chops). There is also a *paella valenciana* and a fine trout dish. Aside from the huge glass expanse facing the mountain, the decor inside could use some sprucing up.

Restaurant Chino
Av Los Chorros de Milla
(Chorros de Milla District)
Open 11 am - midnight daily
☎ 504-508
Moderate

The owner has managed to create an oddity: a first-class restaurant featuring Chinese and international food (both recommended) in a Latin country. Restaurant Chino would do well in San Francisco's Chinatown. If you're hungry for Chinese, stick to the left side of the huge menu, where the dishes range from a delicious *subgum kai tin* (diced chicken with shrimp and almonds) to a marvelous grilled pork and mushroom dish called *mou ku siu pin*. We're hooked on the egg rolls (*lumpias*) and the perennial favorite, wonton soup. International dishes (right side of menu) include an outstanding trout with mushroom sauce dish (*trucha con salsa de hongos*). Any *por puesto* with a blue top will drop you here, but these stop running about 9 pm. A cab is best.

La Terraza
Av Los Chorros de Milla
Open 11 am - midnight daily
☎ 441-133
Moderate

Located in what was once a private home. You cross a small footbridge over a brook to enter.

Your introduction to La Terraza will warm you toward this cozy, comfortable restaurant. You dine on a roofed terrace with the stillness broken only by the running brook. A must here is the *aguacate con camarones*, an appetizer of avocado stuffed with shrimp, as well as the sugared fig dessert (*dulce de higo*). In between, we like the *trucha meunier* and the *parrillada*.

Restaurante Tatuy
Calle 24
(On the Plaza in front of the Teleférico)
☎ 525-245

For homestyle Venezuelan cooking at very reasonable prices, this is a terrific choice. The trout here was simply prepared and delicious. The *arepas* were good too.

Restaurant Los Pinos
Av Urdaneta, Calle 39
Lunch and dinner
☎ 637-116
Inexpensive

Los Pinos is an open-roofed restaurant that is informal and pleasant. Near the Hotel Caribay and the airport, it is a good place to stop for lunch if you're in the neighborhood. They specialize in grilled meats.

Chez Peppino
Av Gonzalo Picón Febres
(near the Colonial Art Museum)
Open 12 pm - 3 pm; 6:30 pm - 11 pm
☎ 634-259
Moderate

With wide medieval chairs, wine racks and Italian Renaissance paintings, Chez Peppino is a dinner haunt serving good Italian food. Ravioli dishes are in demand along with the pizza pies. The gregarious customers also call for the veal parmesan and paella (the chef sneaked that in when the owner wasn't looking).

Restaurant Belensate
Hotel Belensate
Open all day
☎ 663-722
Moderate
This rustic dining choice, while not plush, offers good food in a quiet, pleasant cabin-like setting. The trout, avocado and shrimp dishes are all good.

Lo Stivales
1st Floor, Park Hotel
Calle 37, Av 4
☎ 634-866
Moderate
Lo Stivales is a delightful restaurant located in the Park Hotel. The large dining room is decorated in wood and white stucco with wood beam ceilings, wine racks featuring a variety of vintage wines, and gleaming copper pots. The extensive menu is bilingual and features international favorites ranging from hamburgers and sandwiches ($2-$4) to grilled chicken, beef tenderloin Tio Pepe, sirloin steak, red snapper, and trout Boconoque or Grenobloise ($5-$8).

La Campana
Vía Pan-América (Los Próceres), 21-62
Open all day
☎ 663-068
Inexpensive
Set up similarly to the Casa Vieja, but not as nicely, La Campana is an Italian restaurant with a noisier atmosphere. Featuring great spaghetti, the restaurant is a local favorite.

Los Candiles
Av Andrés Bello at the entrance to
the Law School (Colegio de Abogados)
☎ 791-539
This doubles as a fine restaurant and discotheque. The restaurant itself is excellent and borders on fancy, so dress appropriately. Top choices on the menu include the *cazuela de mariscos, lomito en salsa de manzana* (pork in applesauce), and chicken cacciatore. Live music nightly.

Restaurant Marisqueria Vargos
Av Julio Febres Cordero (Calle 31)
☎ 523-836
Expensive
Small, cozy and formal, with plush chairs and chandeliers. Marisquería is a place for fish, all variations. Lobster is also on the menu.

Restaurant Diamante
Av 3, Calle 34
Lunch and dinner
Inexpensive
For good, quick Chinese food. Chop suey dishes are first rate, as are the egg rolls (lumpias).

Mérida has an abundance of pizza and pasta places, informal like their US counterparts.

Pizzeria Da Peppino
Av Gonzalo Picón Febres
Open all day
Disco and Cervecería (beer hall) on premises.

Cafetin El Buen Gusto
Av 3
Always crowded.

Alfredo's
Av 4, Calle 19
A student hangout. Great pizza and vegetarian food.

Il Bimbo
Calle 23 between Av 4 & 5
☎ 528-950
Located just off the Plaza Bolívar, Il Bimbo is a great choice for pizza and other Italian favorites.

For Excellent Ice Cream

Heladería Coromoto
Calle 29 on the corner of Av 3
Tues. - Sun., 2 pm - 10 pm
On any given day you will be confronted with a choice of at least 110 different flavors, possibly ranging from trout to spaghetti with meatballs or even beer. With 624 flavors in all, the Heladeria Coromoto has earned itself a place in the *Guinness Book of World Records*.

Sunup to Sundown

The countryside here has a beauty all its own and you would be remiss if you failed either to rent a car or to hire a cab for our recommended excursions. The mountain rivers and lakes are stocked with trout and fishermen should make it a point to indulge themselves between March 16 and September 30 (fishing season) when Venezuelans and Colombians throng the area.

A Walking Tour

To get a true feeling for the Spanish colonial flavor of center city Mérida you should stroll through it. As noted earlier, the city is built on a plateau between two rivers and at its widest point is only eight avenues wide; but it is long – 44 blocks in all.

A good place to start your walk is at the **Plaza Bolívar** (Avenida 3 and Calle 22) where you might stroll through the gray stone cathedral (look for its modern clock) that faces the plaza. Those buildings nearby are municipal government structures for the most part. Browse in the shops around the plaza, the city's best.

Streets downtown are narrow and generally hilly.

On the plaza's south side is one of the many structures scattered throughout the city belonging to the University of the Andes (Venezuela's second largest, with 25,000 students). Along one wall of the building on Calle 23 Vargas is the **Boulevard de los Pintores**, an informal outdoor gallery/art market where local painters exhibit their works. The homes you will see, uninteresting from the exterior, are uniformly built with lovely interior patios and red-tile roofs, following Spanish colonial style.

From the plaza, we don't think it matters in which direction you head. To the north (uphill) is the **Plaza Milla**, an after-lunch sunning spot, and the Prado Rio Hotel. To the west along Avenida 2 is the city's **outdoor market area**. It's not uncommon to see people on horseback along Avenida Las Américas. To the south (heading toward Plaza Glorias Patrias) is the **Todos Shopping Center**. Whichever way you choose, we know you will return to your hotel with a better understanding of this unforgettable city.

The many other recommended stops, cannot be reached on foot, and you will have to take a cab, *por puesto*, or rent a car.

The Teleférico (Cable Car)

Ready for a two-mile ascent up to Espejo peak? It's on your own head if you fail to take the world's highest and longest cable car journey, rising well above the tundra line and the cloud line to an incredible level of just under 16,000 feet. That's twice the height of Mexico City, three times the height of Denver and 3,000 feet above La Paz, Bolivia – the world's highest capital.

The cable car was designed and built by a team of French and Swiss engineers and inaugurated by Venezuelan President Rafael Caldera in 1966. It was closed for several years during the late 80s and early 90s.

Thankfully, during our most recent visit in the winter of 1997, all but the top station, Pico Espejo, were back in operation. Hopefully the cable car will be fully operational in time for your visit.

After packing a warm sweater, sunglasses, a camera (with extra film), head to the Teleférico terminal on Calle 25 in the Barinitas section. It's best to get there ahead of the time for the first departure at 7:30 am. That way you'll beat the crowds and make it to the top before the arrival of the clouds, which often obscure the view of the city below.

Once there, you'll board a trolley-like cable car for the first of four legs to the summit. While at some points your car will seem to be traveling vertically, the average angle of ascent is about 30° – steep enough. It is a ride of extremes, going from sunny and hot Mérida to the icy fog of Espejo, 15,634 feet above sea level.

The first segment, from **Barinitas Station to La Montaña Station**, is a steep departure from Mérida and its flat plateau. At Montaña you're at 8,000 feet and the landscape is thick and forested. On a sunny day, Mérida recedes and is reduced to small closely meshed dots, the Chama River becomes snake-like, the sugarcane and coffee fields become aerially expansive and the other peaks seem to shrink. Eventually, all you can make out is the airport, the baseball stadium and the bullfighting stadium. From here you also get an aerial view of the nearby towns of La Parroquia and Ejido to the west, and Tabay to the east.

From Montaña, you'll board another cable car for the ascent to **La Aguada** station, a two-mile rise over a deep valley. A few homes are visible while going up; and one wonders how the residents get their necessities. The terrain becomes less forested. Mérida, at this point, is nothing more than a microscopic dot, if visible at all. This ascent is the most drastic, with its environmental changes as you reach the zone above the timber

It gets quite cold as you reach the top. If you didn't bring a warm jacket or sweater, you can rent one for 50¢. A deposit is required.

level called the "paramo." You'll note that the leaves of the trees get thinner and the mist passing through the air is clear. To the right you'll face the steep walls of "**El Toro**" peak and, looking out the back of the car, you're faced with a panoramic view of the **Sierra Nevada**.

On the sides of La Aguada are two small lakes which water the area. The mule trail, off to the side, is also quite visible. But not much more can be seen. On a particularly clear day, however, several peaks can be seen, including **Pico Bolívar** and **La Concha glacier**.

Now it is time to board a third cable car from La Aguada to **Loma Redonda**, at 13,000 feet. The mist is even thicker, but the Lagunas Negra, Colorada and Anteojos are visible – these lakes are the homes of some of Mérida's famous trout as well as the South American Flannel Flower or "Frailejón."

When the weather is clear, Loma Redonda offers a spectacular view of Venezuela's highest peak, the snow-capped "Pico Bolívar," 16,427 feet above sea level. Be sure to get a look at La Concha glacier to the east. From here some of your fellow passengers may be setting off on a trek to the isolated village of Los Nevados.

Finally, Loma Redonda leads to the ultimate stop at Pico Espejo. It is cold, windy and icy up there. Due to the decreased oxygen, altitude sickness is a possibility. Some people don't acclimate very quickly and so are left breathless. Just take it slow. On a clear day you'll see **La Corona**, with its twin peaks of **Humboldt** and **Bonpland**, the glacier of **Timonchitos**. The Virgin of the Snows, patron saint of alpinists, sculpted in marble, is at the summit. The panoramic view will make conversation superfluous as you move about the summit. If the day is cloudless the views will be incredible and you should be able to see as far south as the **Peaks of the Sierra de Coquy** in Colombia.

That snow-capped peak to the east is Pico Bolívar. All you can hear in the booming silence are the clicks of cameras recording a moment at "the top of the world." There is an observation area as well as pathways. There is a small cabin nearby to walk to, and you can sunbathe on lounge chairs during the sojourn at topside. Pico Espejo has an observatory pathway, a small restaurant and food stalls. You can stay on the peak for hours.

Ultimately, it's time for the four-stage descent. Note once again the changes in vegetation as you move down, the small cascades, mountain streams, the absence of trees, and the Indians who live at each level. Yes, you can remain at any station and pick up the next cable car (perhaps two hours later). In all, the system is seven miles long. That's why two days a week (Mondays and Tuesdays) are required for maintenance.

Cable Car Departure Schedule

Wed. through Sundays, 8 am through 12:30, every half-hour. The last return trip departs from Loma Redonda sometime between 2 and 3 pm. The cable car operates seven days a week during the Christmas, Carnival and Easter Holidays and from late July through early September.

It is advisable to check the schedule and make reservations beforehand (☎ 074-525-080).

Parque Beethoven & Museo De Arte Moderno

Amid North American-style homes in the new northern section of Mérida is a park-like plaza famous throughout Venezuela for two clocks – one planted with fresh red, white, and green flowers, similar to the ones in Interlaken, Switzerland and Viña del Mar, Chile – and the other a glockenspiel inside a quaint German house. On the hour the glockenspiel plays a short Beethoven piece, thus the park's name. Every quarter-hour, listen for the gong and watch the small Bavarian statues beat time.

Opposite the park is the **Museo De Arte Moderno**, which houses the best of Mérida's modern art, including paintings, mobiles and woodcuts – many of which are for sale. Some of Venezuela's most acclaimed artists studied in Mérida. I purchased a beautiful handcrafted wooden rooster there. The two-story white colonial house is open Tues. through Fri., 9 am - noon and 3 pm - 5 pm; Sat. and Sun., 10 am - 5 pm. Closed Monday. Free admission. By the way, this area also boasts the finest homes of colonial Mérida.

Plaza Bolívar

A true relic of colonial days, Plaza Bolívar seems increasingly out of place amid Mérida's rapid modernization. The plaza is so perfect – clean, manicured, and outdated – that it looks like a model. At its center is the ever-present statue of Bolívar; the rest of the plaza is patched with grass and flowers. There is one dominating coconut tree that looms over Bolívar and the park.

On the southern edge of the plaza are government buildings, colonial in style and very fitting for the time warp you experience here in the park. Standing by Bolívar's statue, facing east, you can easily imagine life in his era. Bolívar was then a figure of revolt, not as glorified as he is now. His war meant change and created a split in society – the colonists on one side and the revolutionaries on the other. The colonial-style government buildings (actually built in the 1950's) are symbols of the status quo. Directly in front of you is the church, a figure of the Virgin Mary on its facade. At night this mental time travel is particularly powerful.

Construction of the church began in 1803 and was not finished until 1958. In the crypt below the main altar are a late Renaissance statue of the Virgin of the Apple, and the remains of San Clemente, who was decapitated for being a Christian.

Palacio Arzobispal

Next to the Cathedral, this palace was built between 1933 and 1951 to serve as the residence of the archbishop. The gallery contains portraits of the prelate of Mérida and the Archdiocese Museum, a collection of colonial oil paintings. The museum also has what is considered the oldest bell in the world, built in 909 AD.

Museo De Arte Colonial

Venezuelan religious and colonial art from the 16th, 17th, 18th, and 19th centuries is exhibited here. Paintings, sculptures, wood carvings, furniture, and gold and silver objets d'art are all on display. Located in a private house on Avenida 4 between Calles 17 and 18, the museum is open 9 am - noon and 3 pm - 6 pm, Mon. through Fri., and from 10 am to 5 pm on the weekends.

Jardín Acuario

This aquarium museum, housed in three attached cottages on Avenida Andrés Bello in the city's southern section, features some of the largest rainbow trout (stuffed) we've ever seen, most of which were caught in nearby lagoons. An interesting feature is the number next to each fish, indicating the altitude at which it was caught. Two of the cottages display live fish landed in regional lakes and elsewhere.

To reach the aquarium look for the park called Andrés Bello (one of Venezuela's revolutionary heroes). At the end of the park, on Avenida Andrés Bello, stands the Aquarium. Students often study at the large monument in the park at night. Open 9 am - 11:30 am and 2:30 pm - 6 pm every day. There is a nominal admission fee.

Parque Chorros de Milla

Right outside Mérida, near the La Terraza Hotel, this park was built on a slight incline in the mountain. Housing a small zoo, which has indigenous animals as well as big African cats in cages that are far too small, the park has places for picnicking and barbecuing. Admission is 75¢. The zoo is open Tues. - Sun. from 9 am - 5 pm.

Several gift shops and restaurants are clustered around a plaza in front of the park.

Parque La Isla

Off the Pan American Highway overlooking Mérida, this park is pretty and pleasant. It is nice either at sunset or in the middle of a lazy day. The park has an orchidarium and is open 7 am - 5 pm.

Jamau Children

An amazing collection of life-like dolls created by María Eugenia Dubois and Jane Smith de Garces, who live in Mérida. The dolls are pieced together solely from organic substances – the heads and hands from clay, the bodies from cotton and the eyes from glass. The hair is human. Each doll is dressed in traditional Venezuelan costume. ☎ 347-772.

San Javier del Valle

The propellers from the felled twin-engine plane are mounted on two concrete pillars. They rise from a lovely pond with a small waterfall on the immaculate grounds.

In 1950, 27 school boys (students at a boarding school in Mérida) were killed in a plane crash while returning to Caracas to spend Christmas vacation with their families. Near the site – located in a valley 15 minutes north of the city – stands a memorial, a simple and moving reminder of our mortality. The artist, uncle of one of the boys, has created a masterpiece in the ceiling of the lovely chapel nearby with etched representations of all the professions the 27 young men planned to pursue. Most touching are photos of the lads that are mounted along an exterior walkway. The hushed beauty here, with the Venezuelan Andes majestically encircling you, is a moving experience. A colonial-style house here was formerly used by an order of nuns as a retreat and is now a school. A round-trip cab ride will cost around $5 and it's worth it. A *por puesto* is under $1 per person. Though it was once open to the public, permission is now required to visit the memorial. If you're interested, someone at your hotel may be able to help you make arrangements.

The Hotel Valle Grande, one of our recommendations, is nearby.

Excursions

The regal peaks outside Mérida are the main attraction of the region. The city is primarily a base town for excursions in the Andes. The peaks lure you as you stare up at them. You can actually see the cold up there, the frost and the dark mist.

Leaving Mérida, traveling north on Avenida Los Próceres, eventually you will come to signs for **Barinas** and **Valera**. This is the route to **Santo Domingo, Timotes** and **Pico el Aguila**, three highlights of the Venezuelan Andes. The road is a windy groove, the temperature getting noticeably colder with every mile. The vegetation is woody, very much like the eastern United States. There are many streams, brooks, and small rivers. The architecture becomes more distinctive as you climb, moving away from the generic boxes of the modern world, becoming colonial-rococo and colorfully Indian – wooden patchwork homes that look weatherbeaten but resilient. The road is narrow, and the turns so sharp that it is wise to travel slowly, especially if your eyes wander.

The Inca influence is still alive in the small communities of the Andes. Andes is an Inca word for the small settlements and farms here.

About 12 miles outside town you'll pass Vía La Culata, which leads to the **Páramo La Culata Hotel-Resort**. It may be worth a stop if you fell in love with Mérida and are considering a return visit for a stay of a week or more. To reserve ahead, ☎ (074) 748-601.

On the trip up into the Andes you'll pass many roadside gift shops offering the most unusual shopping available in Mérida. Most specialize in Indian and Andean handicrafts (leather and wooden utensils, kitchenware, toys, small guitars, colorful Indian sweaters or ponchos). Any one of these stalls, and there are many, are worth a look. Also along this route is **Los Aleros**, a replica of an early 20th-century Andean Village. Admission to the village is $3, which includes a bus tour aboard an old-fashioned open-air bus.

Continuing, you'll pass through many small two-street towns, where you'll be forced to reduce your speed even further as you're stared at by men and dogs hanging out in the street. **Macuruba** is the first semisubstantial town you'll encounter, with a small central square and a pretty yellow two-tiered church. The **Hotel Macuruba**, with moderate rates, is functional and clean.

Be sure to visit the Plaza Bolívar.

Mucuchies, the next town en route, is larger. It has many small clothing shops, more like cubby holes, that are interesting to stop in. The hotel/restaurant **Castillo San Ignacio** on Avenida Carabobo has clean, inexpensive rooms and good food (even in the Andes credit cards are widely accepted). In town you will also find the **Hotel Los Andes**, with similar rates, and a restaurant.

Mucuchies was founded in 1596, and achieved fame for its gift to Bolívar. Thinking of his welfare, the town gave him a boy and a dog for companions. They became so connected with Bolívar that, after years of loyalty, they died simultaneously with him. The boy's name was Tinajaca and the dog was called Nevado. Their statues are in the Plaza Bolívar. As you pass through town you may even see some local children

selling furry white Mucuchies puppies along the roadside.

San Rafael, 8.4 miles from Mucuchies, is followed by
Apartaderos, which is the town at the fork before Santo
Domingo and Timotes. Apartaderos is really just a pit
stop. The **Mifafi Hotel and Restaurant** is clean and
friendly and has really good food from $5. Inside the
restaurant is a gift shop, small and somewhat tacky.
The people are nice, and the food genuinely Venezuelan. Across from the Mifafi is an anomaly, the Tudor-
styled **Hotel Parque Turístico**, complete with spires
and a weathervane. It offers clean, comfortable rooms,
and has a restaurant that serves good food. Prices are
moderate.

Heading Toward Santo Domingo

From Apartaderos to Santo Domingo is a slow, twisty
drive until you reach the **Hotel Los Frailes**. The hotel
has a courtyard and a bell tower. Once inside, it is easy
to imagine yourself a monk in medieval times, leading
a life of austerity and prayer. The hotel and grounds
are peaceful, beautiful, and quiet. There is a game
room, library, video and reading lounge, disco and
restaurant, which serves food at specified times. At
night the atmosphere is communal, with guests min-
gling in the library lounge or disco. Rates are moderate.

A monastery built high in the mountains in 1642, Los Frailes is a time-warping wonder. Its dome and cross can be seen from a great distance.

Right before the town of Santo Domingo is the **Hotel
Moruco**, which has 19 rooms, four suites and eight
secluded cabins. Very Swiss in style, with a ski-lodge
structure, wood paneling, fountains and gardens, the
hotel is spacious and modern. The hotel offers eight
secluded cabins on the grounds and a children's playground. There is a pool table and restaurant. Rates are
very reasonable.

In Santo Domingo, there are two hotels you can consider:

Hotel Halcon De Oro
Inexpensive
This very lively, pretty hotel, has a great view of the valley and mountains. Owner Amaldo Willdpret speaks German, French, Spanish and English.

Hotel Trucha Azul International Resort
☎ (074) 88-066
Expensive

The flower is used variously as wrapping for butter, to stuff mattresses, and to make jam.

With 31 rooms, the hotel is very lovely. Its rear end hangs over the cliff above the valley. The terrain at this height in the Andes is called the *páramo*. It is dominated by the fragrant flower, frailejón, which rolls across the earth like a rug. If the weather is dark and uninviting, the majesty of the *páramo* diminishes, but on a clear and transparent day, it is resplendent and alluring.

Near Santo Domingo is **Parque Las Piedras**, a fine spot for walking and picnicking.

Two and a half miles off the main road, outside Santo Domingo, is the **Santo Domingo Trucha Cultura El Baho** (trout farm), a three-tiered waterfall, which hatches, breeds, and ultimately sells trout. It is a key business and culinary delight of the area.

Lake Victoria, invisible from the road, is a beautiful glacial lake. It is reached from the road that leads to Los Frailes.

The **Santo Domingo Hydroelectric Plant**, which opened in 1973, gives a glimpse of Venezuela's technological capacity. The plant's observatory offers a good view of the Paez Dam. The turn-off is marked by Mirador Complejo General José Antonio Paez.

Parque Nacional Sierra Nevada
This is Venezuela's second oldest park, covering 470,000 acres. It was opened in 1952, and is a huge expanse of largely untouched wilderness.

The park's highlights are its *páramo*, glacial topography, and lakes. The *páramo* here is overflowing with plants, brightly hued to lure insects for pollination (insects are few at this elevation). There are also a variety of small animals, the fox being the largest, which roam freely. It would be wise to buy a guide to Andean vegetation if you have an interest in botany, ecology, or gardening.

The park is interspersed with glacial valleys; as anyone who has glimpsed glacial wilderness before knows, the sparkling view is awe-inspiring.

The two most visited lakes are the **Laguna Mucubaji**, locally called Laguna Grande, and the **Laguna Negra**. Laguna Mucubaji is the largest glacial lake in the region and is located near the park's entrance.

The main entrance to the park is on the road between Apartaderos and Santo Domingo, closer to Apartaderos, at the 11,644 mark. There are, however, other smaller entrances used primarily by fishermen in their never-ending quest for trout. Some of these entrances are: Laguna Los Patos, La Cañón, Laguna Seca, Laguna Sur-América, Laguna El Oso.

Paso Pico el Aguila

The highest paved road in Venezuela, the Paso Pico el Aguila, ascends steeply into the mist-ridden Andes. Once again, *páramo* vegetation prevails. The gray on the mountains is sheep's sorrel.

The Pico el Aguila is at over 12,000 feet. There, a statue of a spread eagle pays homage to Bolívar and his legendary independence march to Caracas.

Next to the statue is a lodge for hot chocolate and coffee. Across from the monument, and down, is Los Frailes and its proud white tower. Also seen from this vantage point is Apartaderos Knot, the highest inter-

Laguna Negra can be reached on horseback or by hiking. It is an hour on horseback. If walking, leave early because of fog.

section of the Chama, Mututan and Santo Domingo rivers.

Timotes

Founded in 1691 by the Spanish, Timotes is the name of the Indian tribe that inhabited the area before colonization.

Not far from the border with the neighboring state of Trujillo, Timotes is reached by going in the opposite direction from Santo Domingo at Apartaderos, past Pico el Aguila. The Timotes Church on Plaza Bolívar is unique. It has a four-tiered belltower and an artificial marble finish inside. Its ostentation contrasts with the rugged, hard existence of the Andes. There is a small pre-Hispanic museum right outside the town coming from Apartaderos. It features the artifact collection of José Pío Rondón. Watch for the sign "Museo, Visítalo" (Museum, Visit It) on the left side of the road.

Jají (pronounced Ha-Hee)

In colonial times, the square and its immediate circumference was the center of town, the fulcrum for all activity.

Reached by heading west from Mérida, Jají is a reconstructed colonial village. Completed in 1971, Jají is perfectly blueprinted for colonial times with its church, government buildings and wealthy residences making up the central square. The work on Jají was a mixture of fixing up what was there and building the rest from scratch. The **Posada de Jají** is open to the public and is an example of colonial living in the 16th and 17th centuries. Food of the times is available in the posada.

Jají is 45 miles from Mérida. Its restoration inspired local residents to redo their own homes in traditional style. Hence, much of the town has an antique colonial feeling. It is one of the loveliest in the Andes

Adventure Tourism

Mérida is a sportsperson's dream. Its spectacular location and perfect climate offer wonderful trekking, mountain climbing and biking, fishing and other outdoor activities. If you aspire to climb Pico Humboldt (16,210 feet) or Pico Bolívar (16,423 feet), or if you have something a little less strenuous in mind, you will find several outfitters and mountain guides in town just waiting to be of service. Before opting to go with one, be sure to ask for recommendations from fellow-travelers as well as the management at your hotel. Reliability and experience vary greatly.

If trekking in the Andes is your primary reason for visiting Mérida, you should consider making arrangements prior to your arrival. Caracas-based **Cacao Expeditions** offers several different options. Recreational hikers may want to combine a city tour and lodgings in Mérida with daytrips to nearby villages and short hikes, while more experienced trekkers would find a four-day trek in the Sierra Nevada far more appealing. For information on itineraries and to make arrangements, contact Bernard Kroening, General Manager, Cacao Expeditions, Avenida Caura, Torre Humboldt Piso 22, Office 22-03, Prados Del Este, Caracas (P.O. Apartado 88267). ☎ (02) 977-1234 or fax (02) 977-0110. E-mail 73050.2614@compuserve.com.

Sports

Toreador

If the bulls excite you, then you should spend time at the modern **Plaza de Toros** bullring, not far from the Prado Rio Hotel just off the Pan American Highway. Unfortunately the matadors are here only twice a year – in February during Carnival and in Sept.-Oct., usually on weekends only. Seats range from $7 to $30, and you'll have a choice of *sol* (sun) or *sombra* (shade). Shade is usually preferable, especially in February when the sun can be unbearable. Check with your hotel clerk for arrangements.

Futbol (Soccer)

Between May and October, matches are held on weekend afternoons at the **Estadio Olímpico** in the Santa Juana District. Prices range from $1 to $4. Your hotel clerk can help with tickets.

Beisbol (Baseball)

During the school year, baseball fans can watch their favorite sport at the **Estadio Universitario** near the Teleférico, where the University of the Andes and other teams play regularly. Again, check with your hotel clerk for schedules.

Shopping

While the shops here are not overflowing with unbeatable "native" bargains, you can still find good value wool ruanas that are warm and brilliantly colored. All are handmade by Andean Indians.

The most unusual shopping in Mérida is along the road towards Santo Domingo. At the roadside stalls are many authentic Andean items and crafts. A stop at any one of these places is fun – the myriad designs on the sweaters are tantalizing and the crafts are unique.

In Mérida, shops are closed from 12 noon - 2 pm for siesta. Here are details on some shops and malls.

CDAA Shopping Center
Av Urdaneta
Within the Park Hotel, this mall has several shops that sell North American-style as well as local goods.

Centro Comercial Las Tapias
Opposite el Parque Aquario
Mérida's largest shopping center, the upscale Centro Comercial Las Tapias offers shoppers four levels of boutiques and restaurants. Among the many shops are **Boutique Karina**, which specializes in women's ap-

parel, **Rosy's Shoes** for both men and women and **Artesanos Pinceladas**, a good choice for gifts, although somewhat high-priced. **Tasca Máscaras** is a delightful choice for a light meal. There is also an American Express office, Multi-Cine and ladies' hairdresser.

Los Mercados (Markets)

There are several *mercados* throughout town. A *mercado*, or market, is often one large building packed with stalls and vendors. Usually it specializes in one item or type of goods; i.e., food, clothes, crafts.

Mérida's most important *mercado* is the **Mercado Principal** on Avenida Las Américas at Viaducto Sucre. Here you'll find a lively combination of food vendors and craftsmen selling their goods. I bought a beautifully crafted copper pot at **Artesanía Klever** on the second level. **Artesanías Luff**, also on the second level, offers a wonderful selection of leather items, ponchos, hammocks and paintings.

The selection of fine handicrafts is no less appealing on the third level. A painting purchased at the **Galería De Artesanos** (at the urging of longtime manager Jaqueline, a genuine charmer) is now proudly displayed in our home. In addition to paintings, the Galería also specializes in terra cotta sculptures and ceramics and doubles as a fine restaurant. **La Calle Mayor** on the third level features a great selection of authentic Andean crafts.

Calle 22 between Avenida 4 and 5, near the Plaza Bolívar, is a pedestrian-only shopping street. No cars are allowed and independent vendors sell their goods.

There are also a lot of vendors and small shops outside the entrance of the **Parque Chorros de Milla**.

For Art Aficionados

Works by the internationally acclaimed painter Luis Salas Davila were once exhibited at the Hotel Pedregosa. A native son of Mérida, Salas Davila studied under Latin American masters Tito Salas and Pedro Santaner as well as in Rome, Florence and at the Academia de Belles Artes in Madrid. Salas Davila has since moved to Tampa and taken most of his pieces with him. However, every once in a while you may come across one of his paintings.

The soft-spoken Davila captures the spirit of the Andes in his works of fantasy and of the spirit.

After Dark

Current US and British films – fortunately undubbed – are usually showing at one or more of four theaters, all in the city center. Cinemas include: **Glorias Patrias** on Avenida 2 (☎ 3095); **Multicinema Viaducto** at the end of Viaducto Campo Elias; and **Multicine Las Tapias** in the Centro Comercial Las Tapias on Avenida Andés Bello.

Performances

Concerts, plays and occasionally operas are performed on weekends mostly in the city's main cultural center, **Paraninfo**, which is part of the University of the Andes near the Plaza Bolívar.

Casinos

In 1997 both the **La Terraza** and **Park Hotels** added casinos to their list of attractions. The casino in La Terraza is the larger of the two and features a bingo room as well as roulette, blackjack, and poker. The minimum bet is $5. Patrons at the tables are offered free drinks. The casino is open from 8 pm to 5 am every day.

Discos
El Castillo Tasca – Discoteca
Av Los Próceres
☎ 663-746

Once a private home, this building was cleverly renovated in the image of a rook on a chessboard. The ambience is intimate. There is a large bar, but the dance floor is on the small side. Open evenings till 3 am; closed Sundays.

La Jungla Party & Sports Bar
Av Bolívar at Calle 36
Located near the Park Hotel, La Jungla is one of the newer clubs in town, and has quickly become one of the most popular as well. If you can't get in or are looking for something a little more intimate, try **Club 37** in the Park Hotel

La Basura
Centro Comercial Alto Chama
Semi-Sotáno Level
Vying for top notch, La Basura is always filled-to-the-gills with students. The place is lively and hot.

La Cucaracha
Centro Comercial Las Tapias
This is another highly regarded disco, popular with the younger set. In addition to dancing, patrons enjoy sports videos and pool. Not for the inhibited.

Los Candiles
Av Andrés Bello
(at the entrance to the Law School)
Also listed in the restaurant section, this is another well-recommended night spot.

El Bodegon De Pancho
Av Los Próceres
Centro Comercial Mamayeya
Ground Floor Local C-1
Located next door to La Vuelta de Zorro, the mostly wooden decor makes this an inviting spot for a night out. D.J. Music upstairs and live salsa downstairs. Open evenings till 3 am; closed Sundays.

Tops Dance & Bar
Hotel La Pedregosa
Eighteen- to 25-year-olds are the dominant age group here, attracted by the Top 40-type Latin American music.

La Taberna De Eugenio
Paseo La Feria
Edificio Alto, Local P-4
This is a great place to sit and have a drink with friends after a long day of sightseeing, hiking or working. A popular meeting place.

A few other popular student haunts include the **Piroska Carioca** on Avenida 2 at Calle 24, the **Universidad de La Caña** on Calle Cerrada and Avenida Bolívar, and **La Piraña**.

Bowling

If you're restless some evening and can't get through another moment without a round of bowling, you're in luck.

Oddly enough, this sport might be one of Venezuela's favorite night-time activities. Mérida's alley has eight lanes and is located on Avenida Los Próceres. The hours are 2 pm - 3 am Mon. - Fri.; 10 pm - 3 am Sat. and Sun. There is a disco downstairs.

Mérida Etc.

Airlines

Avensa
Airport: ☎ 637-737; 8 - 9:30 am; 3 - 5:30 pm.
Plaza Bolívar: ☎ 526-232, 527-045; 8 am - noon; 2 - 6 pm.

Aeropostal (LAV)
Airport: ☎ 637-798, open 8 - 11 am.
Park Hotel Shopping Arcade: ☎ 635-555, 8 am - noon; 2 - 6 pm.

Auto Rentals

Since the roads here are excellent and we do recommend a number of one-day excursions, you might consider a car rental.

At the airport are several car rental outlets, all offering Jeeps as well. **National** (☎ 630-722), **Budget** (☎ 631-768), **Avis**, **Hertz** (☎ 632-085), **Oriental**, and others.

Banking

A good local bank is **Banco Unión**, Avenida 4 near Calle 23.

Folklore

The Andean Indians have a rich folklore tradition. The local dances and costumes vary from town to town. Mérida City's fiesta is called "**Feria del Sol**," held in February.

Language

It is very helpful to know some Spanish in Mérida. While many of the University students understand English, you will probably experience some difficulty communicating with the average Mérideño.

If you'd like to take a two-week intensive Spanish course in Mérida, contact the **Venusa Institute of International Language Studies** in West Palm Beach, Florida; ☎ 407-753-3661, fax 407-753-3758. E-mail vnusa@flinet.com.

Medical Help

Centro Médico La Parroquia is on Av Andrés Bello. ☎ 713-812.

Newspapers

El Vigilante and *Frontera* are the local Spanish-language dailies. For a few cents you get listings of films and sporting cultural events. *The Daily Journal*, the English-language daily published in Caracas, is often sold here at the major hotels.

Pharmacies

These are plentiful; a good one is the **Farmacia Moderna**, Avenida 3 and Calle 21.

Population

Mérida's population (250,000) is one third of the total population of Mérida State.

Por Puestos

These jitney-like sedans travel the main streets only, continually picking up and dropping passengers; depending on distance traveled, the cost is always small. Remember these stop running at about 9 pm. Your hotel clerk can tell you the specific line to take for your destination.

Post Office

The Post Office (IPOSTEL) is located on Calle 21 between Avenidas 4 and 5. Open 8 am - 7 pm Mon. through Fri.; and 8 am - 4 pm on weekends.

Safety in the Streets

Provided you exercise the same common sense you would in any city, you needn't be overly wary of street crime while strolling around colonial Mérida.

Casa Scholl

Yes, even in Mérida the good doctor has an office in the Edificio La Quinta on Avenida 4 (☎ 2988). A complete foot treatment runs $2.25. Open 8:45 am - 12:30 pm and 2:45 - 6:30 pm; Sat. 9 am - 5:30 pm.

Taxis

Plentiful in the evening, scarce during the day (when the cheaper *por puestos* are preferred). Rates usually go up to $1.25 within the city and twice that to reach the Chorros de Milla suburb. Since there are no meters, set the fare in advance.

Tourist Information

The **Corporación Merideño de Turismo** has small kiosks in various locations throughout the city where you can pick up maps and other information. Locations include the airport, the Jardín Aquario, in the Mercado Principal on Avenida Las Américas, and the main office, which is at the intersection of Avenidas 1 and 2 across from the Plazoleta Cruz Verde de Milla.

Venezuela

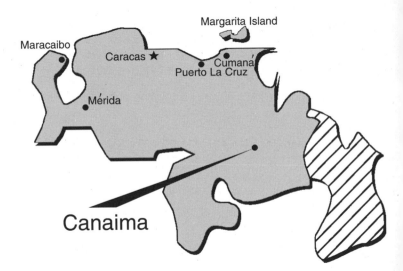

Margarita Island

Maracaibo

Caracas ★

Cumaná
Puerto La Cruz

Mérida

Canaima

Canaima

Not far from Brazil's border, some 800 miles south-east of Caracas, lies Canaima National Park, home of Angel Falls, the world's highest waterfall and 8,000,000 acres of what just may qualify as the world's most spectacular landscape. For many visitors, both the falls and the Park hold the promise of unparalleled adventure. And what an adventure it is, including the 2½-hour Avensa flight there, which passes the legendary Angel Falls.

Just before reaching Angel Falls you will fly over the stark **Auyan Tepuy**, often referred to as Devil Mountain. This towering flat outcropping thrusts upward from the jungle below. Arthur Conan Doyle used this site for the setting of his story *Lost Worlds*. The falls, which thunder down a 3,200-foot ravine on the western face of the Tepuy (Niagara Falls has a 200-foot drop), become visible as your pilot guides the jet through a narrow ravine alongside the Auyan Tepuy. With only slight urging, he will make a second pass, and perhaps a third. Keep your camera ready, and sit on the left side for the best shots. US flier Jimmy Angel gave his name to the falls when he survived the crash-landing of his small plane on the summit of the Auyan Tepuy in 1937 and later wrote an account of his experience. By the way, the falls are rather narrow but, considering the length of the drop, a wider flow of water would long ago have eroded much of the mountain base.

Ten minutes or so after the Angel Falls fly-by, your pilot will be landing at the surprisingly smooth airstrip in Canaima. A jitney will carry you and your luggage to your camp.

Tip: travel light!

Listen for the muffled roar of La Hacha waterfalls from the right side of the lagoon. These falls are fed by the Carrao River, which in turn is indirectly fed by Angel Falls well upriver.

Rain can come suddenly here and disappear just as quickly.

What to do in Canaima? One traveler who comes here for a week each year says tartly: "Nothing! This is the only place I know where you can come and do nothing and enjoy it. That to me is what vacationing is all about." For the more active, there is swimming in the lagoon, boating to La Hacha Falls, or fishing and hiking along little-used Indian trails. Shoppers needn't feel out of their element as there are plenty of opportunitites to visit Indian settlements where local artisans gladly sell their wares. We find fatigue quickly ebbs as the air and waters restore both spirit and energy. Wild flowers, lush vegetation, exotic birds and strange scents tantalize and tease the senses.

The Legend of Jimmy Angel

Jimmy Angel was a typical pre-WW II mercenary. He was paid $5,000, a lot of money at that time, by a wealthy Mexican to fly him into the Gran Sabana for reasons unknown. Jimmy landed right by Angel Falls, but the mist was so intense then that, although the falls were probably audible, they were not visible. The Mexican went into the bush and came out about five hours later carrying bags overflowing with gold. Angel, a professional, asked no questions. A year later, in 1937, Angel with his wife, a geologist named Gustav Heny, and Heny's gardener, went in again to find the "hidden treasure." On this mission Angel crashed and, during their 15 days of being stranded, he found Angel Falls.

Until 1970, Jimmy Angel's original plane was still on top of the tepuy where he landed it. Now the plane sitting there is a replica and the original is in Ciudad Bolívar.

Orientation

Canaima National Park is in the southern section of
Bolívar State, part of which borders Brazil. In fact, a
small portion of the park is on the border with Brazil.
Originally founded in 1962 and expanded to its present
size in 1975, Canaima is the largest National Park in
Venezuela and the sixth largest in the world. The dense
jungles of the Guyana Shield occupy the western portion of the park which, understandably, is the section
least accessible to visitors. The village of Canaima,
located in the northwest sector of the park, is the out-
post of civilization before the vastness of Venezuela's
Gran Sabana overcomes the landscape to fill the eastern portion of the park.

Majestic *tepuies* (mesas) rise out of the savannah, which
is dominated by grassy prairies interspersed with areas
of humid jungle. Over the centuries rivers have wound
their way through the prairies to create otherworldly
grottoes and magnificent waterfalls within the depths
of the *tepuies*. Growing alongside the rivers are green
tropical forests filled with orchids and bromeliads.

Often referred to as "Islands in Time," the *tepuies* are
entities unto themselves with an ecosytem unlike any
other. Though similar to the large rock formations that
are common to Arizona and the Badlands in South
Dakota, their vegetation is decidely distinct. The *tepuies*
are home to hundreds of varieties of ferns, bromeliads
and other plants not found anywhere else in the world.
The largest of the *tepuies* is **Auyan Tepuy** or Montaña
del Diablo, as it is also called. The focal point of virtually all excursions to the park, the majority of Canaima's natural attractions, including Angel Falls and
the grottoes of Kavac, are either within or in the area
surrounding Auyan Tepuy. What makes Canaima so
attractive is that it does still seem like an unexplored
world, a part of the earth that man has yet to penetrate.

*Auyantepuy,
Devil Moun-
tain, was the
setting for
Conan Doyle's
Lost Worlds
and resembles
the Tepuy, rock
mountain, in
Close Encoun-
ters of the
Third Kind.*

This illusion is not shattered by reality, because Canaima, the Gran Sabana, is so isolated, teeming with animal and insect life.

When To Visit

Angel Falls is at its most spectacular during the rainy season, which generally starts in May or June and lasts until September. Rainfall is heaviest in August and September, and the falls are most powerful during that time. However, you also run the risk of hearing the thunderous roar of the falls as you approach, only to find them obscured by heavy, moisture-laden clouds. During the dry season the volume of water lessens considerably and the rivers are often only marginally navigable, making river trips to the falls impossible. Unless you're planning to climb Auyan Tepuy, rainy season is definitely the better time to visit the park.

Climate is warm the year round, but evenings are pleasant for sleeping. As for clothing, be prepared to get wet, either because of a sudden downpour or simply because you'll be spending a lot of time on or in the water. Bring only a bathing suit, walking shorts and T-shirts, comfortable shoes with non-slip soles, slacks, a hat, possibly a lightweight raincoat, and a warm sweater. Also remember to bring suntan lotion and insect repellent.

Visiting Canaima & Angel Falls

Although Jungle Rudy and Avensa once had a monopoly on tourism to Canaima, that is, thankfully, no longer the case. These higher-priced camps (see below) have been joined by many other more reasonably priced, though less luxurious, ones. Several are located on the shores of the Canaima Lagoon, not far from the village of Canaima. Others are in more remote sections of the park. While in the Caracas airport, you will undoubtedly be approached by numerous tour opera-tors offering you packages to Canaima. These usually include transportation to the camp as well as excursions and meals. Although it is preferable to arrive in Canaima with arrangements made in advance, it is usually possible to find accommodations at one of the camps near the airport once you arrive.

The Avensa flight leaves every day at 10:15 am from Simón Bolívar airport in Maiquetía, outside Caracas. The flight stops in Ciudad Bolívar for about half an hour; the entire flight takes 2½ hours. Without a doubt, this flight will linger in your memory long after you have returned home. The views of Angel Falls are incredible.

Jungle Rudy's Camp U Caima

Two miles upriver from Canaima on the Carrao River is a unique experiment in jungle living where a tough character named Rudy Truffino carved a life for himself and his family out of the wilderness. Fortunately for adventurous travelers, the camp can accommodate 16 guests in eight double rooms (half in the main house and the balance in two cottages). How did Rudy wind up in Ucaima, as he called his camp?

The story starts in 1956 when, at the mature age of 27, he decided he had had enough of "civilization," represented by his job as assistant manager of the Hotel Tamanaco in Caracas. Then single, with a degree in veterinary medicine and with experience as a mechanic, architect, photographer, farmer and mountain climbing guide, mostly in his native Holland, Rudy decided he would live his life away from the mainstream and would support himself by operating a camp or jungle hotel for tourists. Simple, right? Hardly, as Rudy found out when he was flown into what is now Canaima and told by his two partners, "Scout the area. We'll be back in two days to get you."

They did not return for eight months. Rudy survived by joining with Indian tribes, foraging in the jungle for small game, and fishing. That was a blessing. For later when Rudy needed Indian construction labor he was able to get it. His partners eventually returned, explaining that they had plane trouble. Rudy flew back to Caracas, raised funds and returned once again to begin building his first camp at Canaima on the shores of a serene lagoon.

In 1959, while in Caracas to buy supplies, Rudy met an attractive blonde Austrian vacationer, whom he married soon after. Gerty joined Rudy in Canaima. Shortly afterwards the couple decided that even this camp was becoming too civilized due to the increasing flow of tourists. He made the decision to establish a new camp two miles up the Carrao which would be a true jungle retreat. With the help of Indians, and using local timber, the Truffinos built a main house, including a kitchen, dining room, bar and lounge area, a workroom, and five bedrooms – one for the Truffinos – the balance for the guests. Thus was born Camp U Caima, commonly referred to as Jungle Rudy's. Still today it is not accessible by water because of the Hacha Falls. There is nothing but an Indian foot trail and a road of sorts that only a jeep can negotiate. Gerty and Rudy have passed away, so now the camp is run by their daughter Lilly.

To reach the camp, you walk along the beach toward the Hacha Falls. After 50 yards or so, you will be guided to the right up a narrow Indian trail that more or less follows the Carrao upriver. While not arduous, the path is steep in parts and sneakers will help. In 15 to 20 minutes you'll find yourself in a small clearing at the river's edge and, as Rudy's daughter Lillie once told us, "Now we wait for the boat." Sure enough, a few minutes later the chug chug of an outboard motor will be heard and a 15-foot canoe will arrive to take you into camp. Five minutes later you will be there.

In our group during one of my last trips were five birdwatchers from North America, the wife and daughter of Marlin "Wild Kingdom" Perkins, and a pathologist from Florida who comes yearly to "unwind." A young Washington couple was working their way through Rudy's "university."

What to Do at Jungle Rudy's

Since it's lights-out at 11 pm, you are up early for breakfast. After a morning swim, there is a boat trip up the Carrao to explore the lagoons and coves. The birdwatchers in our group provided an education on Venezuelan ornithology. After lunch there might be a hike in the wooded areas behind the camp or another canoe trip, this time to an Indian camp where you can bargain for baskets and other handicrafts. By the way, the food is quite good – hearty and filling, geared for North American palates.

To make reservations, contact the camp at ☎ (02) 661-9153 and fax 661-1980.

Campamento Arekuna

Hikers and birdwatchers should consider staying at Aerotuy's Campamento Arekuna. Situated on the summit of a hill overlooking the confluence of the Antabare and Caroní Rivers in the northern reaches of the park, guests are surrounded by spectacular views of the tepuys, jungle and savanna. Experienced guides lead guests on a variety of wildlife excursions both on foot and in dugout canoe, to the Antabare River, the Baba Falls on the Caroní River, and as far away as Canaima and Angel Falls. Most leave early in the morning when the likelihood of seeing parakeets, toucans, monkeys and other indigenous birds and wildlife is greatest. Lodging is in five rustic two-room cabins, each with private bath, which can accommodate up to six persons each.

Rates include airfare on Aerotuy which flies directly to the camp, all meals, lodging and excursions. For reservations (mandatory) and further information, contact Aerotuy at ☎ (02)761-8043, fax (02) 762-5254 (toll free in Venezuela 800-23-736) or visit the Aerotuy office on the fifth floor of the Gran Sabana Building on Sabana Grande in Caracas.

Kavac

Just before landing, your Aerotuy flight will fly over Angel Falls in a spectacular welcome to **Campamento Kavac**. Another Aerotuy camp, Kavac is at the base of the eastern wall of the Auyan Tepuy and is within hiking distance of Indian villages and natural monuments. Led by Indian guides, guests will travel by foot and dugout canoe to visit the mystical Kavac Canyon with its waterfalls and quiet pools; the impressive La Toma waterfalls and the nearby Indian village of Kamarata, which lies nestled in a valley between two tepuys. Guests also visit Santa Marta, an indigenous community of artisans.

Located in the savannah, Kavac offers its guests unrivaled tranquility and rustic accommodations. Guests stay in a traditional Indian-style wipa and have their choice between a room with private bath or with a shared bath. Kavac is only accessible by plane. Rates include airfare on Aerotuy, which flies directly to the camp, plus all meals, lodging and excursions. For reservations (mandatory) and further information contact Aerotuy at ☎ (02) 761-8043, fax (02) 762-5254 (toll free in Venezuela 800-23-736) or visit the Aerotuy office on the fifth floor of the Gran Sabana Building on Sabana Grande in Caracas.

The Avensa Camp

The Avensa Camp is the central lodge, and on its grounds are 57 huts, all with private bathrooms, a central terraced outdoor dining room and a bar. Meals are served cafeteria-style. The camp lies on the banks of the Carrao River, at a point where it becomes so wide that it looks like a small lake. Its source is the roaring Hacha Falls. The sand is tinted red because of the iron ore deposits; the water is warm and swimmable. At the small beach are beach chairs, umbrellas and a volleyball court.

What to Do at the Avensa Camp

There are three tour companies at the camp and one company that runs plane flights to Angel Falls. The tour companies all sell different tours but since they all go into the savannah it is not worth brooding over the choice. All three companies offer half-day excursions, full-day excursions and four-day trips to Angel Falls. All are comparably priced.

The half-day trips combine a boat ride with walking. You will first be driven to a point where you can get on a boat and ride through the small dense waterways that criss-cross the Gran Sabana. The boat ride is fun and exciting. Finally, there is usually a walk of an hour or so to one of the region's many waterfalls. You'll find yourself getting very hot, sweaty and ridden with insect bites as you walk along, yet your discomfort will be quickly forgotten, dissipated by the sight and sound of the pounding waterfall. At the waterfall refreshments are served, and on the way back there is a short stop at a tiny little Indian village.

The whole-day excursions are extended versions of the half-day trips, a bit more rugged and sweaty.

The four-day hike to Angel Falls is truly exciting and unique but is only for people feeling confident about their stamina and willpower. From those we talked to who had made the trip, self-assurance and pride were key motivators and, of course, the beauty of the trek is overwhelming.

The plane ride to Angel Falls in Servivensa's DC-3 is spectacular. The winding paths of the rivers, streams and inlets, the height of the tepuys, and the incredible diversity of the savannah can only be seen from above. The savannah is made up of a myriad of waterways, cutting through the trees like snakes. The trees look like huge broccolis from above. When the sky is clear, you can see for miles.

Visiting the Park on an Organized Tour

If you would like to maximize your time in the park and are willing to rough it, we recommend a camp-to-camp excursion. Rather than bed down in one of the camps near the airport and go on daytrips, you will spend your day hiking and traveling by dugout canoe to your final destination for the night, while visiting different park attractions en route.

Cacao Expeditions offers a six-day excursion to Angel Falls. It departs from Ciudad Bolívar, where participants board a light-engine plane bound for Kavac, an Indian village at the base of the Auyan Tepuy. From there participants hike and travel by dugout canoe along the Acanan, Churun and Carrao Rivers through grassy savannahs and humid rainforests to the Kavac Canyon, the Kamarata Valley, and the Garganta Del Diablo rapids until reaching Angel Falls on the fourth day. Up until that time participants spend the nights in rustic camps and sleep in hammocks. The fifth day will be spent traveling downstream on the Carrao River stopping at the Isla Orquídea, the Pozo de La Felicidad and La Hacha Falls to Jungle Rudy, where participants will spend the night and the next morning. For serious trekkers, Cacao Expeditions also offers a 10-day trek around the Auyan Tepuy. For information and reservations, contact them in Caracas at ☎ (02) 977-1234 or fax (02) 977-0110. E-mail: 730050.2614@compuserve.com. Their address in Caracas is Avenida Caura, Torre Humboldt, Piso 22, Oficina 22-03, Prados del Este (P.O. Box - Apartado 88267).

Less demanding is **Loggage Care** C.A.'s three-day excursion to Angel Falls. Participants arrive in Canaima on the morning flight, and after a short hike, travel via motorized canoe on the Carrao River to their camp on the Isla Ratoncito. En route to the camp, which is in the shadow of the Auyan Tepuy, are the Pozo de La Felicidad, the Isla Orquidea, and the Aonda and Garganta del Diablo rapids. On the next day, participants will hike to Angel Falls, with stops at many of the other falls and pools in the area, and then return to the base camp. On the final day, the group will make its way back to Canaima in time to catch the return flight to Caracas. A separate excursion to Kavac, with a flight over Angel Falls and a visit to the Indian Village of Kamarata, is also offered, either as a supplement or instead of the hike to Angel Falls. Additional side-trips to other park attractions are available. For information and to make arrangements, visit Loggage Care at their kiosk across from the Avensa counter in the domestic terminal of the airport in Maiquetía, or call them at ☎ (031) 551-577 or 551-056. Their fax is (031) 552-564 or 551-055. Loggage Care should be your first choice among the tour operators located in the airport, whether you're making arrangements to go to Canaima or other destinations in Venezuela. Staff members speak Spanish, English, Italian and German. You will find them to be both friendly and helpful.

Canaima, with its wilderness, beauty and peacefulness, is fascinating. Don't miss it!

Venezuela

Maracaibo

Margarita Island

Caracas ★

Cumaná
Puerto La Cruz

Mérida

Canaima

Maracaibo

Boom Town, Venezuela

Oil! When that cry echoing from here was heard around the world more than 60 years ago, it transformed Maracaibo virtually overnight from a drowsy village beside a lazy blue lake into Boom Town. What happened here would be familiar to veteran Texas oilmen who witnessed similar instant urban growth all over that state.

But the difference – and fortunately for travelers there is a difference – is that, apart from the number of foreign oil executives here, signs of the oil industry's strong presence are virtually invisible in town. You must drive well outside the city to see your first oil derrick rising dramatically from Lake Maracaibo. Petrochemical aromas are unknown in this tidy, attractive town.

What, then, has happened to Maracaibo in the last half-century? For openers, the city now boasts almost two million residents. They represent approximately 10% of Venezuela's population, making it second only to Caracas in size. The rivalry between the Maracucho and the Caraqueño is much like the competition between a wealthy oil-rich Texan and a cosmopolitan New Yorker. According to a popular song, an oil derrick repeats the refrain, "Va a Caracas. Va a Caracas" ("It's going to Caracas. It's going to Caracas") – echoing the up-and-down movements of the pump.

In recent years the capital city of the State of Zulia has sprawled out from its original site along huge Lake Maracaibo to encompass comfortable North American-style suburbs. The city, by the way, is at the northern

Maracaibo is the capital of the State of Zulia.

end of the lake which, just a shade further north, runs into the Gulf of Venezuela. The Gulf in turn connects with the Caribbean, not far from Curaçao and Aruba. The magnificent five-mile-long Urdaneta Bridge, which links Maracaibo with Cabimas across the neck of the lake, skims above the lake here and we will guide you on a motor trip across it.

Background & History

Maracaibo lies in the western region of Venezuela, bordering Colombia. Its central geographic, economic and historic feature is Lake Maracaibo, which is 93 miles long, 72 miles wide and three miles deep. The largest lake in South America, it was discovered by Alonso de Ojeda on August 24, 1499. Houses were built on piles over the water and people got around using small wooden bridges and canoes.

Resembling Venice to the Spaniards of the time, the settlement was named Golfo di Venezuela or Little Venice, which eventually led to the name of the entire country.

Maracaibo was lost and then refounded by Alonso Pacheco in 1570, which is considered the true birth year of the city. Pacheco's community was later destroyed by Indians, and the permanent city was not truly established until 1574 by Pedro Maldonado. The city was then named Nueva Zamora de la Laguna de Maracaibo. It lasted over 200 years, but was repeatedly a target for pirates in the early days. They pillaged the city, almost at will, until the completion of the San Carlos Fort in 1683.

Maracaibo, isolated from the rest of Venezuela until modern times, was the last refuge of the colonial Spanish forces during the Independence War. Although Bolívar had declared Venezuela independent on June 24, 1823, Maracaibo and Zulia were held by the tyrannical Spanish General Francisco Tomás Morales. Yet, without the help of Bolívar, the independent forces rallied behind Rear Admiral José Padilla, forced their way onto the lake, effected a blockade and eventually defeated the Spanish Navy in a famous battle on July 24, 1823.

During the 17th and 18th centuries, Maracaibo, as a result of its isolation, conducted most of its trade with the Dutch Antilles. This interaction led to a markedly Dutch architectural influence in Maracaibo's houses, which is most evident in the older part of the city. Geographically, Zulia and Maracaibo were more a part of Colombia and its culture than a region of Venezuela. For Zulians to reach Caracas, the route was circuitous and time-consuming. From the northern tip of Lake Maracaibo, a Zulian would go to Aruba, or Curaçao, and take a ship to Caracas, at times using Margarita as a stopping-off point.

It was only in this century that Maracaibo became connected with the rest of Venezuela by road.

Recognition and influence came with the discovery of oil in Lake Maracaibo. The discovery made the state and city the wealthiest in the country and gave Venezuela a level of prosperity previously unknown. Oil led to an international outlook and the city is an economic flagship for the country. Oil money enabled Venezuela to build the longest pre-stressed concrete bridge in the world, which spans the lake, running five miles from east to west. The boom also financed a channel, built between 1953 and 1956, for oil-tankers.

Maracaibo now has a dual personality. On the one hand is its internationalism, catalyzed by the oil. There are many modern towers, restaurants, and hotels, and several, as you will see, luxury apartment complexes in construction. The infrastructure is impressive.

On the other hand, there is an indolence about the colonial sector which seems timeless. The architecture of the past is preserved widely. And the Guajira Indians are the most visible in Venezuela because of their firm resistance to modernization. Many still wear their traditional costumes. Even in Maracaibo you will still see women in long colorful robes, while outside the

city you may even occasionally see men in loincloths
and cowboy hats. The mixture is exotic and strange.

Arrival

The 400-mile flight from Maiquetía Airport near Caracas puts you in Maracaibo's small modern two-level
airport (**Aeropuerto La Chinita**) in under an hour. The
white stone terminal houses a bookshop, gift shop,
restaurant and four car rental agencies.

Grab a cab in front of the terminal and in 30 minutes
you should find yourself at either of our first two
recommended hotels: the Hotel Kristoff in the center of
the city or the Hotel del Lago on the lake (the fare will
run about $10). Economy-minded travelers should use
the *por puestos*, which pack five passengers into conventional autos and conclude their run in the city center at Avenida 5 de Julio and Avenida 9, not far from
the Kristoff Hotel. The charge is $1.25 per person. Re-
member, though, that you will need a taxi to get to your
hotel and the *por puestos* can handle only limited luggage.

On the way into town via a modern four-lane highway,
you will find yourself passing a complex of stadiums,
the Polideportivo where baseball and soccer games are
held, along with boxing matches. You also pass the
University of Zulia.

Orientation

In general, Maracaibo breaks down into small neighborhoods but, unlike Caracas, these are rarely used in
locating, say, a restaurant. The street address is
enough. The streets (calles) have higher numbers in the
oldest sections and lower numbers in newer areas.

Key Streets

Familiarize yourself with **Calle 77** (also called Avenida 5 de Julio), the city's major shopping thoroughfare – particularly the stretch from the Plaza República (Avenida 3) to Avenida 15. Here you will find recommended shops, restaurants, and shopping centers (called *centros comerciales*). **Avenida 4** (Bellavista) is important since it runs from the lake through the center of Maracaibo. For quick inexpensive transportation along Avenida 4 use the *por puestos* (jitneys). Avenida 4 (El Milagro), which parallels the lake shore, is where you will find the Hotel del Lago and its nightclub and chic restaurant. Further on, near the dock area, are the old markets, which are worth exploring. **Avenida 8** (Santa Rita) is another key commercial street. Oddly, adjacent to Avenida 8 is Avenida 4. Avenidas 5, 6, and 7 do not extend beyond the old part of town.

Although Maracaibo is a large city, the nucleus is a circle spreading out from the intersection of Avenida 5 de Julio (Calle 77) and Avenida 4 or Bella Vista. These two streets are the primary ones in the city, and are either where many of the restaurants are located, or the route used to get there. Inside the circle, the city is overflowing with restaurants, hotels, stores and office buildings. The eastern limit of the city is the lake, to which Avenida 2, or El Milagro, runs parallel. Bella Vista will take you to the lake and Maracaibo's only five-star hotel, Hotel del Lago. The southern inner city boundary is marked by **Paseo de las Ciencias** (Science Walk), which is one of the attractions of the city. The northwestern edge could be said to reach Maracaibo's large and good university, but you will probably not get out that far unless it is to visit the university itself. Traveling north, which is necessary to reach Sinamaica Lagoon, Maracaibo's most exotic sight, you'll have to pass Hotel del Lago, which could reasonably stand as the northern end of the inner city. The area is clean,

Streets also retain their colonial names, which are noted on street signs.

Addresses include the cross street and building number. Avenida 4 number 75-2 means 4th Avenue at 75th St, building #2.

which is true of much of the city, and quiet – which can't be said of the city at large because of its street action. The old sections of Maracaibo are by the docks, south on the lake from the Hotel del Lago, which has an abundance of Dutch-influenced structures, and by the Paseo de las Ciencias. This was the original heart of the city, with colonial government buildings, and 17th-century churches. The airport, which is small and functional, is about half an hour outside the city, and on the trip in you'll get a glimpse of Maracaibo's periphery.

The area around the Hotel del Lago, on the lake and back a bit, is the wealthiest in Maracaibo, with large North American-style homes, protected by gates and alarms – all containing several cars in the garage.

Weather & Dress

Men rarely wear jackets and ties. Unless otherwise indicated, you can forget them when heading out for the evening.

Since it is at sea level near the Caribbean, Maracaibo is quite sultry, with afternoon temperatures in the 90s much of the year and in the upper 70s during the evenings. The hottest months are July-September. Fortunately, humidity is moderate and at mid-afternoon virtually every day a welcome breeze comes off the lake. Thus, late afternoons and evenings are comfortable and, of course, air-conditioning is ubiquitous. Bring lightweight sports clothes.

Getting Around Town

Cabs are plentiful and cheap. It will cost you about $1.25 to reach most of the city. Since there are no meters, be sure to fix the fare in advance.

Por puestos travel the main streets, continually picking up and discharging passengers. Fares vary by destination.

Hotels

Like any big city, Maracaibo has many hotels. They range from the five-star Hotel del Lago to tiny wooden rooms with no bathrooms, if that is your preference (though we don't list these). Most hotels are in Maracaibo's center and all are pleasant, clean and comfortable; the four-star hotels are an inch away from five-star. Tourism is generally light. In general, rates are about 25% lower than in Caracas.

Hotel Del Lago ☆☆☆☆☆
Avenida 2 (El Milagro)
364 rooms
☎ (61) 924-022; fax (61) 914-551
Expensive
Overlooking Lake Maracaibo, this Inter-Continental hostelry is more a resort than a hotel. First-class inside and out, it enjoys a fine reputation among North American executives, who stop here when traveling with their families. With a long horizontal building in front, the central tower soars above. The inside lobby is windy and long, with rows of stores and five restaurants lining its path. There is a coffee shop, snack bar at the large pool, a live music bar and the Windows Restaurant, serving nouvelle cuisine. On the grounds are a gym, sauna, steambath, jogging track, racquetball courts and convention facilities. The hotel has recently added a new wing. If you're trying to keep costs down, request a room in the old section. Rooms there were half the price ($65 vs. $130) at press time.

What makes this special is the lake in the hotel's backyard.

Hotel Maruma ☆☆☆☆☆
Circunvalación 2
☎ 800-62786; fax (61)360-247
Deluxe
Located just five minutes from the airport and the Rafael Urdaneta Bridge, the opulent Hotel Maruma is

a favorite with businessmen traveling on generous expense accounts. Its 180 rooms are luxuriously equipped with central air, mini-bar and satellite TV. The hotel itself boasts a large pool with bar, tennis and racquetball courts, exercise gym with sauna, volleyball and basketball courts, and a small mall with a bank, travel agency, gift shop and beauty salon. When we last visited, Banco Mercantil was building the largest convention center in Latin America right next door.

Hotel Kristoff ☆☆☆☆
Avenida 8 (Santa Rita) near Calle 68
318 rooms
Pool
☎ (61) 972-911, telex (61) 961-396; fax (61) 980-796
Moderate

In a quiet section. The grassy area surrounding the pool gives you a feeling of being out in the country.

Despite its central location, the Kristoff manages to retain a countryside quality. Chirping birds help too. Prices are extremely modest considering the comfortable air-conditioned rooms and the beautifully maintained grounds.

Its pool is large, and the general atmosphere is very quiet. There are two restaurants by the pool, one informal and the other formal, and past them is a disco. The rooms are not overwhelmingly large, but are very comfortable. There is a gift shop and barbershop in the lobby. The staff speaks fluent English.

Hotel El Paseo ☆☆☆☆
Avenida El Milagro at Calle 74
Sector Cotorrera
54 rooms
☎ (61) 924-114; telex (61) 62-581 Paseo VC; fax (61) 919-453
Expensive

With 14 floors and only 54 rooms, this four-star lakeside hotel has quite spacious rooms. A single room is close to the size of a small suite in other hotels, and the suites themselves are extensive. With a lavish lobby,, the hotel also has very good business facilities, including state-of-the art conference rooms. There are four restaurants, including a rotating one on the rooftop. The hotel offers spectacular views of the sunrise and the activity on the lake, as well as an outdoor pool – a must here.

Hotel Maracaibo Cumberland ☆☆☆
Calle 86A, 4-150
☎ (61) 222-335; fax (61) 222-428
Moderate
Just like its counterparts in Caracas, the Maracaibo Cumberland offers the traveling executive comfortable accommodations and a wide range of services. Rooms are spacious, air-conditioned (of course), and tastefully furnished. There is a fine restaurant in the hotel and the Picadilly Piano Bar is a popular nightspot.

Gran Hotel Delicias ☆☆☆
Av 15 Las Delicias Square
Calle 70
185 rooms
☎ (61) 976-111; fax (61) 973037
Moderate
Just a notch below our three previous selections, this is modern, stylish and clean. A tall building with a prominent stone awning, the hotel has a pool, large restaurant, gift shop and parking lot. Request a room in the new tower. Very little English is spoken, but that should not be a deterrent.

Hotel Tierra Del Sol
Avenida 4 (Bella Vista), 87-125
47 rooms
☎ (61) 230-521, 230-781; fax (61) 230-921
Inexpensive
The Tierra del Sol is a very fine, reasonably priced hotel and has done quite well since it first opened its doors

in 1993. Its 49 rooms are spread over one floor. All are air-conditioned and have color television, with reception provided by a parabolic antenna. The hotel also has a small restaurant and offers a view of the lake. Continental breakfast is included in the room rate. The garden setting is lovely and low key.

The Best Restaurants

As befits any good-sized cosmopolitan city, Maracaibo has a number of first-rate restaurants, including one truly great emporium, Mi Vaquita. Unlike in Caracas, informal dress is standard at most restaurants, largely because of the warm climate. Comfort comes first. A recommended local beer, Zulia, is widely served.

Not only will you find the quality of the restaurants here to be quite high, but you will also enjoy their diversity. With its internationalism, Maracaibo's restaurants are predominantly sleek and high-tech – yet the prices are, for the most part, relatively low by US standards.

*Most Ma-
racuchos start
dinner be-
tween 8 and 9.*

Remember, 10% will be added to your bill for service; add another 5% if the waiter has been particularly attentive. See the *Introduction* for descriptions of Venezuelan foods. Prices noted include a four-course dinner, service, cover and tax, but they exclude liquor and wine.

Argentine Steak Houses

Argentina's great tradition of superb beef has carried north to Venezuela, particularly to Maracaibo, which now boasts two restaurants that would thrive in Buenos Aires, or in New York for that matter.

Mi Vaquita
Av 3H No. 76-222
(Off Av 5 de Julio)
☎ 911-990
Open 11 am - 11 pm (closed Sunday)
Moderate

This is Maracaibo's most famous restaurant. The theme of the restaurant is an homage to and glorification of the American Old West. American Indian weapons dangle from the ceiling. There is a poster advertising the capture of Geronimo. There are dolls of John Wayne, Jesse James and other folk heroes. And, of course, swinging doors for the main entrance. It is fantasy, harking back to the days when you would shoot a man for looking at your wife, and respect was only gained behind a gun. The bar, though, is an homage to modernity. Several hanging televisions broadcast the Mets and Yankees, and a giant video screen features either rock and roll, country western, or pop.

It was founded in 1957 by two Americans and the food is exceptional. The parillada mixta Argentina (mixed meats), cooked at your table, is fantastic.

The house specialties – you need journey no further on the bilingual menu – include three dishes, any one of which will linger in memory long after you've returned home. These are the *parrillada mixta Argentina*, cooked at your table on a small grill stove; a marvelously tender T-bone baby beef steak whose size may intimidate you; and, finally, a succulent *churrasco* (strip sirloin) steak. Instead of plates, you dine on thick wooden platters, which heightens the ranchlike ambience. We're partial to the guacamole salad and the mixed salad. Make sure each member of your party orders a different main dish and share in the riches jointly. The mashed potatoes are the best I've ever had anywhere. Ice cream is also available. This is the local watering hole for many North Americans employed in Maracaibo.

Warning: the hot sauces are just that!

El Gaucho
Av San Martín No. 77-22
(near Plaza República monument)
☎ 82-110
Open 5 pm - 2 am (daily)
Moderate
If you favor outdoor dining, El Gaucho should be for you. Of the two dining rooms – one indoors and air-

conditioned – we prefer the terrace, which has only a tree branch between you and the evening sky. Aside from that, beef is the rage here and you should indulge yourself with the filet mignon, the *churrasco*, or the inevitable Argentine *parrillada*. The owner insists that his grilled chicken (*pollo bebe a la parrilla*) is the best in Venezuela. He may be right.

Criolla Food

El Tinajero
Av 3C No. 71-80
☎ 919-020
Open 11 am - midnight (daily)
Moderate
Easily the best "native" restaurant in Maracaibo, El Tinajero is housed in what was once obviously an elegant private house, reconstructed to resemble an underground cave with a colonial Spanish motif. The atmosphere is informal and the food unique and excellent.

But the atmosphere can only carry a restaurant so far. When you try the *camarones* (shrimp) or the *punta trasera* (a steak served with rice and yucca with beans and plantains), the *pabellón criollo* (shredded beef, rice, black beans and plantains) or the *mojito de pescado en salsa de coco Isla de Toa*, (shredded fish in a tangy sauce subtlely flavored with coconut) you will understand why the locals flock here. *Arepas* (corn bread) come with most platters. Watch the sauces, they can bite.

International

Restaurant Girasol
Hotel el Paseo
Dinner only
☎ 919-621
Expensive
Maracaibo's most physically unusual restaurant because it rotates. Girasol also has fantastic food. The

restaurant is spacious and very modern. As with any rotating restaurant, you get a slow merry-go-round view; add that to a few beers and it's a wonderfully tipsy evening. The meats are searing good, and the chicken dishes are also recommended.

Casa Blanca
Calle 67, Cecilo Agosta
Open 12 noon - 11 pm
☎ 919-530
Moderate
Casa Blanca looks expensive but is actually quite moderate. Very chic and modern, the decor is dominated by mirrors and has the elegant feel of a formal European haunt, with its central fountain, modernist and cubist paintings, piano bar and soft colors. Their pork dish is great, as are the beef and pastas.

Windows
Hotel Del Lago
Avenida 2 (El Milagro)
Dinner only
☎ 924-022
Expensive
Windows caters to an international crowd, with a nouvelle cuisine menu. The complimentary eggs stuffed with caviar served as hors d'oeuvres are a great start to a meal here. The fish is outstanding. We recommend the baked bass in banana sauce. Service is excellent and the beautiful view is enhanced by the music of a pianist.

Hotel Kristoff
Avenida 8 (Santa Rita) near Calle 68
Dinner only
☎ 972-911
Moderate
Tucked away in the back hall of the lobby, the restaurant is relatively small yet plush and comfortable. The menu is not overwhelming, but the meats are good.

Italian

La Trattoria del Cesar
Avenida 8, Santa Rita
Lunch and dinner
Moderate
La Trattoria del Cesar has excellent food, and many people know it. It is an informal place, but the simple decor is more than made up for by the high quality of the food. The *insalata cesar* is great, and the *funghe panna* (mushrooms) are also delicious. This may be Maracaibo's paramount Italian restaurant.

El Tavoliere
Av 8, Santa Rita
☎ 975-449
Lunch and dinner
Moderate

Italian restaurants are usually crowded here. Reservations are advised.

This looks like many Italian restaurants in America – pictures of Italy adorn the walls; the tables have checkered tablecloths; it is crowded, unprivate and noisy. Run by an Italian family. The pastas are pertinent, but the fish, particularly the trout, is bravissimo.

Pizzeria Napolitana
Avenida 5 de Julio
Corner of Bella Vista (Calle 77)
☎ 976-214
Open 5:30 pm - 5 pm (daily)
Moderate
This 30-year-old restaurant, practically an institution, is typical of the great old Italian restaurants in the Little Italys of New York, San Francisco, and even Buenos Aires. The house specialties are the pizzas and the enormous pasta dishes. Every dish we sampled could hold its own anywhere, but, oddly, a simple spaghetti dish seemed to mesmerize us. Dine in the rear garden or in either of the two indoor dining areas. Ideal too for

a late night take-back-to-your-hotel pizza. Look for the chefs in front feeding the huge pizza ovens.

Chinese

Mandarin
Avenida 3H (with Calle 68A), 3H-08
In Bella Vista
☎ 930-108
A popular choice of North Americans. Fine Cantonese and Mandarin cuisine is served at this relative newcomer. But the main attraction here is the Karaoke Happy Hour, held every Monday through Friday from 3 pm until 7 pm or from 11:30 pm until 3 am Thursday through Saturday.

Lago Oueste China
76, No. 3H-02
Lunch and dinner
☎ 912-120
Moderate
Across from Mi Vaquita, Lago Oueste China is as formidable for Chinese food as Mi Vaquita is for meats. Its large Oriental facade glitters at night.

Japanese

Samurai
Avenida 20, Calle 69
Dinner
☎ 518-806
Expensive
Well-known and frequented by Maracuchos, Samurai is alone in Maracaibo for Japanese food. The entrance is a bridge over a large aquarium and fountain. The set-up is typically Japanese, with low tables, pillows, grills at each table, and a sushi bar. The staff speaks English. *Camarones Sakura* is their best dish. There are many soup dishes on the menu that set the proper mood. The friendly staff will explain all daily specials.

French

Chez Nicolas
Calle 78, Avenida 18 and 19
Dinner
☎ 511-801
Expensive
Chez Nicolas is formal and proper. The French cuisine rivals any restaurant in the States, and the beef bourguignonne is tremendous. A classy restaurant.

Restaurant Aisko's
Avenida 13, No. 77-40
Lunch and dinner
☎ 78-559
Moderate
This is a fine restaurant in an intimate, elegant setting. Try the duck dishes for a real treat.

Spanish

Casa Paco
Av Bella Vista No. 70-49 (Av 4)
Open 11 am - 1 am
☎ 92-7025
Expensive
The motif is Spanish bullring (circa 1940) but the food, fresh from the sea, is of a high order. In particular, you should investigate the *cazuela de mariscos* (shellfish casserole) and the *pargo* (red snapper), which is a find. The locals clamor for the *mero* (bass), a delectable dish in a tangy sauce. The bilingual menu also features steak and chicken platters.

Taberna Vasca
Avenida 3 (between Calle 73 and 74)
Lunch and dinner
☎ 72-394
Moderate

Very modern and spacious, Taberna Vasca has good snapper, trout and bass. The setting is old Spain. Good second choice.

Restaurant Toledo
Avenida 76 No. 3H-74
Open 11 am - 11 pm
(Closed Sundays)
☎ 74-665
Moderate
A long canopy provides an attractive approach to the inviting and comfortable Toledo, where the *paella* and *arroz marinera* are highly recommended. Another favored dish is the *pargo habanera* (spicy red snapper). Steak lovers should try *lomito al jerez*, steak cooked in sherry. There are two dining rooms, both of which have been crowded when we have stopped here in the past.

Tasca Restaurant "Don Quijote"
Avenida 4 (Bella Vista) with Calle 69
☎ 71014 or 77427
Moderate
The huge figure of Don Quixote out front makes this Spanish tasca hard to miss. The menu features typical Spanish dishes including *paella marinera* and *zarzuela*, as well as the specialties of the house, *pescado escalfado* (poached fish), *lomito Don Quijote* (tenderloin) and grilled meats. The daily buffet is a real bargain. There is a flamenco show and live music most nights.

Rías del Mar
Paraíso Sector, behind Maxie's Dept. Store
☎ 52-7515
Moderate
Rías del Mar was recommended to us as one of Maracaibo's best Spanish restaurants

La Tasca Torremolinos
Avenida 9 at Calle 75
☎ 79-672
Moderate
La Tasca Torremolinos has received equally high accolades.

Swiss Food

Chalet Suizo
Calle 78 Av 3G-65
(near Plaza de la República)
Open 6:30 pm - 1 pm (daily)
☎ 910-496
Moderate
This tiny restaurant, which manages to create a Swiss
atmosphere via decor, paintings and posters, features
a fondue that is outstanding. Regulars are partial to the
bistek chihuahua, a ham and cheese blend on steak that
comes with a tangy sauce, as well as the chuletas with
sauerkraut. Different and pleasant.

Fast Foods

Maracaibo is packed with quick eateries. Anywhere
you walk there will be a snack bar, coffee shop or pizza
joint. Here is a list of several.

Pizza Hut, Burger King
Costa Verde Shopping Center

McDonald's
Avenida del Lago
Avenida Delicias

Tico's Snacks
Avenida 3, Calle 74
Hams, papitas, empanadas.

Heladeria (ice cream)
Avenida del Lago
Avenida Delicias

Habana Lunch
Calle 76, Bella Vista

De Candido
Calle 70, Santa Rita
The supermarket also serves pizza and fast food.

Los Faroles Pizza
Calle 67, Bella Vista

Fuente De Soda Popia
Avenida Bella Vista, Calle 67
Coffee shop, sandwiches, ice cream.

Sunup to Sundown

The way to get to know any city is on foot and accordingly we recommend a walking tour of Maracaibo, beginning with the old colonial section in the downtown dock area.

A Walking Tour

Hop a cab to Avenida El Milagro (also known as Avenida 2) and Calle 100, where the city projects into Lake Maracaibo. This is the heart of the bustling **dock area** and from dawn to dusk shoppers throng the open stalls, which are overflowing with fruits, vegetables, meats and clothing. The stallkeepers vie with hawking salesmen for the attention of bargain-hunting customers. Food odors, particularly oranges and grilled frankfurters, dominate the senses.

When you've had enough of the dock section, stroll away from the lake along Avenida El Milagro for four blocks until you reach the **Indian Markets** on Calle 95. As you amble along the narrow streets, note the brilliantly-painted and seemingly windowless colonial-style buildings. Wisely, the builders put the windows on the inside facing peaceful inner patios.

Be on the alert for pickpockets.

Once at the Indian market, note the handmade *mantas* (long dresses) worn by most of the women. These are

A perfect time to stroll the streets is during the siesta (12:30-3) when stores are closed and all is quiet. If the day is hot, then wait until late afternoon, when breezes make it comfortable.

particularly good buys here. More common in the stalls are *ruanas* (ponchos), pom pom slippers, beaded bags, and miscellaneous inexpensive souvenirs.

Turn left onto Calle 96 and three blocks beyond at Avenida 5 is the city's colonial center – **Plaza Bolívar**. Typically, the plaza is dominated by an equestrian statue of Simón Bolívar and there are benches, greenery, shrubbery and footpaths. Perfect for a rest. So relax for a time. Look around at the government buildings and the **Maracaibo Cathedral**, which faces the plaza. The two white colonial-style structures are the Municipal Building and the Government Palace. Not far from the plaza are two of the city's oldest neighborhoods, **Santa Lucia** and **El Saladillo**, both of which have been designated as national landmarks.

The huge statue at the park entrance is General Rafael Urdaneta, a revolutionary hero born nearby who fought with Bolívar.

When ready, walk along Avenida 5 to Calle 93, turn left, and two blocks down is the beautiful **Urdaneta Park**, which is adjoined by the lovely **Plaza Urdaneta**. Oddly, the park resembles in some ways a Japanese setting, with shooting fountains illuminated at night by colored lights, foot bridges over the fountains and pagoda lanterns. Try to come at dusk when the lights are turned on.

A block up from Urdaneta Park at Calle 91 are the tall gray Grecian-style columns marking the entrance to the block-long **Museo Urdaneta**, erected on the site of General Urdaneta's birthplace. Here you will see colonial weaponry and other war memorabilia, as well as Urdaneta family heirlooms. The hours are: 8 am - 5 pm, Tuesday - Friday; 8 am - 1 pm weekends.

Modern Maracaibo

Avenida 5 de Julio – from the Plaza de la República (Avenida 3Y) to Calle 15 – is considered the commercial center of new Maracaibo. You can walk the stretch in 30 minutes and along the way you will stroll by the city's major shops, restaurants and nightclubs. Another interesting street to walk along is **Bella Vista** (Avenida 4). It runs through the entire city and has many modern office buildings, banks and shops.

Paseo de las Ciencias (Science Walk)

The Science Walk (actually a sculpture walk) stretches from the Cathedral and Plaza Bolívar at one end to the Basilica of Chiquinquirá at the other. The area is bustling and active; the street west of the Walk is lined with shops.

Paseo de las Ciencias was named after a once-important Maracaibo street, and is about seven blocks long. On the walk are many sculptures, modern designs done by Venezuelans. The idea, it seems, is a public art gallery, and there are small parks and benches interspersed. It's an opportunity for artists and non-museum-going citizens to connect. There are also gardens, fountains and a sundial. The street paralleling the Walk to the east is a colonial relic (this part of town was the original heart of Maracaibo); the buildings are ornamental, with wrought-iron balconies and columns in the front. In the middle of the walk is the **Church of Santa Barbara**, with a blue stuccoed fairyland facade and a weathered stone base. The church dates from 1865 and was restored in 1940.

La Catedral

Next to the Plaza Bolívar, the cathedral is associated with a strange tale. One of the relics in the Cathedral is an old and famous cross called Cristo de Gibraltar (Black Christ). Originally in the church in Gibraltar, the town and church were leveled by the Quiriquire Indians in 1600. The image of Christ was so beatific, it is said, that even though the cross it was on burned, the image was only charred. The Christ image was given to the church in Maracaibo for safekeeping until Gibraltar's church was redone. But the image acquired such notoriety that the clergy in Maracaibo broke the contract and kept it. The ensuing dispute went to the top reaches of the Church hierarchy, and their decision was to put the image in a canoe and see which way it floated, towards Maracaibo or Gibraltar. Well, the winner is obvious now. The Cathedral is open 8 am -12 pm; 4 - 8 pm.

Basílica de la Chiquinquirá

Finding a plain white board on the beach never interrupted her thoughts for more than a moment. The woman who found the board took it home to use as a cover for jars. Unexpectedly, noticing a religious painting on the board, she relocated it to her wall as decoration. Then one day the board began banging and, when the woman turned her attention to it, the board was glowing with the image of Nuestra Señora de la Chiquinquirá. She screamed "miracle," and her neighbors witnessed it also (her street was named El Milagro, now Avenida 2). The clergy wanted to put it in the local church but, as they carried it, the weight grew exponentially until it was too heavy to move. Scratching their heads, they surmised that the Virgin might want to be taken to the Church of San Juan de Dios; this was the correct assessment because, as they headed in that direction, the board returned to its original weight.

The revered Crown of the Virgin is made up of gold and precious stones, all gifts from parishoners.

The Basilica of Chiquinquirá, popularly known as La Chinita, at the other end of the Science Walk, was begun in 1686 on the site of the Church of San Juan de Dios. But when Pope Benedict XV, in 1917, decreed the coronation of the Virgin of Chiquinquirá, the church was reconstructed where it is now. The Basilica is large and yellow, with two domed towers shouldering a middle Gothic structure. There are leaf paintings on the facade. Inside the Basilica are complex minute blue and white carvings, and a white pulpit.

The plaza in front of the Basilica was redesigned as part of the Science Walk. There are two fountains.

Concejo Municipal

Constructed on the site of the house in which the last Spanish governor of Maracaibo lived, the Concejo Municipal (Municipal Council) replaced the house in which Maracaibo's Independence was signed. South of the Plaza Bolívar, the Concejo is home to the **Municipal Museum of Graphic Arts** on the ground floor, open Tuesday - Saturday from 8 am - 4 pm.

Plaza Baralt

Formerly the apex of Maracaibo's business, politics and shopping, Plaza Baralt lost that status as a result of oil money, time and demographics. Plaza Baralt is one block south of the Science Walk on Avenida 6, and is now a mall that is closed to traffic. The newly renovated **Teatro Baralt** is on the plaza.

The waterfront **Mercado de las Pulgas,** which was built in 1927, is now home to the city's newly modernized **Lía Bermúdez Art Center.** Its monthly calendar features special exhibitions, concerts, performances and regional as well as international conferences.

Parque Urdaneta

North of the Science Walk at Calle 93 between Avenida 7 and 9, Parque Urdaneta brings you closer to the water and temporarily away from the colonial look and history of the Paseo de las Ciencias. It is a new park, bragging its modernity with a bandshell, several pools crossed by bridges, and fountains that are illuminated at night.

Lake District

Hugged by Avenida El Milagro (Avenida 2), the lake district is where Maracaibo's docks are located and is a shopping center. From dawn to dusk, shoppers throng the open stalls that sell fruits, vegetables, meats and clothing. Also in the area is the Indian Market, which specializes in *mantas* (long dresses) that are worn by the Indian women of the region. Slippers, beaded bags and other crafts are sold here as well.

Plaza de la República

The plaza is in the modern section of Maracaibo between Calle 78 and 77 (Avenida 5 de Julio) and is a good jumping-off point for a walk around this part of the city. In the center of the plaza is a tall obelisk which is supposed to honor all Venezuelan states. The area around the plaza is Maracaibo's economic center. Its infrastructure is near-perfect, the buildings new and the area filled with shops, banks, travel agencies and airlines from around the world. Despite the cosmopolitan air, Maracaibo's spirit remains slow and friendly, here as elsewhere in the city.

Plaza del Buen Maestro

Translated as the Plaza of the Good Teacher, there is a water jet here supposedly able to reach a height of 165 feet – another testament to "black gold" riches. At the intersection of Avenida 4 (Bella Vista) and Avenida 2 (El Milagro), the jet is a bit of a letdown. When they work, there are rotating lights at night.

El Monumento de la Marina – El Mirador

The stages of the battle are depicted on the sides of the Monument.

This, the Marine Monument, commemorates the naval victory that overcame the last obstacle to Venezuela's independence. You will also see here the bust of Commander-Admiral José Prudencio Padilla.

The 164-foot observation tower, El Mirador, offers fantastic views of the lake and city, and is highly recommended for a full view of Maracaibo's sprawl, the enormous lake, and the derricks in the distance. The elevator is open every day from 3 pm - 10 pm.

Centro de Bellas Artes

The Fine Arts Center is dedicated to showcasing all of Maracaibo's artistic facets, with a succession of events and regular shows. On Sundays at 11 am a film or play for children is presented. On Thursdays at 8:30 pm the 100-piece Maracaibo Symphony Orchestra gives a concert.

There is an art gallery here, and on the first Sunday every month the handicraft artists of the area show and sell their work.

The Fine Arts Center has a little theater where concerts, plays and other shows are performed (local papers have the schedules). The Maracaibo Players, who perform in English, use this space.

The Centro de Bellas Artes is located at Avenida 3F and Calle 68A.

Santa Rosa del Agua

If you don't have the time to visit the Sinamaica Lagoon, Santa Rosa del Agua may be a consolation. The small wooden buildings are built on stilts; walkways connect them with each other and the mainland. There are several restaurants here and on the weekends many feature live music. Unfortunately, the squalid conditions you'll encounter here bear little similarity to the natural beauty and tranquility of Sinamaica.

Excursions

Rafael Urdaneta Bridge & Oil Town

This short excursion will highlight the country's monetary mainstay. The bridge is six miles long and wonderful to drive across at sunset. It seems infinite, and gives an indication of the lake's size; it is also the route to oil town. Unexpectedly, the oil rigs do not dominate the skyline and are, in fact, invisible from the center of town. Seeing them from the bridge, or El Mirador, from the top of the Hotel El Paseo, or from the shore of Maracaibo, they can be majestic, strangely regal. For a peaceful, almost surreal experience, see the oil rigs and bridge at night.

Sinamaica Lagoon & Los Filudos

The lagoon is an aquatic community of Creole-Paraguana people who have lived on the lake for centuries. There are about 4,000 of them.

Sinamaica Lagoon is about an hour's ride north of the city on Carrera 2 (Highway 2). The easiest way, but not necessarily the cheapest, is to rent a taxi to Puerto Mar, then catch a launch via the Río Limón to the lagoon (approximately $20).

The boat trip on the lagoon is as long as you want it to be, and if you get as intoxicated by it as we did, you might make it last for hours.

The bohios *are thatched, stilted and surprisingly sturdy.*

The central part of the lake has rows of small well-cared-for clapboard houses, many painted beautiful pastel colors, interspersed with traditional *bohios*, houses made from a papyrus-like reed that grows in the shallows. Gardens are cultivated in hollowed-out logs, ditched canoes, dotting the lake. You'll pass local residents traveling in dugout canoes and children swimming. On the trip you can stop at El Barrio, where there is a general store and school. In the center of the lake is a bar and restaurant for tourists, built in the same style as the *bohios*.

Physically, the lagoon is a slice of dense vegetation – hot, tropical, jungle-like. It is cut to pieces like a maze by the water, with countless sinuous watery threads slipping past the thick overhanging trees. The birds, eagles among them, are abundant and audible; with the water lapping at the sides of the boat, you are in the heart of the jungle.

Though this is one of the most popular attractions, the lagoon is a fine and memorable experience, unrushed and seemingly untouristed

Continuing north from Sinamaica Lagoon, en route to Los Filudos, you will begin to see the houses of the Guajira Indians, some similar to the bohios, the women in their long *mantas*. Cattles serve as currency here, hence the their large numbers.

It is estimated that there are 50,000 Guajira Indians. They live, when not moving, on the Guajira Peninsula, which spans both Venezuela and Colombia. These modern borders are irrelevant to them, as they follow their traditional ways – nomadic, matrilineal, violent. Most of the Guajiras are on the Venezuelan side.

Disputes erupt easily and often; they can be bloody. This way of life has been very lightly touched by the modern world, although some Guajira men hire themselves out to work in construction or on other people's ranches. The men, dressed in loincloths and cowboy hats, are the herders and hunters.

Their constant movement is spurred by the seasonal water supply. When traveling, they take their houses with them.

The women, always robed in their *mantas*, are the power bloc of the society. They do most of the work and are the spiritual mediators of the tribes. Each tribe has its symbolic animal, which is branded on the cattle and tattooed on the women.

The **Guajiro Market**, Los Filudos, an hour or so further from Sinamaica Lagoon, is not a place to buy Guajiro crafts, but a market where the Guajiros buy goods themselves. In essence, it is a chance to see the Guajiro society in action. The market opens at 5 in the morning on Mondays and goes until 10 am. What you will see here are trucks offering plantains, corrals with cows, meat shops, and shops for hides. Women cook for the shoppers.

The sole route to the market is by dirt road, which makes a jeep or truck the only means of transportation.

Spectator Sports

Horseracing

Track fans should head to the new **Hipódromo Santa Rita** on Via Cabimas just after the Urdaneta Bridge in Santa Rita. Admission is 75¢ and the minimum bet is $1. Check the *Panorama* newspaper or your hotel clerk for a schedule. A cab there should cost you $2.

Baseball, Soccer & Basketball

From October to January, baseball fans flock to the Estadio Luis Aparicio at the Polideportivo to catch their local team, Los Aguilas del Zulia, in action. Games are played nightly and on Sunday afternoons. General admission is $2. Hall of Famer Luis Aparicio, the great White Sox shortstop of yesteryear, was Venezuelan.

Soccer (futbol) and basketball are played here as well. Maracaibo has two soccer teams (Los Petroleros del Zulia and the Maracaibo Futbol Club) and one basketball team (Los Gaiteros del Zulia).

Bullfighting

Bullfights are held in the **Plaza de Toros Monumental** on Avenida Ziruhacomguajin in November and December.

After Dark

Unfortunately, Maracaíbo is not a city in which you can wander freely at night. As a result, many nightspots have closed in recent years. Your best bet for evening entertainment may well be the lounge or disco in your hotel. If you do venture out, always phone for a taxi before leaving, and avoid walking the streets.

All the good hotels, in particular the Hotel del Lago and El Paseo, have piano bars and discos. Current US and European films are shown around the city, primarily in the theater in the Costa Verde Shopping Center. Concerts at the Bellas Artes are an option. There is **bowling** at Pin Zulia. Or you can watch the Yankees or Mets at Mi Vaquita.

Concerts & Opera

Longhairs (1950's variety) should haunt the **Centro de Bellas Artes**, Avenida 3F and Calle 67, the city's main cultural hall where visiting artists and troupes regularly appear. Your hotel clerk will keep you informed or you can call the theater directly at ☎ 91-2950.

Bowling

Enthusiasts need go no further than Pin Zulia, in the Centro Comercial Internacional, Avenida 5 de Julio.

Discotheques

There are several in town; each charges $2 - $3 per drink.

Lenvill's Club
Costa Verde Shopping Center
Open 10 pm - 4 am, Tuesday - Saturday
Singles admitted
Lenvill's caters to young professionals in their 20s and 30s. The small club is centered around the dance floor and features merengue, salsa and traditional gaetas. A bar hangs above the floor, and the voyeurs sit there and watch. There are booths for couples and for groups, and seats adjacent to the floor. Strobe lights adorn the walls, and everything feels strangely claustrophobic; but that is the way Marachuchos like it, according to the bouncer/maitre d'.

American music is mixed in with Venezuelan, Brazilian, and other Latin music.

Hotel Kristoff
Avenida 8 (Santa Rita) near Calle 68
Open 9 am - 3 pm
☎ 972-911
Singles admitted
The Kristoff has both a piano bar and disco. The disco, known as **La Boite,** is one of the largest in Maracaibo and contains many booths. Great for dancing. The piano bar is pretty and quiet, good for relaxing and talking.

Plaza Club
Centro Comercial Salto El Angel
Avenida 3Y at Calle 79
☎ 922-538
Tuesday - Saturday until 3 or 4 am
Tuxedo-clad waiters, antique-style city lights, large photos of Marilyn Monroe, Elvis and Frank Sinatra along the walls, and black and white decor characterize the Plaza Club. A fairly cosmopolitan crowd, 25 and over, gathers here most evenings.

Bars & Pubs

Champions
Calle 71 at Avenida 9B
☎ 974-889
This 90s- style sports bar is the most popular nightspot in Maracaibo, especially among fans of North American sports. Large screen TVs permanently tuned in to ESPN, a great bar, darts and a bar-style basketball court guarantee a crowd here every evening.

The second most popular pub is **Luna** on Calle 75 and Avenida 3.

Picadilly Piano Bar
Hotel Maracaibo Cumberland
Another very popular place to spend an evening with friends.

Shopping

Maracaibo has two major highlights for shoppers – shoes and Indian crafts. The city has many shopping areas (one across from the Hotel Kristoff, another in the radius of Bella Vista and Calle 77, and still another by Mi Vaquita). They have international goods that are slightly cheaper than in the United States. Shop hours are 9 am - 12:30 pm and 3 pm - 7 pm. Most shops are open on Saturdays.

Guajira handicrafts and clothes represent the most un-usual shopping available in the city. *Mantas*, the long colorful psychedelic robes worn by Guajira women, carved-out gourds, pouches, duffle bags, Christmas ornaments, and the popular Guajiran hammocks are all available in Maracaibo cheaper than anywhere else. The price range can be vast.

The **Mali Mai** shop, attached to the Centro de Bellas Artes, features all these items. Guajira rugs are com-plex, intricate and beautiful, and can be bought from this shop. The rugs are designed by Luis Montiel, and are made in his small factory north of the Los Filudos market. All the items at Mali Mai are special and will give you an idea of the work that is done, the quality that can be expected, and the price range.

Costa Verde, Avenida 5 de Julio and Calle 65-67, is the primary and largest shopping complex in Maracaibo. It is jammed with stores, but the clothes are somewhat expensive. On the other hand, shoes, including Italian shoes, are relatively inexpensive – a pair that is $150-$200 in America is $50-$60 here.

A new shopping center has sprung up in front of the Plaza República, **El Centro Comercial Salto Angel**.

Turismo Del Tropico
Avenida 2 (El Milagro), 93-25
☎ 223-010
This colorful shop carries such a wide assortment of rugs, wall hangings, masks and other *artesanías* from across Venezuela that it fills two floors to just about overflowing. You'll have a lot of fun shopping here.

Artesanía Nacional
Avenida 5 de Julio
At Santa Rita (Avenida 8)
☎ 52-2595

Heavy in Indian crafts, this small store carries handbags, belts, maracas, and Indian-style long dresses. Prices for the better items run from $10 and up.

Artesanía Del Hogar
Avenida 9 and Avenida 5 de Julio
Operated for charity, the thrifty Artesanía del Hogar sell items such as stuffed rag dolls, stuffed animals, and woven wall hangings, all handmade by Indian women working at home. Prices are quite low, $3 and up. Good values.

Indian Market
Avenida 1C at Calle 96
Indian families gather here daily to sell homemade goods from wooden stalls set up in this old section of the city. Best buys are colorful ruanas (ponchos), shoulder bags, belts, beaded slippers, and pom pom slippers. We purchased a lovely warm ruana for $10. Prices in general start as low as $1. Reportedly this area is slated for leveling as part of an urban renewal project, so check with your local hotel clerk before you journey here.

Maracaibo Etc.

Area Code
The area code in Maracaibo is 061

Auto Rentals
Hertz, Budget, Avis and National have agencies here. Rentals can be arranged through your hotel. You must be 21 and licensed. Renting a car without a credit card can be a problem.

Avis
Aeropuerto - ☎ 83-925

Budget
Calle 76, Avenida 13, No. 13-08
☎ 970-107; fax 983-107
Aeropuerto - ☎ 360-093

National
Bella Vista - ☎ 92-4545
Aeropuerto - ☎ 344-486

Hertz
El Milagro - ☎ 361-126

ACO
Edificio Aco Occidente No. 86A-50
Avenida 4
☎ 22-6405

Airlines

Avensa
Aeropuerto - ☎ 361-554 or 344-419

LAV-Aeropostal
CC Primavera, Calle 75, Avenida 13A
☎ 82-395
Aeropuerto - ☎ 349-363/346

VIASA, Venezuela's international airline, has an office on Avenida 5 de Julio in the Centro Comercial Icuma. ☎ 977-052 through 057 or 976-011 through 013.

Also in Maracaibo: Air France, Alitalia, British Airways, Iberia, KLM, Lufthansa and Varig.

American Consulate

Edificio Materna, Avenida 15, Calle 78-79
☎ 522-605

Banks

First National City Bank of New York has a branch here on Avenida 5 de Julio. **Banco Consolidado** has a branch just off the Plaza Baralt on Calle 99.

Banking hours are 8:30 - 11:30 am and 2:30 - 4:30 pm (Monday - Friday).

Books & Newspapers

English-language books and periodicals are available at the **Hotel del Lago gift shop** and at the **Librería Universal**, Avenida 5 de Julio and Avenida Bella Vista, as well as in other bookstores throughout the city and at the airport. *The Daily Journal*, published in Caracas, is sold at the Hotel del Lago for 20¢ daily and 25¢ on Sundays, same price as in Caracas. The Maracaibo daily newspaper, *Panorama*, lists all sports events, films, and cultural programs in town. Price is 25¢ daily, 50¢ Sunday. The paper's office is in a beautiful, modern downtown building.

Emergency

Dial 171 in case of an emergency.

Horse Racing

Horseracing enthusiasts should visit the **Santa Rita Hipódromo** just over the Rafael Urdaneta Bridge, heading towards Cabimas.

Dr. Scholl's

The foot-weary should see the good doctor at Avenida 5 de Julio between Avenida 4 and 8 (also called Bella Vista and Santa Rita).

Pharmacies

These are plentiful and most carry a full line of North American over-the-counter medicines.

Around Venezuela

In the preceeding chapters, we've guided you through the most frequently visited destinations in Venezuela. As is true of most places, however, to truly experience the wonder and beauty of Venezuela you need to venture off the well-trod path. Thankfully, many of the country's most beautiful destinations are not far off that path, and are either within driving distance or a short flight from Caracas.

Obviously, we don't purport to be a guide for those who want to set off in the wilds with little more than a compass and a Swiss army knife. Our suggestions are more akin to soft adventure where you'll spend the day hiking in a rainforest, gliding through mangroves or fishing in the Orinoco, only to return to a hot shower, comfortable bed and a good meal. While far from exhaustive, the following suggestions should offer a good enough start to keep you returning to Venezuela again and again.

Guides & Tour Operators

Once you get out of the cities and resort towns, heading into the national parks and less developed areas, it's often best to seek out the help of an experienced guide. Not only will you visit places you would not get to otherwise, you will also spend less time getting lost or trying to work out complicated logistics. Instead, your time can be devoted to experiencing local wildlife, traditions and customs, while making new friends along the way.

Conservation-minded **Eco Voyager** specializes in soft-adventure tours to the Amazon Rainforest, Henri Pittier National Park, Los Roques and the Andes, with

Venezuela

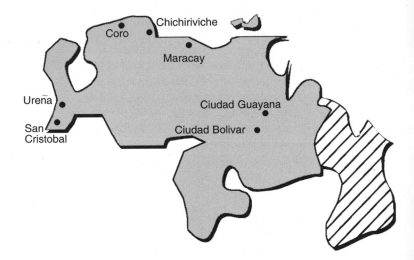

Coro
Chichiriviche
Maracay
Ureña
Ciudad Guayana
San
Cristobal
Ciudad Bolivar

extensions available to Caracas, Canaima and Los Llanos. Groups of no more than 12 persons are led by experienced bilingual guides who rank among Venezuela's most respected naturalists and friendliest people. Accommodations are in comfortable lodges, and deliciously prepared meals reflect the local cuisine. Travelers can customize their plans by combining several destinations in one itinerary and all participants get a detailed pre-departure kit with information on the regions they'll be visiting. Commited to environmental conservation, Eco Voyager adheres strictly to the guidelines for sustainable ecotourism and has worked with local communities to develop and implement conservation programs in Venezuela. With offices in Miami and Caracas, Eco Voyager is one of the most reputable tour operators in Venezuela. For more information, contact their Miami office toll-free at ☎ 800/326-7088 or check out their Web site: www.ecovoyager.com (e-mail: ecotour@ecovoyager.com).

Caracas-based **Cacao Expeditions** offers itineraries throughout Venezuela ranging from soft-adventure tours to rugged multi-day treks in Roraima or the Sierra Nevada. Commensurate with the itinerary selected, accommodations may be anything from a comfy double room with private bath to a tent atop the Auyan Tepui in Canaima National Park. Destinations include locations throughout Canaima National Park, Mérida and the Andes, the Gran Sabana, Henri Pittier National Park, and Puerto Ayacucho, where Cacao Expeditions has their own camp on the banks of the Orinoco River. Tours are led by experienced bilingual, naturalist guides. For more information, contact their Caracas office at ☎ (02) 977-1234, fax (02) 977-1010 or by e-mail at 73050.2614@compuserve.com.

If you'd prefer to travel with a private guide, contact **Dylan Melo** in Caracas at ☎/fax (02) 744-618, or write to him at 1ra Avenida El Casquillo, Edificio Santa Teresita P.B. #1, Alta Florida, Caracas. In addition to specializing in the Henri Pittier National Park, Dylan has a wealth of knowledge and experience to draw from, and speaks English, French and Spanish fluently.

A Wildlife Ranch: Hato Piñero

If your time is limited and you'd like to see some of Venezuela's wildlife close-up, Hato Piñero may be the answer. This private wildlife refuge on 198,000 acres of grasslands and forests is home to over 300 species of birds and native reptiles and mammals, including the often heard but seldom seen howler monkey. Tours are given on horseback, jeep and by boat. Hato Piñero is an hour flight from Caracas or five hours by car. For more information and to make arrangements, ☎ (02) 92-4413 or 924-531 or fax (02) 916-668. Their representative in Caracas has an office in Chuao on the sixth floor of the Edificio General (suite 6b) on Avenida La Estancia.

Choroní: Henri Pittier National Park

Visitors to Caracas would be sorely remiss if they did not make the time to visit the Henri Pittier National Park. One of Venezuela's loveliest and most idyllic national parks, it is a paradise of lush, verdant rainforests, majestic rocky cliffs, quiet colonial towns, and secluded beaches. Best of all, it is just a three-hour drive from Caracas, the perfect getaway for those who are in Caracas for business or pleasure.

Venezuela's first national park, it was founded in 1937 and, like all of the country's national parks, owes it existence to the Swiss Botanist, Henri Pittier. Attracted by the country's lush tropical forests, Pittier settled in Venezuela in 1917 and dedicated the rest of his life to their preservation. Cataloguing over 30,000 plants and writing hundreds of botanical studies, Pittier still found time to lobby the government, and did so unceasingly until 1937 when President Eleázar Lopez Contreras declared Rancho Grande the country's first national park. In 1953, three years after Pittier's death, Rancho Grande was renamed the Henri Pittier National Park.

Starting at the dry xerophytic forests along the Caribbean, the park's 416 square miles climb to the cloud forest peaks of the **Cordillera de la Costa**, the northernmost reaches of the Andes, and descend into the fertile **Aragua Valley**. Within its borders, dense tropical forests open onto wide-open fields of sugar cane, and the towering Mihau shelters the world's most precious cacao. Rivulets bordered by impatiens trickle down moss-covered steps while rivers spill over stone walls into deep pools and man-made canals. More than 520 species of birds, representing nearly 7% of those found throughout the world, have been sighted in Henri Pittier. The park's diverse collection of plants, animals, and insects, including hundreds of different species of butterflies, is without rival. That's not all. Henri Pittier also boasts one of the most beautiful coastlines in the Caribbean, its dramatic coastal mountain ranges and sheltered bays dotted with caves where pirates once hid their booty, and locals smuggled goods to the Dutch traders from Curaçao.

Getting There

If you're driving, take CT 1 out of Caracas to Maracay. Once in Maracay, take Route 6, the eastern route through Henri Pittier, to Choroní and Puerto Colombia, where you will probably be staying. If you're going to Ocumare de la Costa or Cata you should take Route 7, which traverses the Paso Portachuelo as it cuts through the western portion of the park. We urge that you not drive through the park after dark, especially if you will be travelling on Route 6. Not only will you miss out on some of the park's most spectacular scenery as the route climbs up to the cloud forest at 6,000 feet and descends back down again, but the serpentine twists and hairpin turns can be quite treacherous. If you're traveling during the rainy season, be sure to check road conditions before you set out as the road is occasionally blocked by mudslides.

Aeroexpress (☎ 266-3601) offers luxury bus service between Caracas and Maracay, with departures out of the Bello Campo terminal at 7 am, 10:45 am, 3 pm and 6:30 pm. From Maracay there is frequent bus service to Puerto Colombia (approximately every two hours) and Ocumare de la Costa (every hour).

Where To Stay

Highrise hotels and five-star resorts do not mar the skyline in Choroní. Instead, you'll find lodging in small posadas which range from private homes, offering simple rooms with coldwater bath, to beautifully restored colonial haciendas with garden courtyards.

Among the loveliest, and our favorite, is the **Posada Humboldt** in Puerto Colombia. Inconspicuous behind a plain white gate and whitewashed walls at the entrance to town, inside it is a garden oasis. Guest rooms are set around a lovely interior courtyard replete with flowering plants and a fountain under the shade of a huge mango. Birdsongs fill the morning air while evenings are accented by subtle lighting and candlelight dinners. Rooms feature modern baths with hot water, comfortable beds and ample storage space. Reservations are mandatory, and the rate includes a generous breakfast buffet, lunch and dinner, as well as unlimited beer and soft drinks. Picnic lunches are provided. Guests dine together in the evening, enjoying fine wine and expertly prepared continental cuisine in a wonderfully romantic setting. For reservations, ☎ (02) 976-

2222 in Caracas or contact the posada directly at ☎ (043) 91-1050.

Located between Puerto Colombia and Choroní, **La Casa de Los Garcia** offers eight rooms with ceiling fans and private bath in a restored colonial hacienda. Breakfast is included in the rate. For reservations, ☎ (043) 91-1056 or fax (02) 976-8273.

Club Cotoperix has four posadas in Puerto Colombia and offers packages including all meals and excursions. For more information contact them in Caracas at ☎ (02) 952-8617 or 952-2628.

Visiting the Park

Unless you're planning to spend all your time on the beach (a big mistake), it's best to visit the park with an experienced guide. Unlike national parks in the United States, you won't find any detailed trail maps for hiking. Not only are trails not marked or only minimally so, they become quickly overgrown. Under such conditions even experienced hikers may get lost. Your enjoyment of the park will be greatly enhanced by an experienced guide who is familiar with the terrain and can identify wildlife, plants and birds, and alert you to any hazards along the way. Plus, a guide will probably take you to beaches you would be less likely to visit on your own.

Ecovoyager and **Cacao Expeditions** both offer multiday itineraries designed to maximize your enjoyment of the park by combining hiking with snorkeling and time spent relaxing on the beach. Lodging and meals are in a comfortable colonial-style posada. If you'd like to tour the park with a private guide, contact **Dylan Melo** in Caracas (☎/fax 058-2-744-618) or write 1ra Avenida El Casquillo, Edificio Santa Teresa, P.B. Apt. #1, Alta Florida, Caracas). Educated in the United States, Dylan speaks English fluently as well as Spanish and French, and is an expert in the zone.

Park Highlights

Beaches

Several lovely beaches dot the coast. While some are accessible by car, others can be reached only by boat. The most beautiful, most popular, and most developed, is **Cata Beach**. It is located to the west of Puerto Colombia, and you'll need a car to get there. **Playa Grande** is within walking distance of Puerto Colombia, and tends to be crowded on the weekends. The less accessible beaches have no facilities or shade so you will need to pack a picnic lunch, including plenty to drink, along with a tarp or beach umbrella. Beaches, which are accessible only by boat, include those at **Chuao, Café, Aroa, Cepe** and **Puerto Maya.** The owner of your posada should be able to direct you to the best beaches and arrange for transportation. Snorkelers should visit the cove by **Playa Seca**, accessible only by boat.

Colonial Towns

The loveliest of the towns in Henri Pittier is **Choroní**. Set inland from the coast as protection from marauding pirates, this three-century-old settlement is known for its narrow streets and pastel-colored colonial homes. It is home to the **Hacienda Excesiva**, a fine example of 19th-century architecture. Also worth a peek is the parish church on the Plaza Bolívar. The neighboring coastal town of Puerto Colombia is usually referred to as Choroní as well.

East of Puerto Colombia, the coastal settlement of **Chuao** can be reached only by boat. Its residents are the descendants of African slaves brought to work on the plantations by the Spanish during the colonial period. Now, working together as a cooperative, they own their own land on which they cultivate cacao, manioc and yucca. Chuao's cacao is reputed to be the best in the world. It is still processed by hand under the knowing supervision of Señora Layla. If you are lucky enough to be there at the right time, you may be able to sample some. In the village there is a small museum dedicated to the history of cacao production and local traditions. Chuao, along with the western seaside villages of Cata and Cuyagau, are known for their Danzantes Diablantes, or Devil Dances, which originated with the slaves. The dances are still performed during Corpus Christi.

Flora

You'll first experience the vast variety of plantlife in the Henri Pittier as you travel from Maracay to Choroní. As you climb the Cordillera, the semi-dry deciduous forest gradually becomes a humid evergreen tropical forest until you reach the cloud forest at the highest altitudes. Along the coastline, rocky outcrops sprinkled with patches of arid coastal cactus are interspersed with mangroves and coconut groves. Just inland is the xerophytic forest, a dry shrubby deciduous forest. Altitudes in the park range from sea level to 7,800 feet above sea level at the Cenizo Peak.

Hiking is the best way to experience the park. To appreciate the its diversity, you should spend one morning hiking through the cocoa plantation in Chuao and take another day to hike through the tropical forest. In the area surrounding Chuao farming cooperatives cultivate small plots of manioc and yucca along with two types of cocoa, Amazonica and Criollo. Criollo, the rarer of the two, is widely held to be the best in the world. The fields are irrigated by a series of man-made canals that carry water down from the mountains. Fruit trees abound, including papaya, breadfruit, mangoes and avocado, along with hardwoods such as mahogany and mihau. Hawks, kiskadees, bananaquits, hummingbirds, woodpeckers and conotos are just a few of the different birds you can expect to see or hear.

Further inland, the landscape will become more tropical. As the humidity increases, tree trunks widen, many supported by huge roots and buttresses. The moist soil nourishes giant ferns and palm trees with leaves as big as, if not bigger than, a man. Trumpetwood, figs, wild cotton trees, and hibiscus thrive here, as do hundreds of orchids, bromeliads, epiphytes, and several different varieties of ficus, impatiens, and colorful flowers and plants, the likes of which you may have never seen before. If you're fortunate enough to make it all the way to the top, you'll reach the cloud forest, another world altogether.

Birds & Animal Life

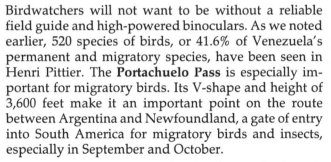

Birdwatchers will not want to be without a reliable field guide and high-powered binoculars. As we noted earlier, 520 species of birds, or 41.6% of Venezuela's permanent and migratory species, have been seen in Henri Pittier. The **Portachuelo Pass** is especially important for migratory birds. Its V-shape and height of 3,600 feet make it an important point on the route between Argentina and Newfoundland, a gate of entry into South America for migratory birds and insects, especially in September and October.

According to studies conducted by the Rancho Grande Biological Station, approximately 75 species live in the lower elevation forests. These include the chachalaca, the palevented pigeon, the orange-winged parrot, the common parrot, the squirrel cuckoo, the common potoo, the rufous-tailed jacamar, tinamous and others. At least 100 different species live in the humid forest, including the grey tinamou, the guan, the lilac-tailed parrotlet, the black and white owl, the green jay, and the cacique. The 200 species that inhabit the cloud forest include the highland tinamou, the helmeted curassow, the band-tailed guan, the buff-fronted foliage-gleaner, the black and white owl, the black-faced antthrush, and the white hawk.

Mammals that make their home in the park include the tapir, the giant river otter, the puma, the margay, the kinkajou, the racoon, the giant anteater, the porcupine, the brocket deer, coral snake, rattlesnake, and the fer-de-lance.

Maracay

Before returning to Caracas or on your way to Choroní, you may want to stop off in Maracay. Situated 60 miles west of Caracas, via excellent highways, Maracay was the home of Venezuelan ruler (1908-1935), General Juan Vicente Gómez, who rose from illiterate cowboy to dictator. His enormous palace on the grounds of the Hotel Jardín is a must for visitors, particularly the fountains and immaculate gardens. A bullfight aficio-nado, General Gómez built a brilliant replica here of Seville's world-famous bullring which still draws Spain's best matadors. Striving for a cultural identity, the general also commissioned an opera house. Open to visitors, his country home, **Las Delicias**, is of special interest to children because of the large zoo on the grounds. Understandably, the tomb of General Gómez – who made Maracay the nation's capital for a time – is another tourist draw. Founded in 1607, the city was named for an Indian chieftain.

Today, as capital of Aragua State, Maracay boasts a growing population of over 200,000 and a steady stream of visitors to the nearby military air base at Palo Negro and to the outlying beaches.

The city's 1,500-foot elevation provides welcome breezes despite a semi-tropical climate with average temperatures of 77°F.

Maracay's best hotels are the 178-room **Hotel Maracay** (☎ 413-111), with a huge pool, golf course, stables and fine horses, and the **El Pipo Internacional** (☎ 413-2022) on Avenida Principal El Castaño.

Coro (Falcón State)

Architecture buffs shouldn't delay a moment in journeying to Coro, some 280 miles west of Caracas on the Caribbean and an easy daytrip by bus or by car from Maracaibo. As Venezuela's first colonial capital, and the departure point for numerous Spanish expeditions to the interior, Coro developed an authentic colonial architecture in its homes, churches, and government buildings.

History

One of the oldest cities in South America, Coro was founded on July 26, 1527 by Juan de Ampiés. Ampiés had good relations with the local Caquetío Indians, but Coro's history changed drastically shortly thereafter.

At the time, the Province of Venezuela encompassed the region of the present-day states of Falcón and Zulia, and the eastern coastal region. Charles V leased the province to the Welsers, a family of German bankers. The first German governor arrived in Coro on February 24, 1529. He immediately set the tone. Using Coro simply as a base for expeditions into the interior, the Welsers were unconcerned with establishing a community, or having good relations with the local Indians. Their interest was profit, and they pillaged and explored the interior for natural resources. It was Charles V's idea, in leasing the area to the Welsers, that they begin a profitable industry. But their attempts failed, and in 1546 their lease was revoked.

Coro languished and became decrepit. It was revived by a growing trade with Curaçao and the Dutch Islands in the 18th century, eventually to become the point of entry for European goods coming into Venezuela.

Coro's economic basis for trade has stayed with it until the present. With a population of 130,000 and the capital of Falcón, Coro has fantastic colonial architecture in bold Spanish and Dutch styles – so much so that it has been declared a National Monument.

Seeing the City Today

If your time is limited, concentrate on these structures:

The Cathedral

Constructed like a fortress as a result of frequent pirate attacks in the 16th and 17th centuries, it is one of Venezuela's oldest cathedrals and the oldest building in the city. Venezula's first mass was celebrated here. It was declared a National Monument in 1957, and was restored to its original design.

The San Clemente Cross and Temple

Though the present structure dates back to the 18th century, it is believed that Juan de Ampíes originally built a temple dedicated to Saint Clement on the same site.

House of the Iron Windows

Considered Venezuela's best example of Spanish colonial architecture, this house dates from the 18th century.

Treasure House

The wealthy stored their gold and diamonds here during pirate attacks.

The Arcaya Family House

Another example of an 18th-century home, the Arcaya House features two floors, massive doors and a balcony that encircles the structure. It is now home to a lovely ceramics museum.

The Jewish Cemetery

South America's oldest Jewish cemetery. Still in use, it was founded by Jews who emigrated to Coro from Curaçao in the 19th century.

Diocese Museum

Home to one of the country's finest art museums. An 800-year-old statue of St. Peter can be seen here as well as a 450-year-old monstrance.

Food & Lodgings

A word about local food. You should sample the goat meat, either in a curry called *talkary* or in a coconut shell dish.

A recommended hotel is the 66-room air-conditioned **Hotel Miranda Cumberland**, with pool and private baths. Located opposite the airport. ☎ (068) 516-732.

The Desert

Just north of Coro on the Paraguana Peninsula is **Los Medanos National Park**, a sweeping desert region that draws many geology students. Be sure to visit – it's almost eery in its hypnotic effect.

Morrocoy National Park

If you're travelling between Coro and Caracas, you may want to consider taking a day to visit the Morrocoy National Park.

Also known as El Golfo Triste, Morrocoy covers 792,623 acres of coastal mountains, mangroves and sandy cays off Venezuela's northwest coast. Though opportunities do exist for snorkeling, scuba and bird-watching, the park's primary attractions are its island beaches. Snorkelers, birdwatchers, divers and beach-goers should opt first for Los Roques, Choroní or Mochima National Park, with Morrocoy a close second.

More popular with Venezuelan families than international tourists, Morrocoy is Venezuela's lower priced alternative to Los Roques, Margarita and Puerto La Cruz. It is located in the State of Falcón, 95 miles east of Coro via highway CT3 and 155 miles west of Caracas.

The park is accessible from the once-sleepy coastal towns of Tucacas and Chichiriviche, which border it on the east and west. In recent years Tucacas and its environs have undergone a major building boom. That area is now dominated by highrise condominium complexes, which you will pass on your way to the park. Though still far less developed, Chichiriviche appears to be following the same course as Tucacas.

Getting There

If you've rented a car, you can easily drive to Morrocoy from Caracas or Coro. From Coro, take highway CT3 east to Tucacas or Chichiriviche. From Caracas, take highway CT 1 west beyond Valencia until you reach the turn-off for Puerto Cabello, where you pick up CT3. A cab from Caracas should cost around $120. A less expensive option is to take an **Aeroexpress** (☎ 2-266-3601) luxury bus from the Bello Campo terminal in Caracas to the bus terminal in Valencia, and then catch a local buseta to Chichiriviche. Travel time between Caracas and Valencia is just under two hours and a ticket is little over $5 US. There are several departures all day long and the air-conditioned buses are far more comfortable than most in the United States. Travel time between Valencia and Chichiriviche is about an hour and a half, and the buseta will drop you off right in front of the two best hotels in town, the Hotel La Garza and the Hotel Mario.

What to Bring

Since the exchange rate is less favorable here than in Caracas and because there is a likelihood that you may not even be able to change money, it's best to arrive with enough bolívares. In a pinch, you can try to change money at the Banco Industrial on the main street in Chichiriviche.

Additionally, you will need insect repellent for the evenings, along with the usual beachware, sunscreen,

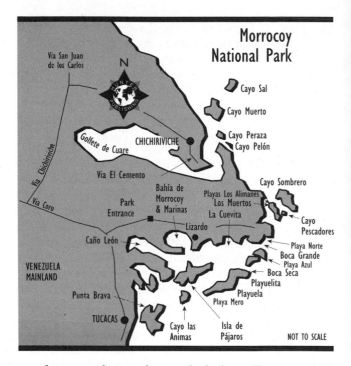

Morrocoy National Park

Via San Juan de los Carlos

N

Cayo Sal

Cayo Muerto

Cayo Peraza
Cayo Pelón

Golfete de Cuare

CHICHIRIVICHE

Via Chichiriviche

Via El Cemento

Cayo Sombrero

Bahía de
Morrocoy
& Marinas

Playas Los Alimanes
Los Muertos

Via Coro

Park
Entrance

La Cuevita

Cayo
Pescadores

Lizardo

Caño León

Playa Norte
Boca Grande

VENEZUELA
MAINLAND

Playa Azul
Boca Seca
Playuelita
Playuela

Punta Brava

Playa Mero

TUCACAS

Cayo las
Animas

Isla de
Pájaros

NOT TO SCALE

sunglasses, a hat and casual clothes. Shorts and T-shirts are fine.

Where to Stay

Dusty and unattractive best describe Chichiriviche and Tucacas. Though Tucacas now sports condominium complexes and 12 casinos, it still has more dirt roads than paved ones. Upon your arrival in Chichiriviche you may even ask yourself why you bothered coming. Its dirt roads, low nondescript buildings and shops, including a few surf shops, look far from promising. Neither Tucacas nor Chichiriviche have an attractive coastline or beach. Don't be misled when you hear Chichiriviche's waterfront referred to as Playa Norte.

There is no beach. Since access to the cays is better from Chichiriviche, we recommend that you stay there.

Given the lack of mainland attractions, it's best to arrive as late in the afternoon as possible or in the early evening. Upon your arrival, or when making hotel reservations, you should arrange to tour the park the following day. Boats to the islands leave in the morning and organized tours are generally booked the night before. If you arrive after 10 or 11 am, your only option may be to spend the afternoon at the hotel pool. However, you may be able to take an independent launch out to one of the beaches (see below).

Lodging and dining are below the standards set in Margarita and Puerto La Cruz, but prices are lower as well. The best hotels in Chichiriviche are the Hotel La Garza and the Hotel Mario which are located across the street from each other on the main road just as you come into town. The larger and more modern of the two is the 120-room **Hotel Mario**, ☎ (042) 86-811. fax (042) 86-096, which has a large outdoor pool, a casino, restaurant and nightclub. The more traditional 73-room **Hotel La Garza** has an open-air garden style restaurant next to the outdoor pool. ☎ (042) 86-126.

Just before press time we received word of two new hotels, four and five stars, that are scheduled to open in Chichiriviche by the fall of 1997. Located on the oceanfront, the four-star **Hotel Playa Sirena** will offer guests a choice of standard or suite-style accommodations. Twenty-five of its 75 rooms are two-bedroom suites with kitchenettes and room for up to six persons. The Playa Sirena also has a pool and rooftop restaurant, as well as a luxuriously appointed casino featuring blackjack, roulette, Caribbean and American-style poker and slot machines.

The **Hotel Coral Suites** will be the first five-star hotel in Chichiriviche. Though it is half a mile away from the beach, door-to-door service to the cays will be provided by hotel launches. The Coral Suites will also feature two swimming pools with a swim-up bar and waterslide, buffet-style dining, a game room with billiards and arcade games, and a Las Vegas-style casino. For a 10% discount on your first night accommodations or a $10 match play coupon in the casino, just show your copy of *Venezuela Alive* to the front desk or casino cashier.

Since dining options are limited, you may want to take advantage of your hotel's meal plan. There is little variety among the restaurant menus, virtually all of which feature the standard pizza, pasta, seafood and chicken dishes. Restaurants are located on the Playa Norte and the main road, and are within walking distance of the hotels.

Visiting the Park

Created in 1974, the national park covers three separate zones. That portion of the park which is on dry land is dominated by the Cerro Chichiriviche, a range of low-lying coastal mountains covered with a dry jungle of oak trees, mountain roses and gumbo-limbo trees. Though rarely spotted, red howler monkeys, fox, opossum and deer inhabit this part of the park. Less elusive are the birds, which include the whitecheeked pintail, the barred tinamou, hummingbirds, and kiskadees.

Mangroves and salt marshes cover much of the coast. Brown pelicans, frigatebirds, great egrets and American flamingos feed and are frequently spotted in the marshes. The park's most popular attractions, however, are the cays, tiny islands with sandy white beaches surrounded by the crystal clear turquoise waters of the Golfo Triste. Most of the cays offer little more than perfect beaches and a few palm trees for shade. Venezuelan families usually pack for the day, bringing coolers stocked with plenty to eat and drink, and a tarp for shade. A tarp or beach umbrella is a must if you plan to spend an entire day on the beach since there is very little shade.

Cays nearest to Chichiriviche include **Cayo Sal, Muerto, Pelón and Peraza.** Further away are **Varadero, Borracho, Sombrero** and **Pescadores. Punta Brava, Paiclá, Playa Mero, Playuela, Playuelita, Boca Seca, Playa Azul,** and **Playa Nortes** are more accessible from Tucacas. There are no comfort facilities on any of the cays, although Muerto, Sal and Sombrero do have small open-air restaurants.

Launches to the cays depart from Playa Norte at the end of the main street in Chichiriviche. Prices to the different cays are posted on the shack and range from $10 to $25 per launch. Most launches hold eight to 10 people. Prices go up as you travel to the more distant cays. Usually, you arrange with one driver to take you out to a cay and to return for you at a specified time. Payment is not expected until you return. The cays are about 15-30 minutes from shore. Departures are from around 7 am until 3 pm. Returns from 1:30 pm to 5 pm.

Refugio de Naturaleza Cuare & the Cays

The best way to see the park is by a guided tour combining the Cuare Wildlife Refuge and a visit to several cays. Cuare is a 33,500-acre wildlife refuge which encompasses the **Golfete de Cuare** – a sheltered inlet made up of springs, lagoons and five coral cays. Most of Venezuela's water birds and about half of the migratory birds that winter in Venezuela can be seen here. The most conspicuous is the dark red cora cora. The coastal caiman, a species unique to Venezuela, also makes its home in the park.

The remains of *La Gaviota*, a fishing boat that sank just outside the mangroves 44 years ago, mark the entrance to the refuge. Fishing is no longer permitted in the area. In the refuge you'll glide through channels in the mangroves jokingly referred to as the *Canal de Amor*, or

Tunnel of Love. After leaving the mangroves, you'll travel in the shadows of the Cerro Chichiriviche, which borders the lagoon. Next you'll visit the area's two most important sites, the **Cueva de los Indios** and the **Cueva de la Virgen**. Both caves are only accessible by water. The Cueva de los Indios is an archaeological site which was sacred to the Indians who once inhabited the area. It is home to stalactites and pre-Colombian petroglyphs. The **Cueva de la Virgen** is a religious shrine and an annual pilgrimage site for the local fishermen. Its nooks and crannies serve as natural alters for religious statues placed there by local worshippers.

Antonio at the Hotel La Garza offers one- and two-day tours of the park, including the Cuare Wildlife Refuge and stops at many different cays. Make arrangements at the reception desk of the Hotel La Garza and request Antonio specifically. He charges about $10 per person and his boat holds six.

Trip to the Yaracuy River

Located 30 minutes south of Tucacas, the shoreline of the Yaracuy River is a favorite afternoon feeding ground for birds and other local wildlife. Visits can be arranged with Luis Guillermo of **Guilica Travel** in Tucacas at ☎ (042) 803939 or cellular (014) 250663.

Scuba Diving

Experienced divers should contact **Submatur**, in Tucacas, ☎ (042) 84082 or ☎/Fax (042) 83-1051; or in Caracas, ☎ (02) 941-4939.

San Cristóbal, Ureña & San Antonio (Táchira State)

South of Mérida and only 34 miles from the Colombian border in the heart of a mountain resort zone is San Cristóbal, a city of 235,000 with a near-perfect year-round climate that draws tourists from both Venezuela and Colombia. The grounds are the site of the San Sebastian International Fair every January and a bull-ring draws first-rate matadors. Shoppers should seek out ceramic and woven straw gifts. It is a lovely town with attractive plazas and parks.

A few minutes from the Colombian border is Venezuela's most famous spa, **Aguas Calientes,** near Ureña, where temperatures of the iron- and sulphur-rich springs reach 123°. Regulars here attest to the restorative powers of the springs. The best hotel here is definitely the 28-room **Hotel Aguas Calientes,** ☎ (076) 871-291, which offers a private thermal pool and air-conditioned rooms.

Your flight lands in the border town of **San Antonio del Táchira**, which is connected to Colombia via the historic Simón Bolívar International Bridge across the Río Táchira. On the Colombian side is the old city of **Cúcuta**, where you should do some crafts shopping since prices are especially attractive.

Stay at the 113-room **El Tama Hotel** on Avenida 19 de Abril, ☎ (076) 558-366, a hostelry with all amenities, including a pool.

Ciudad Guayana & Ciudad Bolívar (Bolívar State)

Understandably, visitors throng here to view Angel Falls, the world's highest waterfall, Devil Mountain, and the jungle camps at Canaima. Many Venezuelan financiers point to the gold, diamond and other mineral wealth of Bolívar as representing the economic future of Venezuela. And that may well be, for this state is huge – larger than all of New England plus West Virginia. It embraces a quarter of Venezuela's land mass, including much of the plains, jungles and mountains. The Orinoco and four other major rivers cut through the region.

The new city of **Ciudad Guayana**, carved out of the jungle much like Brasília in Brazil, was formed in 1961 by joining the towns of Puerto Ordaz and San Felix at the junction of the Orinoco and Caroni Rivers. Key to the city's rugged beauty are the **Cachamay Falls**, which cascade near the city center. Travelers are charmed by **Caroni Park** and by the order of the well-planned streets and highways. Serious hunters and fishermen embark on their trips into the mountains from here. For luxurious accommodations, stay at the 205-room **Hotel Inter-Continental Guayana** (air-conditioned), which offers a stunning view of the La Llovizna Falls. Make reservations at the Hotel Tamanaco in Caracas or the Hotel Del Lago in Maracaibo.

Sixty-five miles west is the old colonial city of **Ciudad Bolívar**. Founded in 1764 by Governor Joaquin Sabas Moreno de Mendez, the city was originally known as Angostura and was the most important city during the Independence War.

Its early history was mainly determined by its location on the Orinoco River, Venezuela's largest. It became a staging point for trade into the interior. Easily reached from the Atlantic, it was and still is an important city for trade.

The city's elegant cobblestoned streets, austere cathedrals, and fine homes have been largely preserved.

Angostura reached its fame during the Independence War as the base of operations for Bolívar and the independence forces. It was finely suited for this role because of its interior location. It was easily defended and really was never threatened. Bolívar and his troops were able to work and plan in peace.

In Angostura on February 15, 1819, the Second Congress of the Republic of Venezuela was held. The Constitution was hammered out here. In fact, most of

Bolívar's and future Venezuela's structure developed in embryo form in Angostura. It was perhaps the most important city during the Independence War.

On May 3, 1846, Angostura became Ciudad Bolívar. The capital of the State of Bolívar, it is a prosperous city because of its trade and location, and its new suburbs are most attractive. The University of the East Schools of Mines and of Medicine are located here, giving the city a cosmopolitan and cultural feel as well.

Today, the city retains a colonial flavor through its architecture despite extensive rebuilding and development. Flights to Canaima stop here for refueling. Sights include the **Talavera Colonial Museum**, the ruins of the **Fortress of the Vulture** and **Orinoco Avenue**, a two-mile promenade along the river.

Amazônas

The name alone evokes images of dense, humid jungle and wide, slow-moving rivers. The mighty Orinoco, the third largest river in South America, originates in Amazônas, the southernmost state in Venezuela and the closest to the equator. It is bordered by Bolívar State to the north and by Brazil to the south, east and west. Brazil shares the western border with Colombia.

Although Amazônas is the second largest state in Venezuela, it is also the least populated, with under 100,000 inhabitants, three-quarters of whom live in Puerto Ayacucho, the state capital. Only 120 kilometers of paved roads penetrate its 68,000 square miles of low-lying savannah, marshlands and thick jungle. Another 62 miles of dirt roads provide access to mining and Indian communities. Some 70% of Venezuela's indigenous inhabitants live in Amazônas. They include the Makiritares, Guahibos, Guaicas, and the Piaroas. Mining is the state's primary source of income.

Given its location, the climate is hot and humid all year long, with an average year-round temperature of 81°. It rains frequently. Showers are most intense from April to November, during which time the Orinoco often rises as much as 50 feet, swallowing up the wide expanses of beaches which line its banks during the rest of the year. Tree tops rise out of the surface of the water like shrubbery. The intense humidity fosters the growth of exotic flora and fauna. Of the 8,000 different species of plants in Amazônas, 7,000 are native to the region. These include innumerable varieties of orchids, many of which are still unknown to man. Portions of the land have been set aside as protected national parks, including: **Serrania de la Neblina**, **Yapacana**, **Duida-Marahuaca**, and **Parima-Tapirapecó**.

Protected naturally formed monuments include **Piedra de Cocuy**, **Cerro Autana**, **Piedra Pintada**, and **Piedra La Tortuga**.

The gateway to Amazônas is **Puerto Ayacucho**, the state capital and one of the few settlements with modern facilities. Many of the city's 75,000 inhabitants are northern Amazonian Indians. It was founded in 1924 by Juan Vicente Gomez and originally served as a camp for the workers who were building the highway to Samariapo. Though the Orinoco provided the primary route for the transport of goods through the Amazon region, an alternate land route was needed between the upper and lower Orinoco at Puerto Ayacucho where the Atures and Maipures River rapids made the Orinoco impassable. Nowadays, Puerto Ayacucho is an important gateway for tourists who want to visit the Venezuelan portion of the Amazon basin.

Getting There

Avensa (☎ 361-554 or 344-419) offers one flight daily to Puerto Ayacucho from Maiquetía. Given the state of the airline industry in Venezuela, additional service may have been added via another airline by the time you visit. The folks at **Loggage Care** in the domestic terminal should be able to help you make arrangements.

What to Bring

Mosquito repellent is a must, as is lightweight clothing, including long pants, shorts, T-shirts, a bathing suit, comfortable walking shoes, sunscreen and a hat.

Where to Stay/What to Do

The best way to visit the region is to stay in a camp on the shores of the Orinoco. The spectacular scenery combined with the river flowing beside you create a magical effect. One of the finest is the four-star **Camturama Amazônas Resort**. Its 52 rooms are in one- and two-room cabanas, all of which are fully enclosed and air-conditioned (a must). They have private baths with hot water. Decor features local handicrafts. The restaurant menu includes international and local cuisine finely prepared and served in generous portions. The riverside setting is lovely and there is even a small lake on the ample grounds, along with a discotheque and game room built into a natural granite ledge.

Camturama offers several different excursions, which can be included in the rate or billed separately. You'll visit the nearby natural monuments, including the **Cerro Pintado**, the largest petroglyph in the country and the **Piedra La Tortuga**, an immense rock formation in the shape of a turtle. A sacred Indian burial ground is nearby. One of the most popular attractions is the **Tobogán de la Selva**, a natural water slide. There is a beautiful hiking trail which continues beyond the Tobogán, passing a couple of small waterfalls, until it reaches a beautiful grotto. You should also try to visit the **Indian Museum** in Puerto Ayacucho as well as the the Indian Market – usually held on Thursday and Friday mornings in the plaza across from the museum.

Not to be missed are the river trips led by experienced guides native to the area. You may visit the **Canyon de Paria**, a quiet lagoon, especially beautiful when the orchids are in bloom; fish for pavón, picua, palometa and other exotic Amazon fish; cross into Colombia at the confluence of the Orinoco, Tomo and Tuparro rivers; or hike through the savannah to a beach just beyond the Maipure and Ature Rapids. For information and reservations, contact Camturama's office in Caracas at ☎ (02) 941-8813 or fax (02) 943-5160.

Cacao Expeditions has recently reopened **Campamento Garcitas Orinoquia**, the camp next to Camturama. Much smaller than Camturama, it is in a secluded setting alongside the Orinoco. Accommodations are four enclosed cabins and four open-air *piruatas* with enclosed bathrooms underneath. Excursions include nocturnal river trips by torchlight as well as a trip to an Indian mission. Trips are led by experienced biologists. For more information and reservations, contact **Cacao Expeditions** in Caracas at ☎ (02) 977-1234 or fax (02) 977-0110. E-mail 73050.2614@compuserve.com.

Also reputable is **Campamento Genesis**. Though not on the river, it offers comparable tours and accommodations. For further information, contact **O.G.A. Tours** at ☎/fax (048) 213-123 or write to them at P.O.Box 54 Puerto Ayacucho, Estado Amazônas.

Indian Tribes – Puerto Ayacucho

The Venezuelan government is protecting the secluded lives of its tribes, though efforts are being made to incorporate them into modern society. It is not easy to visit the tribes because the governors of Bolívar and Amazônas are restricting the necessary permits. The town of Puerto Ayacucho would be a starting point for expeditions to the Indian villages of the area. Some private pilots at the Caracas airport offer excursions. If you are fortunate enough to obtain a permit, it will be an unforgettable journey.